19.95

The Young, the Old and the State

D1458484

GLOBALIZATION AND WELFARE

Series Editors: Denis Bouget, *MSH Ange Guépin, France,* Jane Lewis, *Barnett Professor of Social Policy, University of Oxford, UK and* Peter Taylor-Gooby, *Darwin College, University of Kent, Canterbury, UK*

This important series is designed to make a significant contribution to the principles and practice of comparative social policy. It includes both theoretical and empirical work. International in scope, it addresses issues of current and future concern in both East and West, and in developed and developing countries.

The main purpose of this series is to create a forum for the publication of high quality work to help understand the impact of globalization on the provision of social welfare. It offers state-of-the-art thinking and research on important areas such as privatisation, employment, work, finance, gender, and poverty. It will include some of the best theoretical and empirical work from both well established researchers and the new generation of scholars.

Titles in the series include:

Social Exclusion and European Policy
Edited by David G. Mayes, Jos Berghman and Robert Salais

Social Exclusion and European Welfare States
Edited by Ruud J.A. Muffels, Panos Tsakloglou and David G. Mayes

Restructuring the Welfare State
Globalization and Social Policy Reform in Finland and Sweden
Virpi Timonen

The Young, the Old and the State
Social Care Systems in Five Industrial Nations
Edited by Anneli Anttonen, John Baldock and Jorma Sipilä

The Young, the Old and the State

Social Care Systems in Five
Industrial Nations

Edited by

Anneli Anttonen
University of Tampere, Finland

John Baldock
University of Kent at Canterbury, UK

Jorma Sipilä
University of Tampere, Finland

GLOBALIZATION AND WELFARE

Edward Elgar
Cheltenham, UK • Northampton, MA, USA

© Anneli Anttonen, John Baldock, Jorma Sipilä 2003

All rights reserved. No part of this publication may be reproduced, stored in a retrieval system or transmitted in any form or by any means, electronic, mechanical or photocopying, recording, or otherwise without the prior permission of the publisher.

Published by
Edward Elgar Publishing Limited
Glensanda House
Montpellier Parade
Cheltenham
Glos GL50 1UA
UK

Edward Elgar Publishing, Inc.
136 West Street
Suite 202
Northampton
Massachusetts 01060
USA

NORTHBROOK COLLEGE DESIGN + TECHNOLOGY	
140427	Class No 369. 712 ANT
MACAULAY	10 Oct 2007
Location. 1995	WE B

A catalogue record for this book
is available from the British Library

Library of Congress Cataloguing in Publication Data
The Young, the old and the state : social care systems in five industrial nations / edited by Anneli Anttonen, John Baldock, Jorma Sipilä.
    p. cm. — (Globalization and welfare)
    Includes bibliographical references and index.
    1. Child care. 2. Aged—Care. 3. Human services. I. Anttonen, Anneli. II. Baldock, John, 1948– III. Sipilä, Jorma. IV. Series.

HQ778.5. Y69 2003
362.71'2—dc21   2003040774

ISBN 1 84064 628 4 (cased)

Printed and bound in Great Britain by MPG Books Ltd, Bodmin, Cornwall

Contents

Figures

Tables

Contributors

Dr Anneli Anttonen is Professor of Social Policy in the Department of Social Policy and Social Work at the University of Tampere. Her academic interests include welfare state theory, feminist approaches to social policy, comparative social policy and social care research. She has published widely in both Finnish and English. Recent publications include: *Suomalaista sosiaalipolitiikkaa*, Vastapaino: Tampere, 2000 (with Jorma Sipilä), *Feministejä — Aikamme ajattelijoita*, Vastapaino: Tampere, 2000 (with Kirsti Lempiäinen and Marianne Liljeström) and *Women and the Welfare State: Politics, Professions and Practices*, Jyväskylän yliopisto, Yhteiskuntapolitiikan laitos, Työpapereita No. 87, 1994.

John Baldock is Professor of Social Policy in the School of Social Policy, Sociology and Social Research at the University of Kent at Canterbury. He is particularly interested in the ways in which different industrial societies provide for the welfare of frail older people and has published widely on this issue. He is co-editor of the journal *Social Policy and Administration* and of the textbook, *Social Policy*, published by Oxford University Press.

Dr Adalbert Evers is Professor of Health and Social Welfare at the Justus-Liebig University, Giessen. His research interests include welfare pluralism, the long-term care of older people, developments in the third sector and environmental aspects of welfare. He has published widely in German and English. Recent publications include: *Von öffentlichen Einrichtungen zu sozialen Unternehmen: Hybride Organisationsformen im Bereich sozialer Dienstleistungen* (2002 with Ulrich Rauch and Uta Stitz) and *Wohlfahrtspluralismus: Vom Wohlfahrtsstaat zur Wohlfahrtsgesellschaft* (1996, with Thomas Olk).

Joseph Heffernan is Professor of Politics at the University of Texas at Austin. A prominent researcher in the field of social welfare, social care and the family, he has published on social welfare policies in the United States and has worked in comparative research since the early 1980s.

Dr Teppo Kröger is a Research Fellow in the Department of Social Policy and Social Work at the University of Tampere. He is interested in care in its social contexts and particularly from a comparative perspective. Currently he is responsible, with Jorma Sipilä, for a multi-national research project of the work-life balance (SOCCARE) funded by the European Union. His English language publications include: 'The Dilemma of Municipalities: Scandinavian Approaches to Child Daycare Provision' (*Journal of Social Policy,* 1997); 'The Unique and the General in the Emergence of Social Care Services' (in S. Karvinen, T. Pösö and M. Satka, eds, *Reconstructing Social Work Research*, University of Jyväskylä, 1999); *Comparative Research on Social Care: The State of the Art* (European Commission, 2001).

Dr Christoph Sachße is Professor of the History and Theory of Social Work at the University of Kassel. He has published widely on the history and theory of social welfare and the welfare state. Recent publications include *Sicherheit und Freiheit. Zur Ethik des Wohlfahrtsstaates* (Frankfurt: Suhrkamp Verlag, 1990; co-editor with H. Tristram Engelhardt), *Von der Wertgemeinschaft zum Dienstleistungsunternehmen. Jugend- und Wohlfahrtsverbände im Umbruch* (Frankfurt: Suhrkamp Verlag, 1995; co-editor with Thomas Rauschenbach and Thomas Olk) and *The Mixed Economy of Social Welfare* (Baden-Baden: Nomos, 1996, with Michael B. Katz).

Jorma Sipilä is Professor of Social Policy and Rector at the University of Tampere. He is the author of five books on aspects of Scandinavian social welfare and many publications in Finnish, English, Estonian, Italian, Swedish and Spanish on social policy issues. He has twice been the editor-in-chief of the main Finnish journal of social policy (*Sosiaalipolitiikka,* later *Janus*). He has focused mainly on cross-national social service research since late 1980s and is co-editor of *Social Care Services: The Key to the Scandinavian Welfare Model* (Aldershot: Avebury, 1997).

Dr Mutsuko Takahashi is Professor of Political Science at the University of Shimane in Japan. Her particular research interests and publications are principally concerned with the comparative politics of social welfare and the history of public and voluntary welfare in Japan.

1. The Importance of Social Care

Jorma Sipilä, Anneli Anttonen and John Baldock

THE RATIONALE AND PURPOSE OF THIS STUDY

Our Objectives

The intention of our book is to contribute to the understanding of social care and to the wider field of comparative social research. In particular, we explore how both similarities and differences in countries' social care arrangements are rooted in their cultures and in their social and political histories. We wish to move beyond comparative accounts of national care systems that concentrate on institutional description, available data on expenditure and numbers provided for. Rather, we seek to capture something of the normative and moral qualities of care systems: the degree to which citizens find them desirable, accessible, reliable, fair and trustworthy. These are criteria that are essentially judgemental and lack the specificity and precision that many social scientists and policy analysts would regard as the marks of academic inquiry. However, despite the fact there is now a substantial literature on comparative social care, there can be few who have been involved in cross-national studies who have not been frustrated by the inability of these 'scientific' accounts to illuminate the place of social care in different nations' cultures and social lives. All of us involved in this project were well acquainted with international conferences and meetings on social care where delegates labour to translate the standard terms we all have to use (home care, home help, nursing home, old people's home, sheltered housing, service housing, day care, childcare, nursery, kindergarten) into genuine understandings of how things 'really are' in their own countries. Often the most informative parts of these meetings are visits by the delegates to local institutions and services close to the conference centre. Only then is it revealed how forms of social care with similar names and policy intentions have quite different social and cultural meanings and practical consequences.

Social Care and Welfare Systems

Care is a growing concern in welfare states and an ever more frequent object of social policy reform. Every post-industrial society is confronting anew how to support families in organizing the care of those who need regular help: particularly small children and those adults whose disabilities are linked to age or illness. Nor is this enough, as care must also be found for those people who have no family or who are not members of some close community with someone to turn to in time of need. Established forms of provision are being undermined by economic and social change. Social networks based on kinship have fragmented and even become international. It is more and more common for older people to live alone. The spread of paid female employment has changed the division of labour between the sexes and unpaid work by women at home and in the local community can no longer be treated as a resource to be drawn on freely.

Children, the sick and older people will always need care and support and it can be provided in many ways. In our study we accept the analytic usefulness of the distinction between informal and formal sources of care. Informal care is that given by family members, and by relatives, friends and neighbours, while formal care is provided by public, voluntary and commercial organizations. However, the boundary between formal and informal care is by no means clear or fixed but is rather a broad territory of cooperation, conflict and continuous negotiation. It is a shifting boundary and, moreover, it is disputed for ideological and political reasons. Thus the comparative analysis of social care arrangements cannot be restricted to simple distinctions between the public and the private but must develop methods that are capable of distinguishing changing balances between the sectors.

Social care will become increasingly central to the analysis of social policy. First, a greater focus on social care is necessary to construct a better understanding of the behaviour of modern welfare states and of the consequences for welfare systems of broader economic and social changes. As the globalization of production and consumption have challenged and undermined national welfare settlements, so the differences between countries' welfare systems have become more than just a problem of descriptive historical explanation. They have become central to nations' economic success and even survival. In particular, social care arrangements are being renegotiated and reformed as governments seek new balances between social and economic goals. Second, social care services define a central core of the relationship between state and citizen. As the most personal of social services, the point at which the state often, quite literally, enters the home, they are a barometer of the balance of the public and private worlds within a society. Consequently, for social researchers, the study of social care needs to be the locus of significant theoretical and empirical development. Through the comparative analysis of social care it is possible to illuminate developments and trends in national social policy systems as well as differences between welfare state ideologies and cultures. For social researchers an understanding of the origins and variety of these changes in social care is central to explaining the overall development of social policy.

In this book five different post-industrial societies are compared. Finland, Germany, Japan, the United Kingdom and the United States have been chosen because they are, on one hand, sufficiently similar, in terms of economic and social development and their exposure to the forces of globalization, and, on the other hand, clearly distinct from one another in their social care arrangements. The main purposes of the book are: first, to describe national social care patterns in the five countries; second, to seek explanations as to why they have developed into distinct systems; and third, to understand why countries are now rearranging social care in a variety of ways. Because social care, as both work and policy, is so pervasive in society, we have found it useful to restrict our analysis to the two dominant sectors in terms of the numbers of people involved and the scale of public expenditures: the day care of small children and the care of older people.

WHAT IS SOCIAL CARE?

The Discovery and Dissection of Social Care

Our study draws on many sources in social research. The theoretical approach used is above all indebted to several strands of feminist sociology. In the 1980s care became a key concept in feminist research and an important object of study in its own right as women-centred epistemologies and methodologies were developed by feminist scholars. The shift from structural analyses, often driven by patriarchal values and assumptions, towards theories emphasizing the agency of women raised questions about reproduction as work and about who did that work. The domestic labour debate of the 1970s had focused on the analysis of the economic and subordinating functions of domestic labour, but the idea of care stimulated a more wide-ranging discussion of women's unpaid labour and its relationship to the practices and modes of operation of the welfare state. Care was explored as a single entity, in other words informal and formal care, care of the old and care of children were not treated separately, and this was a step of decisive importance (Ungerson, 1990).

The first feminist studies of care concentrated on the unpaid care of the elderly in the home and family (Waerness, 1978; Finch and Groves, 1983; Ungerson, 1987). Waerness (1978) spoke of an invisible welfare state of care, by which she meant the extent and socio-economic value of unpaid work done by women. Graham (1993, pp. 461–2) observes that it was characteristic of the new currents in feminist research to devote attention to the domestic lives of wives, mothers and adult daughters by highlighting the emotional significance of their labour and its contribution to the welfare of relatives who needed help with the tasks of daily living. In particular British care research was tied firmly to the study of informal care work (ibid.).

Empirical work in the 1980s showed how widespread informal care activities were. The findings undermined a common critique of the welfare state: that it had seized possession of even the most intimate areas of everyone's life (for example, Habermas, 1984). Instead the arduous work of care remained a hidden activity, largely carried out by women and often without remuneration or professional support. Later, in the 1980s, care research was criticized for an excessive concentration on women's roles, particularly those of middle-class women (Graham, 1993; Thomas, 1993). According these critics, class and ethnic perspectives were ignored and so it was sometimes forgotten that care work is also done by servants and by low-paid care employees of the welfare state.

In the 1990s these omissions were tackled by more comprehensive and integrated studies of women's work across all the economic sectors:

- of women's paid care work within the labour market (for example, Borchorst, 1990; Leira, 1992; Lewis, 1994; Eliasson, 1996; Szebehely, 1999);
- by studies of the links between care work and family forms and structures, particularly the lives of single parents (for example, Hantrais, 1994; Millar and Warman, 1996);
- through research on social services and their care contributions and omissions (Anttonen and Sipilä, 1996; Lewis, 1998); and
- by paying attention to the globalization of care (Anderson, 2000; Hochschild, 2000).

Until the 1990s this progress in the understanding of care and care work had been largely ignored by policy studies of social care services. While the sociology, psychology and economics of care had been developing rapidly, policy analysis of how states organized and paid for their social care services had continued to leave the concept of care itself unpacked. As the new approaches began to influence policy studies so their focus widened from the formal to the informal and especially to the analysis of the relationships between these two spheres. In this book, social care, in its newer and broader senses, is used to provide a core foundation for international comparison.

Concepts of Care

It is rare that researchers in the social sciences agree on the meaning and content of concepts. This is often considered a weakness, but there are reasons to see it as a strength. Concepts adapt to changes taking place in society and to the introduction of new perspectives. Concepts that are not contested have either become conventions or else are no longer of any real interest. The debate about how to define social care continues to gain momentum.

Social care is customarily defined by way of pragmatic reduction: by excluding all those things that it is not. For instance, in his original but now well-worn definition, Philip Abrams (1977, p. 146) said that social care 'includes all forms of care and treatment in institutions and elsewhere, other than medical care and direct cash support'. This definition was based implicitly on the convention that social policy consists of income transfers and of services. It is further assumed that education and employment services are excluded, so the services that remain are either health care or social care services. Social care is then identified as everything else that remains outside the categories of income transfers and health care. This may be an easy and convenient way to define social care, but it does involve at least two major problems. First, in so far as social care takes place in institutions, it leaves international comparison very much at the mercy of national administrative boundaries: whatever happens to be defined in each country as health care will also determine the contents of social care. A second, bigger problem has to do with the word 'elsewhere'. How do we identify something that happens outside institutions but which is not 'medical care' or 'direct cash support'? Essentially the point that Abrams seems to be making is that social care may be provided not only formally but also informally. This was a novel insight in the 1970s, but is now one that is generally understood and accepted. Social care is more than just organized services; it is more than 'social services', 'personal social services' or 'social care services', which are terms now used to denote care provided by formal organizations.

It continues to be difficult to say what exactly social care is without starting out from what it is not. One source of this difficulty is the organizational variety that is so typical of social care compared to health care. It is hard to define even formal social care through occupations or through specialized institutions; the terms and functions differ considerably from one country to the next. Another difficulty is that the boundaries between formal and informal social care are becoming more and more blurred with the growth of public support for informal care. A third factor is that within the informal sphere it is virtually impossible to distinguish between health care and social care. Family carers are far less bound by strictures concerning who should carry out 'medical' procedures or make 'clinical' judgements than are professionals.

To understand what is essential about social care, it is perhaps better to start out from the content of the concept of care itself, to attempt positive rather than negative definitions. Again this is a task that has received most attention within feminist research. 'The origins of the concept lie in an attempt to define in its own right the work that makes up caring for others and to analyse how that work reinforced the disadvantaged position of women', write Daly and Lewis (1998, p. 4). It is perhaps precisely the key position that informal activity holds in feminist research and the fact that the distinction between health care and social care is less relevant in this field that have led to the much greater use of the terms 'care' and 'caring' and, in the United States, 'care-giving'.

Even the distinction between care as 'tending' and care as 'being concerned about' has been at first accepted but then found artificial. Tronto (1995, pp. 102–3) concludes that 'care implies some kind of on-going responsibility and commitment...caring is necessarily relational'. Clement (1996, p. 56) argues that the 'care worker acts to promote the well-being of others' and that the 'care-worker's personal relationship with her clients allows her to know them as individuals rather than as abstractions, and thus to provide better care for them'. There is also a sense in which the motivation or goal may determine whether the helping should be called care at all. Anttonen and Sipilä (1996) seek to draw a line excluding personal social services that do not belong to the domain of social care. They argue that actions aimed primarily at controlling the behaviour of others should not be included within caring. On this basis the concept would not, for example, cover the 'treatment' of juvenile delinquency.

Waerness (1984a; 1984b) has distinguished three kinds of relationships between the carer and the care-recipient. Care-giving work is characterized by a relationship between carer and cared for where the cared for, through illness, handicap or youth, is incapable of complete self-care. Spontaneous care arises impulsively and unplanned, for example among neighbours offering each other services without an expectation of continuity. Personal service is characterized by an unequal relationship between carer and cared for. This 'caring for superiors' is something for which Waerness prefers to use the term 'service' rather than that of 'care'. Thus, 'caring' is best not used where there is great asymmetry in the relationship: where there are elements of oppression rather than volition.

Daatland (1992, p. 171), writing of care of older people, stresses ways in which care has no clear state of finiteness or closure: 'The need for care, and the nature of caring, is inherently vague. There is no objective norm, and hardly any commonly agreed upon standard, to evaluate against. What constitutes a need, and who should be considered needy, is unclear and subject to opinion.... No matter what and how much is done, you can always do more — or better'. This applies most particularly to the sphere of informal care.

A more positive definition of care, constructed by Knijn and Kremer (1997, pp. 328–30), allows for much of what has been said so far: 'Care includes the provision of daily social, psychological, emotional, and physical attention to people...This can be provided by paid or unpaid work, on the basis of an agreement or voluntarily, and it can also be given professionally or on the basis of moral obligation'. Daly and Lewis (1998, pp. 6–7) suggest a similar approach but seek definitions that will allow the concept of care to serve as an analytic tool for understanding the welfare state. For them care is a multi-dimensional concept with three aspects meriting most emphasis. The first is care as labour. Highlighting the labour aspect emphasizes care as a verb and the carers as actors. The second dimension of the concept sets care within a normative framework of obligations and responsibilities. Care is not like other work or labour because it is often initiated and provided under conditions of social and/ or familial responsibility. In their third dimension they see care as an activity with costs, both financial and emotional, which extend across public/private boundaries.

For the concept to serve analytic purposes it must also separate health care from social care. One way to do this is simply to list the particular activities that are involved in, for example, the care of children or of older people. This method is however arduous and often arbitrary. An alternative shortcut is to say that the focal concern in social care is with the whole individual. Health care, in contrast, has traditionally concerned itself with parts of the body. This bodily focus has historically determined the specialisms and limits of medicine but these too are under attack from ideas about whole-person health care.

In short, while definitions of social care that are based upon what it is, rather than on what it is not, are to be preferred, they remain fuzzy at the edges. Nonetheless, the very processes of definition construction have helped to reach a deeper understanding of the specific nature of social care. Social care is above all characterized by its flexible boundaries, by the ambiguity of the tasks involved and the uncertainties over the divisions of labour. Much of the process of definition construction that has preoccupied many analysts so far is implicit in a succinct definition suggested by Knijn and Kremer (1997, pp. 323–30), which will suffice for this book: social care means giving informal or professional attention to whole persons who need help in their everyday lives.

THE COMPARATIVE STUDY OF SOCIAL CARE

Related Methodologies

The second major foundation for this study is comparative social research. Current patterns of globalization in politics, economics and culture and the growing

movements of people across borders have raised the significance of comparative social research, a field that already had a long history in social policy analysis. Clasen (1999, pp. 2–3) observes that 'comparative social policy analysis is
becoming an established sub-discipline'. Its theoretical and methodological
development, though, is just beginning. Earlier comparative welfare state
research was largely a matter of explaining differences in development between
welfare states by seeking correlations between overall welfare expenditure and
structural and political variables. The aim was to advance the 'grand theory' of
welfare state development. Instead more recent comparative research has,
according to Clasen, begun to investigate 'the causes of policy changes within
social policy components or programmes, such as health care, pensions or
social care arrangements' (ibid.).

Our study can be placed in a tradition of comparative research in which differences in social policy are neither treated only as quantitative terms nor
reduced to very specific examples. Rather it can be located, in accordance with
the classification made by Clasen (ibid., p. 3), somewhere between large-scale,
cross-national comparisons and contextually rich case studies. The former deal
with welfare systems as whole entities rather than examining particular areas of
social policy (Mabbett and Bolderson, 1999, p. 41). In the latter the object of
analysis is more tightly defined, focusing on provision for similar needs within
comparable environments. Our study takes whole nations as its objects and
seeks to understand national social care patterns in their historical and cultural
contexts. One of our key arguments is that, in the birth and development of
social policy institutions, culture plays a central role. Social care arrangements
do not merely reflect the politico-economic models found in countries, they are
also produced by, and embedded within, deep cultural streams flowing through
their histories (Hantrais, 1999). The method used here might be defined as
cross-cultural social policy analysis.

Our approach has also to some extent been influenced by what has been in
recent years the most influential school of comparative social policy analysis,
the welfare regime approach or large-scale cross-national comparisons usually
aimed at modelling whole social policy systems. Gøsta Esping-Andersen's *The
Three Worlds of Welfare Capitalism* (1990) inspired much interest in developing typologies of welfare states. He distinguished types of socio-political
arrangement defined by the links between forms of welfare provision and the
political organization of the society. This point of departure produced a broad
critical debate about the bases for the formation of regimes. Feminist scholars
in particular have criticized Esping-Andersen and other regime theorists for
concentrating their classifications on the income security of wage earners in
formal employment (Hobson, 1990; Langan and Ostner, 1991; Lewis, 1992;
Orloff, 1993; Sainsbury, 1994). Both the theoretical conceptualization and
empirical analyses of the welfare regimes have focused almost entirely on

social insurance; largely pensions and unemployment benefits. This leads to gender blindness and to the marginalization of welfare goods and socio-political institutions that are important to women.

Developments in Comparative Social Care

The regime debate has since been extended into typologizing comparisons of social services and social care (Anttonen and Sipilä, 1996; Daly and Lewis, 1998; Hill, 2000). The scope of social policy research has thus expanded considerably, bringing new problems for comparative social policy studies to solve. Anneli Anttonen and Jorma Sipilä (1996, pp. 89–91) classified the difficulties that are met when social care services in different countries are compared. The first has to do with concepts and names. Service organizations and care processes with the same names are not necessarily similar in different societies and neither are the relations between them. Besides these problems of name and meaning, there are further difficulties relating to the location and funding of social care activities. The same care activities may appear within different fields of public administration. A comparable service for older people, for instance, may be delivered within one country by means-tested social care services, in another by a universal health care system and in a third by purchase of care through the social security system. In the case of children's day care a key dividing line often separates educational and care provision, but to a different degree and different ways across systems. Data problems constitute a third set of obstacles faced by researchers. It is never easy to produce reliable datasets for cross-national comparison, and this is especially so in the case of social services. Indeed, there is good reason to argue that much of the available data on public social care expenditures is of little validity. As the chapters on the United Kingdom and the United States in this volume both point out, there are complex forms of indirect public spending on social care in those countries that make it difficult to compare them with more universalist forms of state provision: grants and tax reliefs to non-profit providers and to employers; tax allowances and selective needs-based social income additions to households.

As researchers have deconstructed the broad categories of welfare provision so it has become clear that the concepts and methods used, as well as the generalizations drawn, in comparative research have often been too simplistic. There is a need for greater theoretical development if unduly schematic modelling is to be avoided. There is, furthermore, a danger that the categories are constructed in ways that involve in-built hierarchical assumptions about the greater significance of some types of provision relative to others. Some classifications at least imply the developmental and even moral superiority of some systems over others. For example, Kamerman and Kahn (1997) are explicitly judgemental in their evaluation of family support services. Even Anne Helene

Gauthier's (1996) division of national family policy systems into 'pro-family but non-interventionist' (United Kingdom and United States), 'pro-family/pro-natalist' (France), 'pro-traditional' (Germany) and 'pro-egalitarian' (Sweden and Denmark) has an implicit developmental loading with the Nordic model as the apogee. The empirical reality is that we know only that different societies organize and fund care differently, and that therefore both the costs and the workloads are allocated differently too. There is a little, but not much, evidence that those needing care are more likely to go without it in some industrialized societies compared with others.

However, as this volume shows, we certainly cannot conclude that, because there is less public care funding and provision in the United States, the United Kingdom and Japan, that there is therefore also less childcare and eldercare or it is of lower quality than in Finland or Germany. One of the key characteristics of the production of social care is that it is almost infinitely substitutable between home and institution and among family, market and state. Where direct public supply appears low its place may be taken by voluntary, private or family services, possibly subsidized to varying degrees, directly or indirectly, by public expenditure on pensions, welfare allowances or tax incentives. All classificatory models find this quality of transferability across sectors very hard to handle. A recent comparative European Union study of social protection for older people across fifteen nations concluded 'the exact amount of resources that society spends [on] older people is not known. At the same time there is no clear evidence whether systems are being driven to more or less social protection' (European Commission, 1999, p. 135). This is a fairly startling admission of uncertainty: we do not know how much social care there is or whether it is rising or falling in amount. The uncertainty is because 'support and services for the elderly include a wide spectrum of protection systems that can change the relative circumstances of dependent elderly people in each country. The relevant points include not only the perennial protection systems, such as pensions, health insurance and traditional services, but also additional income support, housing benefits and tax spending' (ibid.). Similarly, recorded public expenditure on forms of social care may be useful information for students of public expenditure but they tell us very little of the likelihood that a child or older person will receive care when they need it, of its quality and real social and economic costs. What initially may appear to be 'softer' data, qualitative and individual accounts of social care, may in fact be more informative than official classifications of expenditure and service use.

It has become necessary to develop new kinds of contextual interpretation that are sensitive to cultural, social and psychological differences and not simply organizational arrangements. Social care, in all its complexity and diversity, lends itself fruitfully to research and theorizing of this kind. The intellectual and academic interest in the subject is largely inspired by the fact that there is more variety in ways of arranging social care than there is, for instance, in ways of organizing education, health care or social security. It is quite obvious that this is fundamentally a result of the basic yet simultaneously complex nature of care. Care is everyday work, done especially by women, and this work is governed to a very large extent by cultural conceptions about, among other things, who should be giving care and what it may cost. Nonetheless it appears in a great variety of forms and organization and is loaded with an array of social meanings. In contrast, when it comes to the organization of social security provision, such as pensions, child benefit and unemployment benefit, a greater degree of international uniformity prevails. There are variations in the scale and scope of services rather than in their objectives and outcomes.

DIVERSITY AND DIFFERENCE: THE WELFARE-MIX APPROACH

As the argument so far has shown, our study draws on a theoretical tradition that analyses the interaction of different sources of social provision, a tradition characterized by the concepts of the 'welfare mix', 'welfare pluralism' and the 'mixed economy of welfare'. The welfare-mix approach (Evers and Wintersberger, 1990), as well that of welfare pluralism (Johnson, 1987), underlines the role of the agent: it is a matter of significance whether social care is provided by a private enterprise, a local authority or a neighbour. In contrast, the mixed economy approach is more often concerned with the funding mechanisms and how demand and supply are reconciled. In debates about the welfare mix it is frequently suggested that the production of welfare functions better when there are many providers and a sustainable division of labour and funding emerges among them.

Studies in comparative social care have featured large in the development of the welfare-mix approach because social care is particularly likely to exhibit variety of form and source. There are national differences in the scale, scope and targeting of formal social care services as well as in the operational practices used and normative rationales that drive them. One and the same function may be arranged through services provided by government, by private businesses, by voluntary organizations and associations or through various combinations of these public and private sources. For example, carers and care recipients in some welfare systems may be offered cash benefits or tax concessions instead of services. Alternatively, a whole system may rely largely on social care being provided by relatives, family members, friends and neighbours, supported and encouraged by state policy to different degrees and in various ways. Social provision in the United States can be under-rated if voluntary, denominational and communal forms of provision are ignored, that in Japan if corporate employment-based supports are left out.

Thus comparative analyses built round the organizing themes of welfare pluralism and the welfare mix have helped to elevate personal and social care from a minor afterthought in the understanding of welfare systems to a far more central position. The routine and menial characteristics of social care (tending, feeding, bathing, watching over) obscure both its universal importance and its complexity. In contrast, social security and income maintenance systems, while much more often studied by comparative social policy, are both less universal (they do not exist at all in many countries) and far more homogeneous in their organization. It is slightly odd that welfare typologists have mainly built their categories on forms of welfare more rather than less likely to be similar.

However, while the complexity of social care services may better represent the real world of welfare, it also brings with it larger problems of analysis and classification. Two fundamental approaches to the modelling of social care arrangements can be distinguished: the managerial and the sociological. The first, particularly associated with the literature on the mixed economy of welfare, is broadly economistic in its approach. It generally seeks to separate out who pays for and who provides a service (Knapp, 1989, p. 230; Wistow et al., 1994). The analytical variables are the spectrum of funding sources (taxation, tax exemptions, price subsidies, social insurance, private insurance, compulsory purchase, voluntary purchase, barter and exchange, donations and gifts) and the hierarchy of providers (state, non-governmental organizations, voluntary organizations, private firms, paid professionals, communities, neighbours and families). The strength of this approach is that it emphasizes the almost infinite variety of combinations of funding and provider that can in principle be used to meet a particular social need. Its limitations are those generally associated with economic and managerial analysis. All the factors that have actually determined the service arrangements are left out of the account. These are the dimensions of taste, values, culture, ideology and history, the variables with which economics is most uncomfortable. The second approach to modelling the welfare mix is the one adopted here. These are broadly sociological analyses; they seek to relate process, agency and meaning. They try to explain why particular social care arrangements have emerged and how they have been sustained. Table 1.1 is no more than an example of this approach. It demonstrates the categories of analysis that typically inform these approaches, set out in terms of four modes of provision of social care.

Simply setting out in tabular form the now widely accepted division of social care into a typology that distinguishes formal from informal and public from private reveals both its strengths and weaknesses. It is a framework into which most social care can be fitted; in this sense it approximates well to the real world of services and can be used to make comparisons between countries. At the

Table 1.1 A typology of social care arrangements

	Informal	Voluntary	Commercial	State
Rationale or motive	Love, guilt, obligation, tradition, religion, gift, reciprocity	Charity, volunteerism, social norms, public esteem, religious principles	Profit, fee	Entitlement, rights, statute, political goals, social control
Agency	Household, family, friendship, neighbour-liness	Voluntary organization, charities, churches, communities	Firms, professionals, independent care workers and contractors	Central and local government bureaucracies
Recipient	Member of household or family, friend or neighbour	Person defined as object of charity	Customer or client	Entitled citizen
Carer	Unpaid member of household or family, friend or neighbour	Volunteer, employee or contractor	Employee or professional	Civil servant, public sector worker

same time it highlights the problems that have to be surmounted in making cross-national comparisons. How is one to measure or weigh the degree to which a country's social care services are preponderantly of one mode or another? Even within a mode, the range of variables that fall with in the dimension labelled 'Rationale or motive' is likely to be very large. Allocating instances of social care to one or another mode is both a matter of evidence and one of judgement. Nonetheless, in carrying out this study, we found, as researchers from each of the countries involved, that we could fairly readily apply the following categories to our national systems of social care:

Household and home: here social care is usually the responsibility of family members. The rationales that drive it are complex: tradition, religion, reciprocity, love. Where families fail in terms of these codes of responsibility, or

seek support from other sources such as the state, shame and stigma may
follow.

Communities based on shared values: often social care is the 'duty' of religious or other value-based communities. Members provide care for each
other. Giving help brings moral and psychic rewards and even commercially
or politically useful publicity to individuals and organizations. It raises the
status of the people who act as helpers and helps sustain forms of social
order and cohesion. Local voluntary organizations may or may not be supported by the wider community through state subsidies or joint working with
public agencies.

The market: here social care is a commodity exchanged for money or for
other goods. Commodity exchange is based on contracts and it can take
place between strangers. Prudent people may prepare for future needs by
accumulating savings or taking out insurance. Inequalities of income are
likely to be reflected in the quantity and quality of care.

The state, particularly local government: social care is frequently a statutory
duty of the most local state authority. Such provision often has historical
roots in public poor relief. More universal modern forms help integrate the
local community and legitimate local governance and politics. Local government may receive support from the central state, usually finance.

Most social care is produced by complex and changing combinations of
these forms and motives. The modes of provision presented in the table are
essentially ideal types. In practice welfare-mix studies show that actors in the
field of social care often creatively mix forms and motives (Evers, 1993). However, the typology does illuminate aspects of welfare in a society that are less
perceptible in the larger more universal services: patterns of entitlement and
obligation; the implicit contracts between citizen and state and between one citizen and another; the inequalities in social care and their roots in class, religion
and the wider culture.

COMPARING SOCIAL CARE PATTERNS IN THE FIVE COUNTRIES

The chief purpose of our book is to delineate the welfare mixes that are more
'typical' in each of five industrial countries and to explain their sources and the
ways in which they are expressed in the care of children and older people. To do

this we focus mainly on the evolution of social care arrangements since the 1960s.

Social care arrangements are an integral part of the wider order and structure of a society. In particular, social care patterns vary because of their close association with the histories of local welfare institutions (for example Higgins, 1981; Stjernø, 1995). The norms and assumptions that govern social care in a locality are also the products of cultural, political and particularly religious values. People accept, almost unquestioningly, the ways in which social care is organized within their own culture and have a preference for it (Erler et al., 1994; Bodiuzzaman et al., 1995). Thus forms of provision vary considerably even within Western Europe (see Anttonen and Sipilä, 1994, 1996, 1997). On the other hand, in times of major social and political change, social care arrangements can be among the first aspects of welfare provision to be questioned and 'reformed'. Historically, public opinion tends to swing back and forth between two extreme positions, one stressing the responsibility of individuals and families for their own welfare and the other expecting the wider society to take responsibility for at least some elements (Midre, 1995, pp. 115–35). More explicit welfare ideologies, those presented by political parties for instance, usually locate themselves between these poles, though not necessarily with great consistency.

In affluent nations, social care is based on combinations of formal and informal provision. Countries have very different kinds of welfare mixes. In this book we construct national profiles of social care which include both formal and informal arrangements. In particular, we focus on variations in support for carers and family care. In none of the countries we have studied are data on informal care collected or presented in systematic ways. Formal care, because it is generally accounted for in financial budgets such as national accounts, lends itself much more readily to comparison. The limited availability of data on informal provision, and its relative non-comparability, has severely limited our efforts to map social care systems.

While anchored to its national and normative contexts, social care is exposed to many pressures when societies are changing. This is not just a matter of ideological changes taking place in the arenas of the economy and politics, changes that generally arise from structural adaptations to economic competition. Some ideological shifts, at least, appear to be relatively isolated from material changes in the economy and patterns of employment, for example the never-ending moral debates about family responsibilities. Others are more clearly rooted in changes in everyday life, such as the discrepancies between social policy assumptions and the growing participation of women in paid employment. Although the forces of change are, to some extent, pushing in the same direction, they have not yet produced much cross-national uniformity in social care policies. Unlike social security systems, social care arrangements remain distinctly national and local innovations are common.

Social care arrangements have growing political salience as dependency ratios in industrial societies rise, driven by population ageing, extended education and earlier retirement. In all affluent countries care systems are undergoing reassessment and reorganization. The competitive pressures of economic globalization and the continuing crisis in the public sector are increasing the need to find low cost but politically acceptable social care solutions. However, it will be argued here that there are poorly understood limits to change, set by the internal logic of caring itself, and by the constraints created by its normative and material history in each country. In order to understand these limits this study suggests ways of moving on from descriptions of social welfare systems and from empirical generalizations towards theory construction. We perceive a need to develop categories that embed social care arrangements in their cultural, political and social contexts.

Finland, Germany, Japan, the United Kingdom and the United States exhibit a variety of forms and principles in the provision of social care for children, the frail elderly and the disabled. Underlying the choice of countries was the observation that in providing social care Finland makes greater use of the municipalities than other countries, Germany of voluntary organizations, Japan of the family and the United States of the market. The pattern is less clear in the United Kingdom where the balance of public and private provision appears to be under almost constant negotiation. The broad formal differences in these countries' welfare systems are well documented. But these in turn rest on less well-explicated and deeper national differences than comparative research has generally noticed. Implicit social models influence the relationships between the individuals and state institutions.

Which social factors most influence social care arrangements? It is easier to understand the influence of institutions that are closely related to social care than it is to identify those with apparently only remote connections. But it is the role of social science to question obvious links and discover the less obvious. The existing literature suggests causal influences of various sorts:

- legislation which both reflects and changes norms about family obligation (Millar and Warman, 1996),
- women's access to paid employment and other arenas of public life such as politics (Hernes, 1987; Anttonen, 1997),
- the degree of older people's economic independence (Baldock and Ely, 1996; Sipilä et al., 1997),
- the birth rate, which both reflects and affects the caring capacity of a society (Esping-Andersen, 1996),

- the administrative structure of public services and their responsiveness to changes in social need (for example, Jamieson, 1991; Alber, 1995; Kröger, 1997).

All of these factors are primarily historical in the manner in which they impact on social care. Consequently this study pays particular attention to highlighting the historical sources of current arrangements.

In any international comparison it is important to have a suitable balance of difference and similarity. The ideal is one where the societies selected are fundamentally more or less similar, but differ primarily in relation to the phenomenon under study. The choice of countries here was designed to maximize historical and cultural variety, but to minimize differences in economic organization, demography, morbidity and mortality. All the countries are affluent market economies. Greater cultural diversity was sought by including Japan and the United States as well as three western European nations. It was also important that reasonably comparable data would be available. Although data on social care are still very much in their infancy, national statistics in all these countries are highly developed and research into social welfare quite extensive.

Social care institutions are notoriously difficult for people from other countries to understand. Therefore each of the country-specific chapters in this volume is written by one who lives there. However, the content and structure of the chapters was also the product of two lengthy meetings of all the authors at which we sought to develop consistency and relevance across the chapters. We have sought to avoid simplistic stereotypes of national systems but at the same time enable real comparisons to be made by examining the same questions and exploring common themes. Each chapter contains a historical interpretation of the development of care, a description of how children's day care and care for older people is arranged and an evaluation of recent developments. The emphasis on history was necessary because social care patterns evolve slowly and they are affected by unique and often surprising events (see especially the chapters on Finland and Germany). The detailed accounts of social care provision focus mainly and deliberately on the 1990s.

Finland

The chapter on Finland demonstrates particularly the almost accidental effects of politics on social care policy. The present-day high levels of support for childcare and, to a lesser extent, eldercare are not primarily the product of a communitarian or welfarist consensus but rather the outcomes of relatively brief and opportunist political coalitions in a society until recently divided by sharp social differences. The yearning for independence during the period of Russian rule, the defeat of the working class in the Civil War, the alignment with Scandinavian countries after the Second World War and fundamental shifts in public opinion in the 1960s all played their parts in determining social care policy. The country's late industrialization and the widespread poverty that persisted well into the twentieth century meant that support for older people was slow to emerge from its poor law origins. Children though were of great importance to the young republic and this can be seen both in the early support given to kindergartens and, more recently, in the unique guarantees of universal day care for small children. The development of care institutions has been strongly influenced by the early shift, by international standards, of women into paid employment outside the home. Temporary strategic coalitions between the traditionally opposed political representatives of town and country played a role in producing radical, innovative solutions to support care in the home. Localism too has been a fundamental force.

Germany

Germany presents a contrasting story to that of Finland. Despite enormous political trauma, defeat in two world wars, dictatorship and division between East and West, there is a pattern of continuity in the evolution of social care for both children and older people. Both the kindergarten and social insurance systems emerged after unification in 1870 and have remained core institutions ever since. In the chaotic economic and political conditions after the First World War compromise was finally achieved, allowing national welfare associations a central role supported by the state. This pluralist model was reinstated after the Nazi period and extended to the East after reunification in 1990. Under Bismarck, Germany was the pioneer of social insurance. Similarly in the late twentieth century, when health insurance proved to be insufficient for the care for older people, Germany was the first nation to develop long-term care insurance. Nonetheless, the German chapter provides a good illustration of how much the essential nature of social care undermines attempts to impose on it the same forms of organization and professional control that work in other sectors of the welfare state.

Japan

Social care patterns in Japan strongly reflect the contradictions inherent in modernization. On one hand Japan has long clung to the idea that care is the duty of the family. This is in part the reality too. Japanese people live in three-generation family units more often than people in our other countries and the norm still exists, although it is weakening, that women should care for their parents and parents-in-law. On the other hand, Japanese women participate in paid work as much as women do in Germany. The role of women, and therefore of the family as producers of care, is undergoing profound change. By no means all old people want to be cared for by their families. Because state policy has stressed the family's responsibility for care, public care services have been seen as stigmatizing. However, families have often been able to avoid this by arranging for the long-term care of their older people within the health care system. The principle of social care without stigma and available for everyone who needs it, was introduced in the legislative reforms of 1990. The 'Golden Plan' care insurance legislation in 2000 was a further development of this idea.

The United Kingdom

In the United Kingdom the policies and provision that affect the care of older people and childcare present as a series of expedient administrative arrangements rather than a coherent story. They belie the image of Britain as a universalist welfare state. The Beveridge Report and the associated legislation that created the post-war 'welfare state' made no provision for pre-school childcare or the non-institutional care of older people. Both remained essentially private, family responsibilities. Only the destitute old and abandoned or delinquent youth were objects of consistent social care policies. In this respect the British experience most closely resembles that of Japan. State intervention took place only selectively where private provision failed. Thus neither state nor private (for-profit) services were explicitly supported by public policy. The result was a great variety of ad hoc solutions and huge inequalities in access to help. At the turn of the century both childcare and the needs of older people have at last received a degree of systematic political attention, but in quite different ways. The 'New Labour' administration is the first post-war government to put in place a comprehensive childcare policy but it is one determined not by welfare criteria but the perceived need to encourage more women into paid employment. In England and Wales the government has rejected, on grounds of cost, the recommendation of the recent Royal Commission on Long Term Care to establish a system of universal state payment for the social care of older people, while the Scottish assembly, behaving increasingly like a Nordic parliament, has agreed to it. Unlike the United States, Britain has a mixed economy of social care by default rather than by intention.

The United States

The case of the United States is that of a largely market-driven system of social care heavily supported by voluntary and denominational provision. The state plays a minor role even in terms of financing. Traditional hostility towards state intervention and the cultural heterogeneity of the population has led to people relying on combinations of family and for-profit providers in children's day care. The high proportion of children in day care is the result of the structure of the market: wages and tax rates are low and so are the wages of the care staff. There are also limited subsidies in the form of tax reductions for parents and public financial support for providers. Only in the United States is the future direction of childcare clear: 'growth ... outside of the public sector and outside of the informal sector, is certain to continue' (Chapter 6, p. 164). In the case of care for older people, the United States is paradoxically generous. While the first Clinton administration was dominated by the failure to agree on reforms of the health care system for people of working age, there is a secure political consensus that allows expenditure on Medicare, the key source of health and social care for both poor and middle-income older people, to grow inexorably. In this respect the United States has created a form of non-stigmatizing and substantially redistributive universalism.

At the end of the book we build on these national accounts and attempt a more theoretical understanding of how care for children and the elderly varies between societies. Why are there both similarities and the wide differences in the ways in which industrial societies, at the beginning of the twenty-first century, provide for needs as fundamental and inevitable as child-care and dependency in old age? Under what conditions and in what ways does care develop from a family problem to a public issue?

REFERENCES

Abrams, P. (1977), 'Community care: some research problems and priorities', *Policy and Politics*, 5 (6), 125–51.
Alber, J. (1995), 'A framework for the comparative study of social services', *Journal of European Social Policy*, 5 (2), 131–49.
Anderson, B. (2000), *Doing the Dirty Work? The Global Politics of Domestic Labour*, London and New York: Zed Books.
Anttonen, A. (1997), 'The welfare state, women and social care', in T. Gordon and K. Kauppinen (eds) *Unresolved Dilemmas, Women, Work and Family in the United States, Europe and the Former Soviet Union*, Aldershot: Avebury, pp. 9–32.
Anttonen, A. and Sipilä, J. (1994), 'Viisi eurooppalaista sosiaalipalvelumallia. Sosiaalipalvelut hyvinvointivaltiomallien näkökulmasta', *Janus*, 2 (3), 226–48.
Anttonen, A. and Sipilä, J. (1996), 'European social care services: is it possible to identify models?', *Journal of European Social Policy*, 6 (2), 87–100.
Anttonen, A. and Sipilä, J. (1997), 'Cinco regimenes de servicios de atencion social', in L. Moreno (ed.), *Union Europea y Estado del Bienestar*, Madrid: CSIC, pp. 431–58.
Baldock, J. and Ely, P. (1996), 'Social care for elderly people in Europe: The central problem of home care', in B. Munday and P. Ely (eds), *Social Care in Europe*, London: Prentice Hall, pp. 195–225.

Bodiuzzaman, Md, Kulmala, A., Li, B. and Tuurna, T. (1995), 'Who cares? Discussions about the care of the frail elderly in Bangladesh, China and Finland', Unpublished masters dissertation, University of Tampere: International School of Social Sciences.

Borchorst, A. (1990), 'Political motherhood and child care policies: a comparative approach to Britain and Scandinavia', in C. Ungerson (ed.), *Gender and Caring: Work and Welfare in Britain and Scandinavia,* New York: Harvester Wheatsheaf, pp. 160–78.

Clasen, J. (1999), 'Introduction', in J. Clasen (ed.), *Comparative Social Policy: Concepts, Theories and Methods,* Oxford: Blackwell, pp. 1–12.

Clement, G. (1996), *Care, Autonomy and Justice. Feminism and the Ethic of Care,* Boulder: Westview Press.

Daatland, S.O. (1992), 'The public–private mix: the roles of families and the public care system in the welfare state', *European Journal of Gerontology,* 1 (3), 170–83.

Daly, M. and Lewis, J. (1998), 'Introduction: Conceptualising social care in the context of welfare state restructuring', in J. Lewis (ed.), *Gender, Social Care and Welfare State Restructuring in Europe,* Aldershot: Ashgate, pp. 1–24.

Eliasson, R. (ed.) (1996), *Omsorgens Skiftningar. Begreppet, Vardagen, Politiken, Forskningen,* Lund: Studentlitteratur.

Erler, G., Jackel, M. and Sass, J. (1994), *Auswirkungen und Einschätzung Familienpolitischer Massnahmen für Familien mit Kindern Unter 6 Jahren im Europäischen Vergleih,* München: Deutsches Jugendinstitut.

Esping-Andersen, G. (1990), *The Three Worlds of Welfare Capitalism,* Cambridge: Polity Press.

Esping-Andersen, G. (1996), 'Welfare states without work: the impasse of labour shedding and familialism in Continental European social policy', in G. Esping-Andersen (ed.), *Welfare States in Transition. National Adaptations in Global Economies,* London: Sage, pp. 66–87.

European Commission (1999), *Social Protection for Dependency in Old Age in the 15 EU Member States,* Directorate General for Employment, Industrial Relations and Social Affairs, Unit v/E.2, Luxembourg: Office of Publications for the European Communities.

Evers, A. (1993), 'The welfare mix approach. Understanding the pluralism of welfare systems', in A. Evers and I. Svetlik (eds), *Balancing Pluralism. New Welfare Mixes in Care for the Elderly,* Aldershot: Avebury, pp. 3–31.

Evers, A. and Wintersberger, H. (eds) (1990), *Shifts in the Welfare Mix,* Vienna: Campus.

Finch, J. and Groves, D. (eds) (1983), *A Labour of Love: Women, Work and Caring,* London: Routledge & Kegan Paul.

Gauthier, A.H. (1996), *The State and the Family: A Comparative Analysis of Family Policies in Industrialized Countries,* Oxford: Clarendon Press.

Graham, H. (1993), 'Social divisions in caring', *Women's Studies International Forum,* 16 (6), 461–70.

Habermas, J. (1984), *The Theory of Communicative Action: Reason and the Rationalization of Society,* London: Heinemann Educational.

Hantrais, L. (1994), 'Comparing family policy in Britain, France and Germany', *Journal of Social Policy,* 23 (2), 135–60.

Hantrais, L. (1999), 'Contextualization in cross-national comparative research', *International Journal of Social Research Methodology,* 2 (2), 93–108.

Hernes, H.M. (1987), *Welfare State and Women Power. Essays in State Feminism,* Oslo: Universitetsforlaget.

Higgins, J. (1981), *States of Welfare. Comparative Analysis in Social Policy*, Oxford: Blackwell.

Hill, M. (2000), 'Who pays? Who provides? Towards a comparative approach to the study of social care', in B. Hudson (ed.), *The Changing Role of Social Care*, London: Jessica Kingsley Publishers.

Hobson, B. (1990), 'No exit, no voice. A comparative analysis of women's economic dependency and the welfare state', *Acta Sociologica*, **33** (3), 235–50.

Hochschild, A.R. (2000), 'The nanny chain', *The American Prospect*, **11** (4), 32–6.

Jamieson, A. (1991), 'Community care for older people. Policies in Britain, West Germany and Denmark', in G. Room (ed.), *Towards a European Welfare State*, Bristol: SAUS, pp. 107–26.

Johnson, N. (1987), *The Welfare State in Transition: The Theory and Practice of Welfare Pluralism*, Amherst: University of Massachusetts Press.

Kamerman, S.B. and Kahn, A.J. (eds) (1997), *Family Change and Family Policies in Great Britain, Canada, New Zealand and the United States*, Oxford: Clarendon Press.

Knapp, M. (1989), 'Private and voluntary welfare', in M. McCarthy (ed.) *The New Politics of Welfare: An Agenda for the 1990s?*, London: Macmillan, pp. 225–52.

Knijn, T. and Kremer, M. (1997), 'Gender and the caring dimension of welfare states: toward inclusive citizenship', *Social Politics*, **4** (3), 328–61.

Kröger, T. (1997), 'The dilemma of municipalities: Scandinavian approaches to child day care provision', *Journal of Social Policy*, **26** (4), 485–508.

Langan, M. and Ostner, I. (1991), 'Gender and welfare: Towards a comparative framework', in G. Room (ed.), *Towards a European Welfare State*, Bristol: SAUS, pp. 127–50.

Leira, A. (1992), *Welfare States and Working Mothers. The Scandinavian Experience*, Cambridge: Cambridge University Press.

Lewis, J. (1992), 'Gender and the development of welfare regimes', *Journal of European Social Policy*, **2** (3), 159–73.

Lewis, J. (ed.) (1994), *Women and Social Policies in Europe: Work, Family and the State*, Aldershot: Edward Elgar.

Lewis, J. (ed.) (1998), *Gender, Social Care and Welfare State Restructuring in Europe*, Aldershot: Ashgate.

Mabbett, D. and Bolderson, H. (1999), 'Theories and methods in comparative social policy', in J. Clasen (ed.), *Comparative Social Policy: Concepts, Theories and Methods*, Oxford: Blackwell, pp. 34–56.

Midre, G. (1995), *Bot, bedring eller brød? Om bedømming of behandling av sosial nød fra reformasjonen til velferdsstaten*, Oslo: Universitetsforlaget.

Millar, J. and Warman, A. (1996), *Family Obligations in Europe*, London: Family Policy Studies Centre.

Orloff, A.S. (1993), 'Gender and the social rights of citizenship: the comparative analysis of gender relations and welfare states', *American Sociological Review*, **58** (3), 303–328.

Sainsbury, D. (ed.) (1994), *Gendering Welfare States*, London: Sage.

Siim, B. (1994), 'The gendered Scandinavian welfare states: the interplay between women's roles as mothers, workers and citizens in Denmark', in J. Lewis (ed.), *Women and Social Policies in Europe: Work, Family and the State*, Aldershot, UK and Brookfield, USA: Edward Elgar, pp. 25–48.

Sipilä, J., Andersson, M., Hammarqvist, S.-E., Nordlander, L., Rauhala, P.-L., Thomsen, K. and Warming Nielsen, H. (1997), 'A multitude of universal, public services: how and why did four Scandinavian countries get their social service model?', in J. Sipilä (ed.), *Social Care Services: The Key to the Scandinavian Welfare Model*, Aldershot: Avebury, pp. 27–50.

Stjernø, S. (1995), *Mellom kirke og kapital*, Oslo: Universitetsforlaget.

Szebehely, M. (1999), 'Omsorgsarbetets olika former: nya klasskillnader och gamla könsmönster i äldreomsorgen', *Sosiologisk Forskning*, 36 (1), 7–32.

Thomas, C. (1993), 'De-constructing concepts of care', *Sociology*, 27 (4), 649–69.

Tronto, J.C. (1995), 'Women and caring: what can feminists learn about morality from caring', in V. Held (ed.), *Justice and Care: Essential Readings in Feminist Ethics*, Boulder: Westview Press, pp. 101–15.

Ungerson, C. (1987), *Policy is Personal: Sex, Gender and Informal Care*, London: Tavistock.

Ungerson, C. (1990), 'The language of care: crossing the boundaries', in C. Ungerson (ed.) *Gender and Caring: Work and Welfare in Britain and Scandinavia*, Hemel Hempstead: Harvester Wheatsheaf, pp. 8–33.

Waerness, K. (1978), 'The invisible welfare state: women's work at home', *Acta Sociologica*, Special Congress Supplement, 'The Nordic Welfare States', 21, 193–225.

Waerness, K. (1984a), 'Caring as women's work in the welfare state', in H. Holter (ed.), *Patriarchy in a Welfare Society*, Oslo: Universitetsforlaget, pp. 67–87.

Waerness, K. (1984b), 'The rationality of caring', *Economic and Industrial Democracy*, 5, 185–211.

Wistow, G., Knapp, M., Hardy, B. and Allen, C. (1994), *Social Care in a Mixed Economy*, Buckingham: Open University Press.

2. Social Care in Finland: Stronger and Weaker Forms of Universalism

Teppo Kröger, Anneli Anttonen and Jorma Sipilä

INTRODUCTION

This chapter seeks to place Finnish social care provision in its social, cultural and political contexts. There are particular factors in Finland's twentieth century historical and cultural development that have impacted on the evolution and character of its social care services: war, both civil and external; rapid urbanization; high levels of women's participation in the labour market and in political life; and a distinctively consensual national culture.

Finland is usually classified as one of the Scandinavian (or Nordic) welfare states together with Denmark, Norway and Sweden. Although geographically and linguistically separate, Finland is indeed politically and culturally Scandinavian. Compared with other 'welfare states', Scandinavian systems have been characterized as going beyond a reliance on income transfers to placing greater emphasis on public production and consumption (Kosonen, 1987). Most of all they are presented as distinctive in providing universalist social care. They are 'social service states' rather than merely 'social insurance states' (Anttonen, 1997). Public social care services, largely provided by local authorities, are widely available, particularly for children and older people, and are used by all classes including the better off (Sipilä et al., 1997). While describing how Finnish social care services have developed out of the particular circumstances of the nation's social and political history, this chapter questions the degree to which they are uniquely Finnish and, in addition, how far they are truely universalist.

Many definitions of universalism are available in the social policy literature. For example, according to Therborn (1995, p. 97), *universal rights* 'entitle all citizens or residents to social services and income security, determined only by their position in the human life-cycle'. In contrast, *particularist rights* are specific to occupational and other distinct social groups, usually defined as more needy or more deserving than others. An essential characteristic of universalist programmes is that they are intended not only for the poor but provide for all citizens in a society. Within the universalistic programmes of social democratic welfare regimes 'all benefit, all are dependent, and all will presumably feel obliged to pay' (Esping-Andersen, 1990, p. 28). Thus a distinctive quality of universalist social policies is that, once adopted, they become highly popular and reversing them is politically impossible, or at least problematic. However, constructing universal policies is equally complicated, requiring near consensus between the main political players at key historical turning points. The compromises necessary are rare in any nation's politics.

What exactly does universalism mean in the particular arena of social care? The concept is often used loosely, without specifying its detailed content. Here, building on a definition originally provided by Sainsbury (1988), we suggest that, within the provision of social care services, universalism requires six qualities:

1. there is a public system providing social care services,
2. this system offers uniform services across the nation,
3. services are available to all citizens, irrespective of their economic status, gender or ethnic background,
4. access to services is guaranteed in terms of explicit social rights,
5. services are delivered free at the point of use; and
6. the services are actually used by a clear majority of the citizens who need them.

Universalism is strong when all or nearly all of these dimensions apply and, correspondingly, it is weak where only some are fulfilled. The main question addressed in this chapter is the extent to which the Finnish system meets these tests of universalism in two key areas: the care of small children and support for older people. Is the Finnish model universalist and to what extent? A brief historical analysis will argue that services for older people still carry the legacy of poor relief, while services for children and families are entirely modern, having been constructed almost from scratch in the 1970s.

THE HISTORICAL ROOTS OF FINNISH SOCIAL CARE

The Emergence of the Nation and the State

Contemporary patterns of social care in Finland are mainly products of the post-war period, but key foundations developed much earlier. Some aspects can be traced back to the Reformation. Other important sources include the chronic historical persistence of large-scale poverty, the distinctive agrarianism of the society and the specific character of Finnish nationalist movements. The formation of the modern nation state was also influenced by the class-based civil war of 1918. Of particular significance has been the role of central government and the municipalities. The poor law tradition brought the municipalities into the centre of social service development. Overall therefore, there are many historical roots to the Finnish welfare state in addition to the consequences of social democracy and the influence of trade unions, the two sources most frequently mentioned in explanations of the 'politics matters' variety.

As in much of northern Europe, the Reformation was the origin of the development of state responsibility for welfare, separating civil authority from the church and also encouraging the growth of mutuality in the form of guilds and fraternities which set up early types of social insurance. However, the Finnish experience was distinctive in that the development of the nation state was delayed, first by the hegemony of the Kingdom of Sweden which lasted from the twelfth century until 1809 and which created a small Swedish-speaking ruling élite, and second because this was followed by Russian domination until the collapse of the Russian empire in 1917. Finnish nationalism therefore developed in a specific context which encouraged solidarity among all Finnish speakers and an identification of the state as potentially representing the interests of all the people. Élites were small and wealth a rare phenomenon. Most people lived in poverty in rural areas and practised agriculture either as independent or tenant farmers. The class that grew most rapidly during the nineteenth century was the so-called 'landless people', most of whom were itinerant farm workers (Jaakkola, 1994, pp. 85–6; Pulma, 1994, pp. 51–5). Famines were frequent and the labour of women was crucial for the incomes of families (Markkola, 1990). The famines of 1867 and 1868 were national disasters that embedded in the culture an awareness of the value of collective action.

In the second half of the nineteenth century a variety of people's movements and collective organizations developed, including the temperance movement, numerous workers' associations, youth clubs and women's societies. This period in Finland's history is generally seen as the source of strong civic activity leading finally to national independence (Alapuro and Stenius, 1987). The cooperative movements were synonymous with nationalism and ultimately with the state. Sulkunen (1990, pp. 48–9) describes how women took an active part in nationwide popular movements. In this way the concept of a democratic citizenship providing equality for all members of society developed. It was expressed not only in terms of civil and political rights, but included a strong moral commitment to the welfare of the whole nation. The Fennomanian nationalist movement was strongly influenced by a Hegelian conception of state that looked beyond the civil society and its egoistic individuals.

A central achievement of the nationalist movement was the parliamentary reform of 1906 whereby all adult men and women were given universal and equal suffrage in national elections and the right to stand for elective office as well (Sulkunen, 1996). Finnish women were the first to win the vote in Europe (and third in the world). However, these gains, in terms of an association of nationalism with civic and gender equality, received a major setback as a result of the civil war of 1918 in which the mass of the population was effectively defeated by the ruling class and its supporters. Consequently, the influence of trade unions and left-wing parties was severely constrained during the 1920s and 1930s. The ruling class was able to use the state apparatus, at both central and local levels, to maintain a society that reflected its own, untypical, hierarchical ideals. The full fruits of national solidarity were thus delayed.

The Welfare Mix of the Late Nineteenth Century

The famines of the 1860s obliged the state to construct more coordinated forms of poor relief. As in many other European countries, the model was that of the Victorian Poor Law: the construction of poorhouses with admission determined by a harsh 'workhouse test'. In the three decades from 1880, 240 workhouses were constructed by the municipalities, funded by cheap loans from central government (Jaakkola, 1994, pp. 113–17; Kröger, 1996, pp. 36–41; Pulma, 1995, pp. 102–4). An older practice of contracting out to farmers the care of orphan children and dependent older people fell into decline.

The workhouse quickly created new problems, particularly the mixing of a wide variety of the dispossessed, and they became out of date almost as soon as they were built. In 1922 a new poor law reflected changes in moral and professional, largely medical, perspectives and the workhouses became 'municipal homes' and increasingly occupied only by older people. Other and growing areas of social welfare were left to the charities and to the central state. As in Britain, the golden age of charitable giving and organization coincided with the industrialization and urbanization processes of the second half of the nineteenth century. Many voluntary organizations were run by the wives of the bourgeoisie, others were funded and managed by working-class self-help societies (Jaakkola, 1994, pp. 144–5).

Social services that were later adopted by the public sector were first set up through voluntary initiatives. The charities took the lead in establishing children's services, mainly in the form of institutional care. In the 1860s full-day crèches appeared in Helsinki to help working-class mothers take up paid work (Pulma, 1987, p. 90). The first kindergartens appeared in the 1880s, run by private individuals and voluntary associations, some influenced by feminist ideals. The voluntary sector also began to expand into provision for older and disabled persons.

After the trauma of the civil war of 1918, the 1920s and 1930s were a time of stagnation for Finnish social policy. Local social welfare services were limited to the building of 'municipal homes' for older people and the stigmatizing means testing of poor families (Satka, 1995). Initiatives in social services, where they occurred at all, took place within the voluntary sector. By the end of the 1920s, almost all of the few crèches and kindergartens had been set up by the voluntary sector (Pulma, 1987, pp. 173, 190). Yet by 1939 many of the crèches had been taken into municipal control (Jaakkola, 1994, pp. 143–158; Pulma, 1987, pp. 173–4; Satka, 1994, pp. 261–89). Public day-care provision existed only in the larger towns. In the rest of the country the only source of care services for children were those provided by large employers such as some lumber companies (Koskinen, 1989; Kröger, 1999).

However, these historical facts describing the relative roles of the state, municipal, voluntary and private company sectors in the provision of social services do not carry the same meaning as they would in Britain or the United States. Within the Finnish conception of nationhood the perceived gap between government and citizen was much smaller. Hegelian political theory, always strong in Finland, conceives of the state as essentially a community joined by equal citizens and as having a fundamental integrative function above individuals and class interests. Voluntary associations worked closely with local government and were often largely funded by it. These close ties, particularly at the municipal level would, after the Second World War, make the country particularly responsive to the ideals of Scandinavian social democracy and their emphasis on the role of the state as the main, even sole, source of social care services for all citizens.

POST-WAR CARE FOR OLDER PEOPLE: WEAK UNIVERSALISM

Incremental Policy Change

The Second World War accustomed the population to high levels of taxation, greater direction and intervention in all aspects of life by central government and increased mutual responsibility among citizens. During the war Finland was forced to make two disadvantageous peace treaties with the Russians. The need to defend their country tended to unite the people. Class cleavages were sharply reduced and a new, more corporatist 'contract' emerged between employers and workers, represented through their unions and other forms of association. Communists were readmitted to domestic politics and the parties of the far right were outlawed. The Social Democratic Party (SDP) and the agrarian Centre Party would govern for the next four decades. Conservatives lacked sufficient electoral support to play a role in government until the late 1980s.

At the end of the war the care and financial support of older people who continued to live in the community, rather than in a municipal home, remained essentially a family responsibility. The 1950s saw the beginning of changes that would redefine obligations between older people and their adult children. The state began to assume a larger role in both economic and social support for older people. The changes took place slowly and incrementally through a complex evolution of legislation and implementation practices. However, by 1970 adult children were no longer legally obliged to support their parents and retirement and old age were accepted as a phase of life which included rights to financial and social independence which were guaranteed by the state (Rauhala, 1996, pp. 114–19).

The economic independence of older people was founded on reforms in social insurance (Urponen, 1994, pp. 233–7). A new state pension scheme was introduced in 1956. It combined a universal flat-rate benefit with a means-tested supplement. By the 1960s this pension was substantially enhanced for many by earnings-related occupational pension schemes and the economic independence of most older people was secure. This was particularly true for men; widespread economic equality for women in retirement, based on full earnings-related pensions, is a very recent achievement.

One sign of their independence has been the rise in the number of older people continuing to live in their own households. In 1950 more than half of people over 65 lived with their children. Four decades later this had dropped to one in seven and the proportion of older people living alone had increased from one in five to one in three (Rostgaard and Fridberg, 1998). Most of these are women, particularly since life expectancy for men in Finland is markedly lower (OECD, 1996, pp. 18, 27). Clearly, when grandparents live separately from their children and grandchildren, the demand for both childcare and social care services is increased. This was so even among better-off families who had traditionally used privately hired domestic help or maids. The numbers of female domestic servants peaked in 1950 but by the 1970s they had effectively disappeared from Finland (Kauppinen, 1986).

From the 1950s public welfare institutions began admitting more than just the destitute. The Social Assistance Act of 1956 introduced a category of 'self-paying patients' to accompany 'welfare patients' in municipal homes. 'Self-supporting patients' paid a proportion of their fees while 'welfare patients' had most of their limited assets confiscated by the welfare authorities. However, the old poor relief thinking was not fully abandoned until 1982 when legislation required all care-home residents to pay up to 80 per cent of their pension and other income in fees for institutional care. In determining such fees, the assets of the resident (or of relatives) are not taken into account.

For a long time the municipal residential homes received little financial support from central government. This was in part because of the fact that they were not solely occupied by older people; in 1950, almost half the residents were under 65 (table 2.1). Consequently these institutions became increasingly old-fashioned and under-modernized. As local health care received generous central subsidies in the1960s and 1970s, a significant part of care responsibility for older people was transferred to the health sector. Unlike municipal residential institutions, privately run residential homes were from the beginning designed almost exclusively for older people (Table 2.1). In the 1950s and 1960s the number of places in private homes grew rapidly but private provision has remained limited, now contributing fewer than 15 per cent of all residential places for older people.

Table 2.1 Residents in publicly and privately run residential homes in Finland, 1950–1998 (in parentheses the proportion of residents over 65)

Year	Residents in public residential homes	Residents in private residential homes
1950	18,526 (53%)	1,024 (89%)*
1960	25,328 (64%)	2,531 (93%)
1970	31,696 (81%)	4,965 (na)
1980	31,597 (91%)	4,966 (na)
1990	27,821 (96%)	na
1998	21,423 (98%)	3,028 (96%)

Note: * 1951.

Sources: Kauppinen, 1998, pp. 3, 4; Rauhala, 1996b, p. 131; SOTKA.

The Integration of Voluntary and Informal Care

In the 1930s one of the voluntary organizations specializing in childcare began experimenting with home help. At the time, the 'home helps' were particularly used to support poor farming families, caring for the children and doing housework at times of childbirth or where mothers were in difficulty. Legislation allowed central funding for local authority home helps from 1950. After 1956 they began to be used to assist older and disabled people as well as families.

The service was further expanded by a key piece of legislation, the Municipal Home Help Act 1966, which permitted increased funding including that of 'home help assistants' to supplement the more expensive and professionally trained home helps. The work of the assistant home helps was particularly focused on older people (Simonen, 1990). Rauhala (1996a, pp. 153–64) has analysed the political history of the act and shown how it won the support of all the main political parties. Rauhala describes the Municipal Home Help Act as the first truly universalist piece of social care legislation permitting help to be provided to all families with small children and to older people in need of support in their everyday lives.

Home help services, together with home nursing, 'meals on wheels' and other auxiliary services have become the core of community care services for older and disabled people. The numbers of home help personnel have grown steadily (Table 2.2). The expansion is a product of the rising numbers of older people over 65, particularly of older women living on their own. While the municipal home help services are of great importance to many older people the universalist ideology behind them has never been completely realized. Demand

Table 2.2 Publicly employed home helps, home help assistants and households receiving home help services in Finland, 1971–1998

Year	Home helps	Home help assistants	Households receiving home help
1971	2,327	1,581	108,490
1980	3,427	4,356	167,762
1990	6,063	5,983	201,837
1998	13,700*		126,422

Note: * Figures are not available separately for home helps and home help assistants for 1998.

Sources: Rauhala, 1996b, p. 142; SOTKA database; STAKES, 2000, pp. 9, 26.

has always grown faster than supply. Consequently home help services have continued to be rationed and targeted by professionals through the use of needs tests. Assessments continue to take account of people's access to informal, family support. In practice, therefore, there is no absolute entitlement either to domiciliary or residential care services for older people in Finland.

The role of non-state providers has remained significant, not in volume but in terms of new initiatives and innovations. Voluntary non-profit organizations have led the development of new forms and methods of services, which tend then to be taken up by central and local authorities. In the 1950s comparisons with standards in private residential homes encouraged the reform of the municipal welfare institutions. The very idea of home help services was originally developed within the voluntary sector. More recently, the concept of service housing has been successfully marketed by not-for-profit providers.

Non-profit organizations have always worked in close cooperation with the public sector. Since the early 1980s these links have become even closer as most services provided by voluntary organizations are now purchased by local authorities and not by individual users. Many of the not-for-profit service providers are also supported by funds from the quasi-independent Slot Machine Association.[1] In these ways, voluntary service provision for older people has become heavily integrated with, and often indistinguishable from, public provision.

Home care allowances (HCAs) have become an important source of support allowing older, disabled and chronically ill people to remain in the community. These benefits are delivered by local authorities who have wide discretion in how they do so. No law actually requires local authorities to pay HCAs, but from the late 1970s municipalities began paying them to relatives of frail older and disabled people who needed regular help and attendance. By 1989 the allowances were in use in every Finnish municipality. Sipilä and Simon (1993, p. 128), have argued that Finnish payment-for-care policies are particularly open and non-restrictive. Care-givers and care-receivers need not be related in any way. There are no income or capital tests limiting payments. However, in practice, the carers are almost always either spouses (one-third) or other close relatives (two thirds). Four-fifths of HCA payments are to women (Antikainen and Vaarama, 1995).

By the 1990s Finnish home care allowances for carers of older people were among the most comprehensive in Europe (Sipilä and Korpinen, 1998). Yet, they still reach the carers of no more than 2 per cent of the over 65 population. Most informal caring continues to take place without any financial support from central or local authorities and the coverage of HCA payments is much less than that of home help services or residential care. The payments are too modest to motivate anyone to become a carer (the average monthly payment was €290 in 1998). In practice, the effect of HCAs is to encourage relatives to continue with care-giving work they have already begun without financial support and so limit demand for formal services. It has been estimated that two out of three of those whose care has been supported under the scheme would otherwise have entered an institution (Antikainen and Vaarama, 1995).

Commenting on the Finnish home care allowance scheme, Glendinning and McLaughlin (1993, p. 245) have made the interesting observation that, in principle, it offers a cheaper alternative to direct service provision and therefore a route to real universalism. This 'universalism' is to an extent undermined by the large variations in the ways in which municipalities implement the HCA policy. The limited coverage of the benefit also means that its contribution towards universal provision remains, at most, mediocre. However, the potential for universalism is at least implicit in the idea of combining formal service provisions with payment-for-care benefits.

Overall the pattern of development of Finnish social care for older people has been one of growing variety and flexibility. The early emphasis on institutional care for poor and isolated older people, has given way to care in the community often based on innovations developed in the voluntary sector. No strong ideological or political constraints exist to limit the integration of public provision with that provided by the informal and the voluntary sectors.

THE CURRENT PATTERN OF SOCIAL CARE FOR OLDER PEOPLE

At the start of the 1990s, Finland entered a deep economic recession. A rapid rise in unemployment substantially increased state expenditure on social security payments. The jobless rate quickly reached a record level of 20 per cent. Losses in the banking sector were substantial and had, in large part, to be met by the state. All this caused a significant state budget deficit requiring restrictions on central and local government expenditure. The speed of the downturn, caused by a combination of world recession and the loss of Finland's markets in the Soviet Union, was deeply shocking to both the electorate and politicians. By the mid-1990s many social policy experts were suggesting that the era of the 'generous' Scandinavian welfare state was over.

However, economic recovery after 1994 was almost as fast. By 2000, the unemployment rate had fallen back to the average OECD level at around 10 per cent and the public sector accounts were in better balance than in most other EU countries. The political climate and the public's spending behaviour had regained much, if not all, of their former optimism. One result of this experience is that Finnish social and economic statistics for the 1990s can be very misleading. The patterns they 'reveal' depend very much on the base years used.

Institutional care has traditionally been the core of welfare services for older people in Finland. Thus the proportion of older people living in institutions has been somewhat higher than in most other European countries. In the early 1990s the figure was around 7 per cent of those aged 65 and over (including long-term hospital care but excluding those in 'service housing' (OECD, 1996, p. 48) but by 1998 it had dropped to 5 per cent (Table 2.3). The fall was the result of a determined deinstitutionalization policy.

The figures show that in 1998 there were almost equal numbers of older people in the long-term 'hospitals' run by the public health care authorities as there were in care institutions run by municipalities. This balance is continuing to shift away from hospital care.

Table 2.3   Use of care services for older people in Finland in 1998 (per cent of age group)[a]

Type of provision	65–74 year-olds	75–84 year-olds	85+ year-olds	All 65+ year-olds
Hospitals	1	2	7	2
Residential care	1	3	14	3
Service housing	1	3	8	2
Home help[b]	7	26[b]		15
Home care allowance	1	2	5	2
Total	11	42[b]		24

Notes
a   Includes services purchased by local authorities. An older person may receive more than one service.
b   As a proportion of older person households.

Source: SOTKA.

In the case of domiciliary home help, until recently Finland appeared to provide the most generous provision in the world. In 1990 more than 20 per cent of the over 65 population were in receipt of service (OECD, 1996, p. 62). By 1998 this figure had fallen to 15 per cent (Table 2.3). The volume of resources has not been reduced but eligibility criteria and needs assessments for these services have become considerably stricter. Domiciliary home care services are now focused on the very old and frail people whose numbers are rising. Consequently those who earlier might have expected services can no longer obtain them. Within the home help sector, non-governmental provision is increasing its share. Non-profit and for-profit providers now provide about 20 per cent of all home help services in Finland (Kauppinen, 1998).

The only publicly funded service for older people that expanded rapidly in the 1990s was 'service housing'. It has tripled in a decade, covering over 2 per cent of the over-65 population in 1998. The nature of this provision varies but largely consists of serviced flats where residents can make use of those aspects of the provision they need or prefer. The flats may be owner-occupied or rented. Half are provided by the independent sector, mainly non-profit organizations supported by grants from the Slot Machine Association. A large proportion of the supply of service housing is rented directly by the local authorities. Genuinely commercial social care provision has been very rare in Finland. Most 'independent' provision is by the voluntary sector. However, even in many of these cases finance has been arranged by the local authorities in the form of building grants from the Slot Machine Association. Thus, a large part of this provision is really no more than 'quasi-private'.

Despite the generosity of the care system in terms of international comparisons, most help for older people continues to come from immediate families and close relatives. The perception of a comprehensive public system has meant that research into informal care was neglected, resulting in a lack of information compared with that available in some other industrial nations. There is recent evidence that the decline in coverage of formal provision is leading to more informal help. Forss et al. (1995) discovered that children are by far the most important source of help for older people (Table 2.4) though the home help service remains particularly important for women. Men are more likely to have a living spouse to help them.

Further research in 1994 and 1998 has demonstrated the growing importance of informal care (STM, 1994; 1999). Among those over 60 in 1994 only 26 per cent of those who needed daily help said they got it primarily from their spouses. The proportion had risen to 50 per cent in 1998. Moreover, the same study confirmed the changing role of home help services. As a primary source of help, the domiciliary services had dropped from the second to the third place. Among the over 80s the use of home care and home nursing services had dropped by 13 per cent; among those 61–70 it had fallen by 70 per cent (STM, 1999, p. 51).

The degree to which older people enjoy universal social care support is therefore ambiguous. While there are no explicit rights to these services,

Table 2.4 Sources of help named by people 65 and over, Finland, 1994

Source of help*	Women	Men	All
Children	59	52	57
Home help	36	23	33
Relatives	21	14	19
Spouse	9	39	17
Neighbours	15	16	16
Friends	16	10	15
Total	156	154	157
Number	311	100	411

Note: * Respondents could name several sources.

Source: Forss et al., 1995, p. 61.

provision is generous in international terms and those with high needs can always turn to public or publicly supported assistance. Charges are made for services but the interaction of these with the pension systems means that users are not pauperized through their use. However, it is also true that those with lesser needs are more often using only family and spouse support as formal services are increasingly targeted on those with higher needs.

There are other ways in which the classic Scandinavian universalism has been modified in the 1990s. Local authorities have been given more discretion in devising needs tests and in setting charges, leading to greater regional variation in the supply of publicly supported services. As access to public services has become more conditional so a small market in care consumerism is beginning to appear. There is now greater public awareness that informal and family support plays a main role. In these senses a universalism, which may never truly have existed, has been modified.

POST-WAR CHILDCARE: A STRONGER UNIVERSALISM

The Construction of a Comprehensive System of Public Day Care

Universalism in support for children and families emerged after the Second World War. It appeared in the form of universal child allowances in 1949. Administration and payment of the allowances was delegated to local authorities, taking their responsibility beyond the tradition of poor relief. This was a significant step change in administrative function. From then on, central government started to view local authorities as appropriate for the implementation of nationwide welfare policies (Kröger, 1996; 1997).

Nevertheless, it was a long time before universalism was to dominate childcare policy. Arguments for public day care were first presented at the turn of the century (Rauhala, 1996). But by the 1950s the provision of municipal kindergartens and crèches was still fragmented. As in much of Europe, the provision of crèches was limited to a form of preventive poor relief, allowing single mothers and those from low-income households to do paid work. Kindergartens, where they existed, had educational goals and were usually run by the voluntary sector.

However, the situation changed dramatically in the 1960s in the wake of rapid economic and social change. The country moved quickly from a predominantly agrarian to an industrial/service society. Industry and the service sector boomed absorbing more of the available workforce, both male and female. The 1960s and 1970s changed the geographical distribution of the population. At the start of the 1960s only a third of the Finnish population lived in towns. A decade later the urban population exceeded that in the country.

The 1960s also saw heated debate about gender roles. The new women's movement demanded opportunities for women to engage in paid work on equal terms with men and public childcare was regarded as a precondition for this. However, Raija Julkunen (1994, p. 195) has shown that mothers with small children were moving into the labour market before child support became available. By 1973, 64 per cent of women aged between 14 and 65 years were in the active labour force and only 11 per cent of those had part-time jobs. An unusually low percentage of part-time employment among women has been a distinctive and permanent characteristic of the Finnish labour market. In this respect, Finland differs from Sweden and Norway as well as most other countries (Miettinen, 1997). Full-time paid labour of women forms the essential context of Finnish childcare policies.

Vappu Tyyskä (1994, p. 98) has pointed out how Finnish politics has been characterized by women's ability to exert pressure from within the state political structure. This is linked to the comparatively strong representation of women in parliament. During the 1960s, the proportion of women in the Finnish parliament rose from 15 to 22 per cent. This appears to be related to the system of proportional representation and its effects on the distribution of power among political parties. No single party has been able to govern alone. No party has won the hegemonic position of social democrats in the other Nordic countries. Instead, a continuous search for coalitions and consensus has characterized the Finnish political life at the national level. Most welfare state reforms have been produced by coalitions of the agrarian-based Centre Party and the Social Democratic Party, often supported also by far-left socialists. These patterns appear to have provided special opportunities for women and women's issues to come to the fore.

Another characteristic of policy making in Finland has been that social policies have, to a large extent, been negotiated between the state and the labour market organizations. Trade unions, employer organizations and agricultural cooperatives have all sought to secure particular social policy interests. Because women have formed almost a half of the workforce and half the membership of trade unions, these have, to some extent, had to advocate women's interests.

From the 1960s onwards finding ways to assist working women with young children became a priority. Childminders were difficult to find because of the other employment opportunities available. Migration from the countryside to towns and cities made it difficult to rely on grandparents or other relatives. Women wanted paid work and employers needed them for skilled and unskilled jobs. All these factors combined to make day care one of the most debated social policy issues of the 1960s and early 1970s.

Two forms of proposal dominated the debate. Social democrats, supported by women's organizations, argued for a nationwide network of children's day-care institutions (literally 'day-homes'). These were to provide mainly full-time care to pre-school children of those families where both parents were in paid work, professional education or vocational training. Unlike the kindergartens, the day-care centres would combine educational goals with the need for all-day, everyday care, and unlike crèches, they would address their services to all families with small children not just those with special needs.

The Centre Party proposed a 'mother's wage'. This would be a flat-rate allowance to be paid to all mothers of small children. Using the allowance, families would be able to decide themselves who they wanted to have looking after their children. By arguing for a mother's wage, the Centre Party was trying to safeguard the interests of its rural constituency, which remained largely outside waged labour. The proposal also appealed to low-paid mothers.

Following a series of political bargains and compromises, the first National Day Care Act of 1973 came to include elements of both ideas: local authorities were required either to set up day-care centres or 'supervised family day care', that is, to employ and manage childminders working from their own homes. Local authorities were free to choose between these two service forms. Many rural districts favoured family day care. However, most municipalities eventually provided both options.

The National Day Care Act was legislated by a coalition that excluded the Centre Party and their demand for a flat-rate care allowance (Rauhala, 1996a, pp. 164–75). Instead in rural areas municipal day-care provision was heavily subsidized by central grants that could cover as much as 80 per cent of the running costs. In major cities the grant was only 35 per cent.

The act led to the rapid expansion of provision (Table 2.5). By the 1980s no needs tests were applied for the use of municipal day care. By 1990 provision had almost reached the levels of Sweden and Denmark (Kröger, 1997, pp. 492, 496–7). However, the recession of the early 1990s caused a clear, if temporary, break to this development and family day care declined sharply. Growth had resumed by 1998.

Generous local authority childcare services have left very little room for private provision. In 1974 private providers employed 20 per cent of all personnel in children's day care. This had shrunk to 3 per cent by 1990 (Päivärinta, 1993, p. 51).

The Extension of Public Funding to Support Parenting

In 1985 further legislation took Finland a unique step further than any other nation in public support for childcare. By moving from the funding of childcare in nurseries and by childminders to paying parents directly, the state arrived at a position where it actually funds parenthood itself. At the time, there were still some shortages of day-care places as local authorities could not fully meet the

Table 2.5 Places in publicly funded day care for children in Finland,
1965–1998

Year	Day-care centres	Family day care	Total
1965	19,750	0	19,750
1970	28,195	0	28,195
1975	60,220	21,800	82,020
1980	83,670	47,970	131,640
1985	103,400	76,670	180,070
1990	118,030	95,850	213,880
1995	125,031	65,580	190,611
1998	142,776	75,746	218,524

Sources: Ilmakunnas, 1993, p. 17; Muuri and Vihma, 1991, p. 2; Muuri, 1994, p. 15; SOTKA;
STAKES, 1998, p. 7.

demand. This was largely because trained staff were hard to find. The debate
about the fairness of the 1973 Act had rumbled on. In particular the Centre Party
argued that families who did not use public day-care services should be compensated for doing their own childcare. In place of the older demand for a
mother's wage appeared the idea of a children's home care allowance.

The 1985 Act consisted of two major parts. In addition to requiring local
authorities to provide day-care places, the law created a legal entitlement to a
day-care place for all children under three. This right became effective in 1990
and in 1996 it was extended to all children under school age, that is under seven.
The second part of the reform was no less radical. In return for supporting the
first part, the Centre Party secured the backing of the other parties for a Child
Home Care Allowance (CHCA) for those who did not take up a day-care place.
Parents could choose the CHCA cash instead and use it to support their own
day-parenting or to pay for private care (Sipilä and Korpinen, 1998, p. 263). To
enable the first option either parent also won the right to take care leave until the
child reached three, after which the parent is entitled to return to her/his previous work.

CHCA quickly became popular (Table 2.6). By 1987 the number of families
choosing the allowance surpassed the number of children in the age group in
public day care. The peak years in the popularity of the CHCA were in the early
1990s, when unemployment was rising and the allowance was at its highest
value. Fifty per cent of children under three were then covered by the CHCA
(Sipilä and Korpinen, 1998, pp. 267–8).

Table 2.6 Childcare support for children under three in Finland, 1985–1998

Year	Children in day care	Children in family day care	Day care total	Families on CHCA	Children under 3 on CHCA
1985	13,103	27,299	40,402	25,890	na
1990	17,594	25,173	42,767	81,210	na
1993	15,488	16,139	31,627	95,820	103,360
1995	16,392	16,296	32,688	84,476	89,807
1998	18,745	22,245	40,990	74,359	80,683

Note: The 1997 reforms mean later figures are not wholly comparable. Until 1992 figures are for families and not children.

Sources: Sipilä and Korpinen, 1998, p. 268; Kela, 1996, p. 207; 1997, p. 54; 1998, p. 57; STM, 1998, p. 2.

Families were able to use the CHCA to buy private childcare though only 5 per cent of the recipient families did so by 1997 (Rostgaard and Fridberg, 1998, p. 250). In that year a new benefit was created, the Children's Private Care Allowance (CPCA) to be used by those families who preferred to purchase privately. The introduction of the CPCA demonstrated that private childcare provision was now openly encouraged by the Finnish welfare state — a novel step in that country if not in many others. However, only 1 per cent of childcare places are currently provided by the private sector.

THE CURRENT PATTERN OF CHILDCARE PROVISION

In Finland, childcare support is now universally available and since 1996 has been a social right for parents (or guardians) of children under school age. Yet nothing close to every Finnish child is cared for in publicly funded day care: in 1998, 65 per cent of those aged between three and six and 24 per cent aged up to three (Table 2.7).

In the European context, the second figure is quite high, even though in Sweden and Denmark nearly half of children under three were in public day care in 1996 (NOSOSKO (Nordic Social-Statistical Committee), 1998). However, in the older age group the coverage of Finnish day-care provision is internationally low, not only in comparison to Scandinavia but also to countries like France, Belgium, Germany and Italy where nearly all children over three are provided for (Rostgaard and Fridberg, 1998).

Table 2.7 Pre-school children in publicly financed day care in Finland, 1998 (per cent of age group)*

Type of care	Part-time	Full-time	All	Part-time	Full-time	All	Part-time	Full-time	All
	0–2-year-olds			3–6-year-olds			All 0–6-year-olds		
Day-care centres	0.4	10	11	9	36	46	6	26	31
Childminders	1	12	13	2	17	19	2	15	17
Total	1.4	22	24	11	53	65	8	39	48

Note: * Due to rounding up, the totals do not always match.

Source: SOTKA.

Nevertheless, the Finnish provision is distinct from the (often part-time) pre-school provision of those other countries. The Finnish services are a specific sort of 'educare' where schooling is present but secondary. The primary aim is social, to provide adequate care for children whose parents (or the sole parent) are working or studying full-time. Consequently, full-time care clearly outnumbers part-time provision. Nursery care is also complemented by publicly organized childminding that is an integral part of the day-care provision. Most of the under threes are with childminders.

On the other hand Finnish parents have had two quite exceptional rights: a choice between municipal day care or, if they decide not to use it, the right to a payment for care, the CHCA. The use of the CHCA has fallen from its peak in the early 1990s. As a result of the improving employment situation, the demand for day care has risen again and correspondingly, the number of children on the allowance has fallen. Moreover, in 1996 the government, led by the Social Democrats, cut the level of the CHCA by more than 20 per cent and this reduced its appeal considerably. However, even by the end of 1998, 45 per cent of children under three were cared for through this benefit and mainly at home (Table 2.6). Day care covered 24 per cent.

Thus, a clear majority (three-quarters) of Finnish children under three are cared for at home as are a third of those aged three to six. Family care remains the dominant form. Furthermore, although one of the explicit aims of the childcare reforms was to promote gender equality, very few men take parental leave or claim CHCA. Most pre-school children in Finland are looked after by their mothers. This is a somewhat surprising result that seems at odds with the image of Finland as a woman-friendly, Scandinavian welfare state based on the dual-breadwinner model.

However, the dual-breadwinner model is indeed alive and well, because Finnish social and labour market policies have been drafted to make women's temporary absence from paid work feasible. Under the current rules, a worker may leave work until the youngest child turns three and the whole period the parent is supported by either maternal/parental leave benefits or home care allowances. The right to return to one's job is guaranteed. Effectively the parent never leaves the labour market completely and is merely absent from work for a few years.

In principle, these policies are supposed to be gender neutral but in practice they have not attracted men. Gendered assumptions about male and female roles and responsibilities in society have directed the choices of parents. Although full-time paid work is a well-established part of the female role in Finland, full-time informal childcare has not become an accepted part of the male role. Men still on average earn more than women and thus disadvantageous labour market effects still accumulate for women as temporary absences from paid work weaken career prospects and entitlements to earnings-related social benefits.

Finnish mothers are, however, more likely to return to work than those in many other nations. The number of women staying at home after their youngest child turns three is internationally very low (Salmi, 2000). Moreover, as the option of part-time work does not really exist in Finland, women re-enter full-time work and so need to use children's day-care services.

It is clear that the provision of public support for childcare constitutes a strong form of universalism. Most of the criteria set out at the beginning of the chapter are met: near uniformity across the country; support available to all who wish to use it; and a right to day care if not to a particular facility. However, the day care is not delivered free of charge. Parents pay an income-related fee, though it is heavily subsidized (in 2001 the maximum monthly fee for day care was about €185).

It is the parents themselves who undermine the universality of Finnish childcare provision. Only a minority of families with children under three actually use day care. Of children aged three to six, whose counterparts in many European countries are universally in some form of early schooling, a third are still at home. Thus, daycare provision does not cover a clear majority of young children. In this sense the universalist character of the Finnish child daycare provision is reduced, but only because of the universal availability of another benefit which is almost unknown elsewhere — guaranteed payments by the state to cover the costs of childcare at home.

COMPARING THE CARE SYSTEMS FOR CHILDREN AND FOR OLDER PEOPLE

The Finnish experience highlights the limitations and paradoxes that can be thrown up by the classic distinctions between *universalist* and *particularist* social care systems. Finland is among those nations where a relatively high proportion of the retired population use social care services or facilities (Anttonen and Sipilä, 1996). Yet its social policies for older people appear backward compared with those directed at childcare. In the Nordic context Finland has been a laggard in extending social entitlements to older people (Sipilä et al., 1997, p. 36). And in terms of its childcare policies, it also distinct from Denmark and Sweden in providing universal payments that result in a high proportion of children being cared for at home by their parents.

Table 2.8 seeks to highlight some key differences in provision for childcare compared with that for elder-care.

Table 2.8 Key characteristics of social care for older people and for children

Care for older people	Care for children
Roots in nineteenth century local poor relief	Roots in late twentieth century centralism
Evolutionary historical development	Clean-break historical development
Policy consensus	Policies contested
Larger role for non-state providers	Minimal role for non-state providers
Few legal entitlements	Clear legal entitlements
Supplier-led rationing of services	Demand-led supply of services
Poverty tests	Income-related charges
Social class bias in take-up	Cross-class take-up
Weak universalism	Strong universalism

Similarities, Differences and Explanations

Comparing the development of social care for older people and day care for children in Finland, obvious similarities can be identified. Both sets of services originated in one way or another within the poor relief tradition, although voluntary organizations have also played a major role in starting and developing

services. Both service traditions have subsequently sought to break with stigmatizing and residualist ideology and values.

In the case of care for older people, the Second World War clearly disrupted
the system of poor relief and opened the way for a more universalistic provision. Wartime brought shared risks and greater social harmony. National pension schemes were introduced, admissions to old-age homes became less class
based and the growth of domiciliary community care services represented an
even clearer break from the poor relief tradition. From their inception these services were, at least in principle, services for all in need of them. In the case of
childcare the modernization process took place later, as the political turbulance
of the 1960s resolved into alliances in support of universalist childcare provision. The 1970s then saw an expansion of day care for children but little change
in services for older people. In the 1980s both sectors again went through fundamental change. The volume of community-based social care services grew
fast and the significance of informal care was recognized by the introduction of
home care allowances in both fields. Non-profit organizations were more
closely integrated with the public provision, particularly in social care for older
people. In childcare, public support evolved to cover all pre-school children.

Nonetheless, there are also significant differences between these two sectors. When looking at the modernization of care for older people, it is obvious
that the historical connection to poor relief was never totally cut. The coverage
of care services has remained far from universal, professional assessments have
increasingly been used to target the limited resources to those most in need and
to exclude others. Users have no clear legal rights to these services. The reforms
have been piecemeal and cautious, and built incrementally on existing provision. Even support for informal care has remained discretionary and subject to
needs testing. In contrast, childcare reform was radical and fundamental. It
started from an almost clean sheet, old policies and practices were abandoned
and entirely new ones created. Something close to universalism has been
obtained.

Why should the two systems of social care have evolved so differently in the
context of one society and its political and ideological development? One reason was that the post-war municipalities inherited a substantial commitment to
care for older people but almost no role in the provision of pre-school care.
Crèches and kindergartens were a much smaller, more voluntaristic and middle-class system. By the 1960s and 1970s the issues of day care for children
were more relevant to the rapid economic and social changes in a predominantly youthful population. Indeed the provision of day care was actually a significant element in constructing the new Finnish society built on a dual-breadwinner and dual-taxpayer family model (Julkunen, 1994). In this version of the
protestant work ethic, both women and men are expected to work and thus to
contribute to the construction of a richer society (Sipilä, 1996). From the 1960s,

women were badly needed by the labour market and they themselves wanted to join it. Social policy developments reflected these preoccupations of a significant voting bloc. The women's movement campaigned for day care but largely ignored the needs of older people despite the fact that more of them were women. Paradoxically, because there was little conflict between the two main parties on issues to do with older people's care, it became a political backwater. Day care, on the other hand, was an arena of political conflict that had to be resolved through innovation by coalition governments. Within a consensual political culture policy differences rather than agreements may be a source of reform.

As a result there is no common Scandinavian universalism reflected in the rather different histories of services for older people and for children. Universal social entitlements to pre-school care, which support equal labour market participation by men and women, evolved not primarily for ideological reasons but out of a series of pragmatic political compromises. At the same time care for older people, while spoken of in high-minded 'Scandinavian' tones in many policy documents, remained an area of particularist practices and significant underfunding by Scandinavian standards.

FUTURE TRENDS IN FINNISH SOCIAL CARE

A conservative forecast would suggest that the following trends will continue:

- local authorities will seek to limit unit costs in public social care by increasing selection, targeting, subcontracting, deprofessionalization and fragmentization;
- some public sector costs will be shifted to service users by raising user charges and developing more expensive, higher-quality services for the middle and upper classes;
- as needs expand, informal care-giving will substitute for public social care, particularly for home help (see Ungerson, 1999).

All these tendencies are bad news for women. Women are a majority in all groups likely to be disadvantaged by these changes: social service employees, informal carers and older people. Thus the development of genuine gender equality in labour markets will be hampered.

However, once rights are institutionalized and patterns of service provision are established there are limits in any democracy to how far they can be cut. In the recession of the early 1990s families with children and older people with minor or moderate care needs lost a major part of the home help they previously received. Now that care in residential homes includes only 2 per cent of people over 65, there is little room left for reductions. Hence, the costs of Finnish public care of older people are at a surprisingly low level. During the 1990s the stressed health care service tended to shift responsibilities for older people to social care services (Lehto et al., 1999). Social care is needed more than ever as a less expensive alternative to health care.

Institutional Provision

In general, we expect that the present trends will continue, but, because of uneven economic development and local autonomy, there will be growing regional differences. Reducing the amount of expensive residential care will still be a core objective for local authorities. The detaching of serviced housing from institutional care makes it more attractive and, at the same time, less expensive than traditional old-age homes. In Finland the owners of the service home estates have usually not been municipalities but voluntary associations. This arrangement has released new sources for funding. Older people can now invest their own money in a service flat, possibly subsidized by funding from the Slot Machine Association.

The costs of day care for children have risen as more employment has increased demand for formal provision. Local authorities have not entirely replaced those places lost during the recession of the early 1990s. Fewer people wish to provide childminding in their own homes. Consequently the right to day care has been challenged within some municipal councils. However, cancelling the social right to day care would be politically very difficult, partly because that would undermine the right to the alternative home care allowance and the political compromise reached after two decades of negotiations would be breached. Thus, only minor adjustments can be expected.

Finland has put much effort into day care but its continental alternative, the pre-school, has not been developed. People have preferred care to education; school traditionally begins when children reach seven. This is slightly unexpected in a country where education is generally highly valued. However, transforming day care into educational provision would further strain the public budget. Nonetheless, pre-school programmes are increasing in Finland. From 2001, universal and free half-day pre-schooling will be provided to all six-year-olds.

Private businesses produce only a tiny share of Finnish social care. Still a 30 per cent yearly growth during the 1990s has been impressive (Lith, 1999). Small private enterprises increasingly provide home help services. They have been helped by the availability of tax reductions. Municipal subcontracting has also opened the market to larger companies, which have started to operate in all the major fields of social care. Furthermore, a specific new benefit was recently launched to support private day-care provision. Allowances for informal care have acquired a major role in the Finnish social care system. The number of recipients of home care allowances for older people has been growing since the recession ended (STAKES, 2000, p. 10) and they are likely to continue to do so.

Reorientation without Convergence

What is the likely impact of all these current and future changes on the Finnish social care pattern? Is Finland taking part in a worldwide convergence process where global economic competition and rising needs and demands drive all nations to residualist social policies (see Mabbett and Bolderson, 1999, pp. 48–9)? Public services are less dominant in the formal sector than they were in the 1970s and 1980s in Finland. Municipal social care offers fewer direct services than before and the ideal of universal public service provision has been partly undermined. Nevertheless, a new universalism had been obtained by extending public finance and regulation to private and informal care. Local social service authorities are actually involved in more activities now than before and they have spread their influence into new areas in social care. In addition to local government as a regulator and a controller of informal social care, it has constructed a significant role as a funder that collaborates with informal carers and voluntary and commercial providers.

The implications of this new intersectoral and pluralist universalism are controversial and ambiguous. Private organizations may weaken universal principles in service provision and in the social care pattern at large. On the other hand, when, for example, public day care is replaced by public education (preschool), universalism is strengthened. However, when public health care responsibilities are shifted to the social care sector the consequences for universalism are less clear. In general, the Finnish and Scandinavian social service model has lost and will continue to lose some of its distinctiveness. Private purchase now has a growing role. Nevertheless, Finnish social care remains quite unlike that in Japan or the United States. Local authorities still provide the lion's share of formal social care and very much coordinate the rest. Families do not bear the burden of social care in Finland nearly as much as they do in the other four countries in this study. Families do provide a major contribution to care in Finland, but usually with financial help from the welfare state.

Convergence theory (Mabbett and Bolderson, 1999, pp. 48–9) suggests that all public social care will become similar in time. In our opinion, this is an exaggeration. First of all, a basic mistake this theory makes is that it comprehends social care only as consumption and forgets that it is investment as well. Social care services constitute an essential social investment that rationalizes care-giving and releases women into the labour market, where they can be more productive than in individually organized caregiving.

Second, social care will always be a cost to somebody. There is no wholly free care from any source. If the costs are not paid directly by the government, then they will be paid by breadwinners, who will need higher wages, or by employers, who may have to provide services for their employees. In short-term analysis, the costs of care, whether borne by the public sector or by others, may look like a reduction in competitiveness in the global market, but in the longer term, care is a prerequisite for reproducing society. A key to long-term competitiveness is not the level of state expenditure on care but the general efficiency of a care system.

The Finnish pattern of social care underwent great changes in the 1990s. Private provision grew, municipalities played a new strategic role in financing and coordination. But finally, the major trend was unexpected — the share of formal social care diminished during the recession and informal care had to replace it. After the recession children's day care experienced a fast recovery but both residential care and home help for older people is more limited now than in 1990. This may continue in the near future. However, we have to be cautious with generalizations and forecasts. The 1990s were such a turbulent period economically in Finland that it is too early to assess whether it constitutes a short break in the development of a Scandinavian welfare state or was the beginning of a more fundamental reorientation.

CONCLUSION

A national social care pattern is the outcome of numerous social, economic and cultural choices. The diversity of possible forms makes social care an institution with exceptional cross-cultural variety. The integrative character of the Finnish welfare state can be seen in its approach to informal care. Parental care of small children has become universally assisted by welfare benefits. Similarly, informal carers of older people are supported by municipal services and public respite services. A situation where the whole sphere of formal and informal care sources is assisted by local and central authorities represents a very strong universalism. In Finland this is the case in childcare. In care for older people, the principle is there but its realization is less developed.

A key question is why a society adopts a particular pattern of care and in our analysis the care pattern in Finland is explained by its social, political, religious and economic history and is closely related to gender relations and institutional continuity. The part of political history has been decisive: we could hardly speak of a Finnish pattern if the country had never gained its independence. But politics, of course, is important in many other ways. For instance, it has provided the forum in which women have influenced the functions and practices of the public sector. Politics has also provided a means for changing public attitudes. It has been the arena in which care policies have been created through compromises between parties. That politicians have reached universal solutions reveals a relative absence of antagonistic contradictions within the society. Religion too has informed the development of the national social care pattern. The Lutheran church has always accepted the primacy of the state and it does not compete in education or social welfare.

The continuity of institutions tends to be a central explanation in social policy analyses. 'Institutions create interests, as well as being created by them', as Freeman (1999) says, but institutions create frameworks for action as well. One source of this continuity in Finnish social care has been the stock of buildings that post-war social welfare inherited from poor relief. These premises afforded an inexpensive opportunity to provide residential care provision for older people, so slowing the development of care in the community.

These macro-level explanations of social care development may help us to understand not only the rise of a 'social service state' but also why the rising curve was suddenly ruptured in the 1990s. The crisis of the public economy was certainly the main reason for the break, but many other factors impacted with it: labour power was less in demand during the recession so service support for it weakened. The rapid growth of social expenses created a critical debate about the misuse of social welfare. Yet most important was perhaps the breakdown of the principle of equity: the growing inequalities between the employed and the unemployed, the well paid and the more poorly paid. These forces began to dissolve the image of an egalitarian and united Finnish society.

ACKNOWLEDGEMENTS

We are grateful to Anna Kulmala for providing us with the statistical information used in the tables. Juhani Lehto provided useful comments on earlier versions of the chapter.

NOTE

1   The Slot Machine Association is an independent organization running the monopoly in slot machines and gambling in Finland. In practice, it is at least semi-public in its character as its policies must be approved by government and its finances are included in the national budget. Annually, it hands out about €250 million to non-profit organizations providing health and social care services.

REFERENCES

Alapuro, R. and Stenius, H. (1987), 'Kansanliikkeet loivat kansakunnan' (Peoples' movements created the nation), in R. Alapuro (ed.), *Kansa Liikkeessä* (People on the move), Helsinki: Kirjayhtymä, pp. 7–49.

Antikainen, E. and Vaarama, M. (1995), *Kotihoidon tuesta omaishoidon tukeen: Valtakunnallinen selvitys omaishoidon tuesta sosiaalipalveluna* (From home care allowances towards a more comprehensive home care scheme: a national inquiry into home care schemes as a social service), Jyväskylä: STAKES.

Anttonen, A. (1997), 'The welfare state and social citizenship', in K. Kauppinen and T. Gordon (eds), *Unresolved Dilemmas: Women, Work and the Family in the United States, Europe and the Former Soviet Union*, Aldershot: Ashgate, pp. 9–32.

Anttonen, A. and Sipilä, J. (1996), 'European social care services: is it possible to identify models?', *Journal of European Social Policy*, 6 (2), 87–100.

Esping-Andersen, G. (1990), *The Three Worlds of Welfare Capitalism*, Cambridge: Polity Press.

Forss, S., Karjalainen, P. and Tuominen, K. (1995), *Mistä apua vanhana? Tutkimus vanhusten avuntarpeesta ja eläkeläisten vapaaehtoistyöstä* (Where does help for the old come from? A study of the needs of older people and the voluntary work of pensioners), Helsinki: Eläketurvakeskus.

Freeman, R. (1999), 'Institutions, states and cultures: health policy and politics in Europe', in J. Clasen (ed.), *Comparative Social Policy: Concepts, Theories and Methods*, Oxford: Blackwell, 80–94.

Glendinning, C. and McLaughlin, E. (1993), 'Paying for informal care: lessons from Finland', *Journal of European Social Policy*, 3 (4), 239–53.

Ilmakunnas, S. (1993), *Kotihoidon tuen faktat ja visiot* (The facts and aspirations of home care allowances), Helsinki: Helsingin kaupunki.

Jaakkola, J. (1994), 'Sosiaalisen kysymyksen yhteiskunta' (Society and the social question), in J. Jaakkola, P. Pulma, M. Satka and K. Urponen, *Armeliaisuus, yhteisöapu, sosiaaliturva: Suomalaisten sosiaalisen turvan historia* (Charity, mutual aid and social security: the history of social protection of the Finnish people), Helsinki: Sosiaaliturvan Keskusliitto, pp. 71–161.

Julkunen, R. (1994), 'Suomalainen sukupuolimalli: 1960-luku käänteenä, (The Finnish gender model: the 1960s as a turning point), in A. Anttonen, L. Henriksson and R. Nätkin (eds), *Naisten hyvinvointivaltio* (The women's welfare state), Tampere: Vastapaino, pp. 179–201.

Kauppinen, S. (1998), *Yksityiset sosiaalipalvelut 1997* (Private social services in 1997), Helsinki: STAKES.

Kauppinen, U.-M. (1986), *Piiasta kotiapulaiseksi, kotiapulaisesta kotitaloustyöntekijäksi* (From a female farmhand to a maidservant, from a maidservant to a domestic worker), Tampere: University of Tampere.

Kela (1996), *Kansaneläkelaitoksen tilastollinen vuosikirja 1996* (Statistical yearbook of the Social Insurance Institution 1996), Helsinki: Kela.

Kela (1997), *Kansaneläkelaitoksen tilastokatsaus 1997/3* (Statistical Review of the Social Insurance Institution 1997/3), Helsinki: Kela.

Kela (1998), *Kansaneläkelaitoksen tilastokatsaus 1998/4* (Statistical review of the Social Insurance Institution 1998/4), Helsinki: Kela.

Koskinen, T. (1989), 'Metsäsektori suomalaisen muutoksen veturina ja jarrumiehenä', (The forest sector, logging and social changes in Finland), in P. Suhonen (ed.), *Suomi — muutosten yhteiskunta* (Finland: a society of change), Juva: WSOY, pp. 181–90.

Kosonen, P. (1987), *Hyvinvointivaltion haasteet ja pohjoismaiset mallit*, (Challenges to the welfare state and nordic models), Tampere: Vastapaino.

Kröger, T. (1996), 'Kunnat valtion valvonnassa', (Municipalities under the control of the state?), in J. Sipilä , *Sosiaalipalvelujen Suomi* (Social service Finland), Juva: WSOY, 23–85.

Kröger, T. (1997), 'The dilemma of municipalities: Scandinavian approaches to child day care provision, *Journal of Social Policy*, **26** (4), 485–507.

Kröger, T. (1999), 'Local historical case study: the unique and the general in the emergence of social care services in Finland', in S. Karvinen, T. Pösö and M. Satka (eds), *Finnish Reconstructions of Social Work Research*, Jyväskylä: University of Jyväskylä, 54–88.

Lehto, J. , Moss, N. and Rostgaard, T. (1999), 'Universal public social care and health services?', in M. Kautto, M. Heikkilä, B. Hvinden, S. Marklund and N. Ploug (eds), *Nordic Social Policy: Changing Welfare States*, London: Routledge, 641–59.

Lith, P. (1999), 'Sosiaalipalvelualan yritykset uskovat kasvuun', (Social care businesses believe in growth), *Sosiaaliturva*, **87** (15), 14.

Mabbett, D. and Bolderson, H. (1999), 'Theories and methods in comparative social policy', in J. Clasen (ed.), *Comparative Social Policy: Concepts, Theories and Methods*, Oxford: Blackwell, 34–56.

Markkola, P. (1990), 'Women in rural society in the 19th and 20th Centuries', in M. Manninen and P. Setälä (eds), *The Lady with the Bow*, Helsinki: Otava, pp. 17–29.

Miettinen, A. (1997), *Work and Family: Data on Women and Men in Europe*, Helsinki: The Population Research Institute.

Muuri, A. (1994), *Lasten päivähoito 1.1.1994* (Day care for children, 1 January 1994), Helsinki: STAKES.

Muuri, A. and Vihma, L. (1991), *Kuinka siinä kävikään? Lasten päivähoito ja kotihoidontuki vuoden 1990 alussa* (How did it turn out? Day care and home care allowance for children at the beginning of year 1990), Helsinki: Sosiaali- ja terveyshallitus.

NOSOSCO (Nordic Social-Statistical Committee) (1998), *Social Protection in the Nordic Countries 1996: Scope, Expenditure and Financing*, Copenhagen: NOSOSCO.

Organization for Economic Cooperation and Development (1996), *Caring for Frail Elderly People: Policies in Evolution*, Social Policy Studies No. 19, Paris: OECD.

Päivärinta, T. (1993), *Jaettu vastuu. Tutkimus sosiaalipalvelujen organisoinnista Suomessa vuosina 1974–1990* (A shared responsibility: study on the organization of social services in Finland in 1974–1990), Helsinki: Suomen Kaupunkiliitto.

Pulma, P. (1987), 'Kerjuuluvasta perhekuntoutukseen' (From begging licenses to family rehabilitation', in P. Pulma and O. Turpeinen, *Suomen lastensuojelun historia,* (The history of child protection in Finland), Helsinki: Lastensuojelun Keskusliitto, 7–257.

Pulma, P. (1994), 'Vaivaisten valtakunta' (The realm of the miserable), in J. Jaakkola, P. Pulma, M. Satka and K. Urponen, *Armeliaisuus, yhteisöapu, sosiaaliturva: Suomalaisten sosiaalisen turvan historia* (Charity, mutual aid and social security: the history of social protection of the Finnish people), Helsinki: Sosiaaliturvan Keskusliitto, 15–70.

Pulma, P. (1995), 'Valtio, vaivaiset ja kuntien itsehallinto' (The state, paupers and local self-government), in *Virkanyrkit ja muita hallintohistoriallisia tutkimuksia*, Helsinki: Hallintohistoriakomitea & Painatuskeskus, pp. 99–125;

Rauhala, P.-L. (1996), *Miten sosiaalipalvelut ovat tulleet osaksi suomalaista sosiaaliturvaa?* (How have social care services become a part of social security in Finland?), Tampere: University of Tampere.

Rostgaard, T. and Fridberg, T. (1998), *Caring for Children and Older People: A Comparison of European Policies and Practices*, Copenhagen: The Danish National Institute of Social Research.

Sainsbury, D. (1988), 'The Scandinavian model and women's interests: the issues of universalism and corporatism', *Scandinavian Political Studies*, **11** (4), 337–346.

Salmi, M. (2000), 'Analysing the Finnish homecare allowance system: challenges to research and problems of interpretation', in L. Kalliomaa-Puha (ed.), *Perspectives on Equality: Work, Women and Family in the Nordic Countries and the European Union*, Copenhagen: Nordic Council of Ministers, pp. 187–207.

Satka, M. (1994), 'Sosiaalinen työ peräänkatsojamiehestä hoivayrittäjäksi' (Social work from lay watching to a caring business), in J. Jaakkola, P. Pulma, M. Satka and K. Urponen, *Armeliaisuus, yhteisöapu, sosiaaliturva: Suomalaisten sosiaalisen turvan historia* (Charity, mutual aid and social security: the history of social protection of the Finnish people), Helsinki: Sosiaaliturvan Keskusliitto, pp. 261–339.

Satka, M. (1995), *Making Social Citizenship: Conceptual Practices from the Finnish Poor Law to Professional Social Work*, Jyväskylä: University of Jyväskylä.

Simonen, L. (1990), *Contradictions of the Welfare State, Women and Caring: Municipal Homemaking in Finland*, Tampere: University of Tampere.

Sipilä, J. (1996), 'Are Scandinavians lazy or hard-working?', *Scandinavian Journal of Social Welfare*, **5** (3), 143–47.

Sipilä, J., Andersson, M., Hammarqvist, S.-E., Nordlander, L., Rauhala, P.-L., Thomsen, K. and Warming Nielsen, H. (1997), 'A multitude of universal, public services: how and why did four Scandinavian countries get their social service model?', in J. Sipilä (ed.), *Social Care Services: The Key to the Scandinavian Welfare Model*, Aldershot: Avebury, pp. 27–50.

Sipilä, J. and Korpinen, J. (1998), 'Cash versus childcare services in Finland', *Social Policy and Administration*, **32** (3), 263–77.

Sipilä, J. and Simon, B. (1993), 'Home care allowances for the frail elderly: for and against', *Journal of Sociology and Social Welfare*, **20** (3), 119–34.

SOTKA, Sosiaali- ja terveydenhuollon tilastotietokanta (SOTKA: Statistical Data Base on Social and Health Care in Finland), Helsinki: STAKES.

STAKES (1998), *Sosiaali- ja terveydenhuollon taskutieto 1998* (Facts about Finnish Social Welfare and Health care 1998), Helsinki: STAKES.

STAKES (2000), *Sosiaali- ja terveydenhuollon taskutieto 2000* (Facts about Finnish Social Welfare and Health Care 1998), Helsinki: STAKES.

STM (1994), *Vanhuusbarometri 1994* (Old Age Barometer 1994), Helsinki: Sosiaali- ja terveysministeriö.

STM (1998), *Lasten päivähoitoselvitys- syyskuu 1998* (A Report on Day Care for Children, 1998), Helsinki: Sosiaali- ja terveysministeriö.

STM (1999), *Vanhuusbarometri 1998* (Old Age Barometer 1998), Helsinki: Sosiaali- ja terveysministeriö.

Sulkunen, I. (1990), *History of the Finnish Temperance Movement: Temperance as a Civic Religion*, Lewiston, NY: Edvin Meller Press.

Sulkunen, I. (1996), 'Finland — a pioneer in women's rights', *Finfo*, **7**, 9–16.

Therborn, G. (1995), *European Modernity and Beyond: The Trajectory of European Societies 1945–2000*, London and New Delhi: Sage.

Tyyskä, V. (1994), 'Women facing the state: childcare policy process in Canada and Finland, 1960–90', *NORA: Nordic Journal of Women's Studies*, **2** (2), 95–106.

Ungerson, C. (1999), 'The production and consumption of long-term care: Does gender matter?', Paper presented at 4th European Conference of Sociology, Amsterdam, 18–21 August.

Urponen, K. (1994), 'Huoltoyhteiskunnasta hyvinvointivaltioon' (From a poor relief society to the welfare state), in J. Jaakkola, P. Pulma, M. Satka and K. Urponen, *Armeliaisuus, yhteisöapu, sosiaaliturva: Suomalaisten sosiaalisen turvan historia* (Charity, mutual aid and social security: the history of social protection of the Finnish people), Helsinki: Sosiaaliturvan Keskusliitto, pp. 163–260.

3. Social Care Services for Children and Older People in Germany: Distinct and Separate Histories

Adalbert Evers and Christoph Sachße

INTRODUCTION

The German welfare state, like those of most western (post-)industrial societies, is based on twin foundations of different size and age. On one hand, there are the relatively recent nationwide systems of social protection such as contribution-based health care and pensions and the tax-funded services such as education. On the other hand, there are the welfare benefits and services that grew out of the older inheritance of the local poor laws and the forms of social assistance they provided. The main features of services built on the first pillar are a high degree of centralization, standardization, statutory detail and professionalism. The services which developed on the basis of the second pillar are typically decentralized and more discretionary and variable in their impact. This raises the question why some needs, like health and education, are met in one way while others, such as care needs, are met quite differently?

This chapter will begin by seeking to answer this question by using a historical approach. First, key features of the German welfare system are sketched out. Later sections deal with the early roots of social services in Imperial Germany, developments during the Weimar Republic, the Nazi period and, after the Second World War, in the Federal Republic of Germany. It will be shown how current patterns of social provision for children and older people in Germany largely grew out of aspects of the poor law which remain embedded in the modern welfare state. Although there have been numerous changes and innovations since, for the social care services certain basic features remain: a less than comprehensive role for the public authorities, a greater influence of local and voluntary sector organizations, and less well-articulated and clear-cut entitlements for clients and citizens.

More recently the sector providing social services for children and older people has become the subject of an intensified process of centralization, standardization and professionalization. But at the same time, both childcare and social care have followed their own distinct paths of development. Key recent reforms are the introduction of a legal right to *Kindergärten* care for all children aged three to six and a half and the establishment of a national system of long-term care insurance to cover the care needs of older people. Are the 'big brothers' of the welfare state, health and education, then to be seen as role models, showing the path to be followed by the smaller and possibly weaker systems of elderly care and childcare? These questions will be returned to at the end of this chapter with a brief look at possible future developments.

THE CURRENT PATTERN OF CHILDCARE PROVISION

Day-care Facilities for Children

The legal basis for the German system of day care for children is the Child and Youth Act, *Kinder- und Jugendhilfegesetz*, of 1991, in particular its articles 22–26. Local authorities, *Kreise* and *kreisfreie Städte*, are formally responsible for the provision of day care for children. The actual organization of the system, however, is based on a plurality of public and non-profit providers or *Träger*, which are publicly subsidized. There is a tiny fraction of private for-profit providers. The most important of the non-profit providers are the big nationwide welfare associations, *Wohlfahrtsverbände*, a peculiarly German type of non-profit organization. Among these the protestant *Diakonisches Werk* and the catholic Deutscher Caritasverband are by far the largest. The German Child and Youth Act distinguishes between four types of day care for children:

- crèches *(Kinderkrippen)* for children aged one and two;
- 'Kindergärten' for children from three to the start of school at about six and a half;
- day-care facilities for school-aged children *(Kinderhorte)*;
- family day care or childminding *(Tagespflege)*.

Kinderkrippen, *Kindergärten* and *Kinderhorte* are found either as separate institutions or as combined institutions which may take children of some or all ages up to six and a half. As of 31 December 1994 there were 5,596,368 children aged up to six and a half in Germany and Tables 3.1 and 3.2 illustrate the number of institutions and the number of day-care places available to them.

Between them two of the nationwide non-profit welfare organizations provided 50 per cent of all kindergärten in Germany and 80 per cent of the non-

Table 3.1 Numbers of day-care institutions for pre-school children,
          Germany, 1994

	Age range	Public institutions		Non-profit institutions		For-profit institutions	
Crèches	0–3	396	46.3%	455	53.1%	5	na
Kindergartens	3–6½	10,735	36.1%	18,966	63.7%	56	1.5%
Other daycare	0–6½	8,388	67.9%	3,905	31.6%	60	1.5%

Table 3.2 Day-care places for pre-school children, Germany, 1994

Age range	Total places	Public provision	Non-profit provision	For-profit provision
0–3 only	150,753 100%	108,994 72.5%	41,306 27.4%	na
3–6½	2,471,688 100%	1,094,706 44.3%	1,372,189 55.5%	na

Sources: Tables compiled from data available in: Beher, 1998; Statistisches Bundesamt 1996a,
1996b, 1996c; Deutsches Jugendinstitut, 1998; BSFSJ, 1998.

profit sector provision; the Protestant *Diakonisches Werk* provided 6,647 institutions and the Catholic *Deutscher Caritasverband* provided 8,565. For-profit providers, by contrast, play only a minimal role in German childcare. A total of 121 institutions for pre-school children make up less than 1 per cent of all provision in 1994.

The pattern of day care for children in Germany is characterized by relatively generous provision of kindergarten care. The rate of provision by the end of 1994 was 77.2 per cent of eligible children. Legal entitlement to a kindergarten place for every child between three and the beginning of school was introduced in article 24 of the Child and Youth Act in 1992 and fully implemented on 1 January 1999. The availability of places for children aged under three, by contrast, is low. The rate of provision was only 6.3 per cent by the end of 1994. Thus, pre-school day care for children in Germany is predominantly kindergarten care, and it is overwhelmingly part-time.

The pattern of childcare was completely different in the former East Germany where the system of day care for children in general, and for infants and small children in particular, was much more developed than in West Germany. Since 1990 the system in the East has successively adopted the structures of the

West. Thus, there are currently two contradictory trends in the development of childcare in Germany: declining provision in the East parallels a trend towards expansion, particularly of kindergarten care, in the West.

Family day care
Family day care, or childminding, is a significant alternative source of care. Since official registration of family day care is no longer required under the new Child and Youth Act, there are no recent statistics available. According to the most recent data we have, there were 43,615 places available in family day care in 1990. It has been estimated that this number should at least be doubled because of an extensive 'grey market' in childminding. However, we can assume that family day care is predominantly for children under three and that almost as many children are cared for in this way as are cared for in formal crèches.

Funding
Day care for children is part of the social welfare system and is therefore generally subsidized out of general taxation but with means-tested charges paid by users. Contributions to costs have to be paid, but can be reduced or even cancelled according to the income of parents. As a result the financing of the German system of day care for children consists of a complex mix of public tax money and private contributions. Total public expenditure on day care in 1994 amounted to over 18 billion DM. Two-thirds of the expenditure was on public provision and about a third was paid as subsidies to non-profit providers. Only about 14 per cent of this expenditure are recouped in charges to users. The sector is also a significant employer. On 31 December 1994 a total of 344,909 people were employed in the 42,966 institutions providing day care for children aged up to six and a half, of whom over 96 per cent were women.

THE CURRENT PATTERN OF CARE PROVISION FOR OLDER PEOPLE

The most important legal basis for the system of elderly care is the Long Term Care Insurance Law (LTCI) which was passed in April 1995. Organized similarly to health insurance, the care insurance system covers needs for care due to disability and entitles those covered to benefits in cash or in kind, a choice the user can make, according to their degree of need and independently of their income situation. While the LTCI covers all people in need of care, the main clientele is to be found among older people. In the same way as the national system of health insurance, care insurance covers nearly 99 per cent of the population, about 80 million people in 1999 (BMG-*Pressemitteilungen*, 2000).

The provision of services, in institutions and the community is by both commercial and not-for-profit organizations, usually operating under the auspices of one of the big national welfare associations. These providers are paid by the LTCI funds on the basis of general contracts.

About 5 per cent of the German population who are over 65 live in institutions compared with nearly 19 per cent of those over 80 (BFSFJ, 1997). In 1999 some 656,000 people received care of some kind in an institutional setting compared with 661,000 in 1996 and 95 per cent of these were over 60 years old (http://www.bmfsj.de, 1999). Just over half of these people were in nursing homes and the rest in residential homes. Most but not all of them were covered by the new care insurance system. In addition, at any one time about 1.3 million people are eligible for care services at home in that they meet at least the minimum definitions of need defined by the LTCI. The assessments of need are made by doctors according to fairly strict criteria. Estimates of eligibility using a more generous definition of 'being in need of help and care' suggested this group could be as large as 3.2 million people, of whom 2.1 million required some form of home help (BFSFJ, 1996, p. 16). In 1999 half of those supported in some way under the LTCI were over 80 and 68 per cent were women (http://www.bmgesundheit.de, 1999). However, only a minority of older people are dependent on help at any one time: 0.5 per cent of those under 60; 3.5 per cent of those between 60 and 79; and 28 per cent of those aged 80 and over. Even among people over 90, two-thirds living at home manage without specialized help (BAS, 1998, p. 52ff.).

Table 3.3 sets out the pattern of provision of home and institutional care in Germany. While charitable, not-for-profit organizations still dominate the sector, the share of the for-profit sector is currently growing. An unusual feature of the staff of institutional care homes is that approximately 15 per cent are young people doing a job as an alternative to compulsory military service. Overall staffing is now growing fastest in the home care sector, where 10 per cent of the staff at any one time are working as an alternative to military service (Wissenschaftliches Institut der AOK, 1998). As is the case in all the countries described in this study, most care for older people in Germany is provided by informal, usually family, carers among whom, in 1995, 73 per cent of main carers were women (26 per cent daughters; 24 per cent spouses; 14 per cent mothers; 9 per cent daughters-in-law). Among male carers, spouses form by far the largest group (BFSFJ, 1996, pp. 129ff.).

The demand for care will grow as the numbers of older people continue to rise. Between 1995 and 2010 the number of people aged 60 and over in Germany will grow by 3.6 million (BAS, 1998, pp. 52ff.). However, the impact on the pattern of supply of services remains uncertain because the LTCI rules allow users to opt for cash rather than services, which they may, within certain limits, use to pay relatives rather than professional providers. Most but not all

NORTHBROOK COLLEGE LIBRARY

*Table 3.3 Institutional and home care provider organizations, Germany,
1998*

	Institutional care providers	Home care providers
No of providers	8,300	11,900
Non-profit	55%	49%
For-profit	29%	46%
Public	16%	5%
Total employees	216,000[a]	83,000

Note: a 35% part-time.

Sources: Wissenschaftliches Institut der AOK, 1998; Alber and Schölkopf, 1999, pp. 97ff.; htttp://www.bmgesundheit.de, 1999.

expenditure under the LTCI system goes to support older people. Total expenditure in 1999 was almost 32 billion DM. Table 3.4 shows the ways in which this expenditure was taken up by the beneficiaries.

More than 10 billion DM, or a third, of the total expenditure under the LTCI system simply replaced that which was formerly spent on dependent people through the social assistance benefits. In addition about 2 billion DM pays the social insurance contributions of family carers who can show they spend above a minimum number of hours on social care. As a result the additional expenditure incurred as a result of the creation of LTCI was running at some 20 billion DM a year in 1999 and of this total only about a quarter is spent on home care services (http:/www. bmgesundheit.de, 1999). One reason for this is that the cash payments opted for by the majority of those eligible for home care are set at a much lower level that the costs of the alternative services in kind provided

Table 3.4 Beneficiaries of LTCI benefits, Germany, 1999

	Home care	Institutional care	Total
No of beneficiaries	1,310,000	550,000	1,860,000
Of which			
Cash payments	983,000		
Cash and services	193,000		
Services only	134,000		

Source: http://www. bmgesundheit.de, 1999.

by professionals. Where users opt for cash, most of it is used to pay family carers rather than for hiring help from outsiders.

Payments from the care insurance funds for both institutional and home care are graduated according to needs assessments made by doctors employed by the Association of Care Insurers, which operates the LTCI system. There are three levels of need leading to different amounts of payment as set out in Table 3.5.

Table 3.5 LTCI payments per month by level of assessed need, Germany, 1999

	Type of benefit	Level I DM per month	Level II DM per month	Level III DM per month
Home care	Cash payment	400	800	1,300
	Services	750	1,800	2,800
Per cent of recipients		50	39	11
Institutional care	Services	2,000	2,500	2,800
Per cent of recipients		37	41	22

Source: http://www. bmgesundheit.de, 1999.

At the time of writing (2002), the care insurance funds are in surplus, receiving more in contributions than they are paying out in benefits. It is expected that this balance will change as the population ages. There is also the possibility that as the system matures the balance of take-up between services in kind and payments in cash will change too, but, at present, there are no clear indications of the direction of change (Rothgang and Schmähl, 1996).

THE ORIGINS OF SOCIAL CARE SERVICES IN WILHELMINE GERMANY

Poor Relief and the Growth of Social Services

The modern welfare state in Germany was established by the end of the nineteenth century and its main features endure to the present. Rapid industrialization and urbanization following German unification in 1871 led to the growth in numbers of the urban, industrial proletariat and to their political organization. The 'question of the working class' (*Arbeiterfrage*) became a central social issue in Wilhelmine Germany. The new social policy of the Reich sought a solution to this question and in the 1880s a system of social insurance was set up. Though the benefits were initially low and only a minority of workers was covered, Germany was the first country to have two systems of social security side by side; of local poor relief and of social insurance. The question of the working class (*Arbeiterfrage*) was thereby clearly separated from the traditional question of the poor (*Armenfrage*) by both legislation and administrative organization. Though in practice the constituencies of both systems overlapped in the beginning, the two sectors developed in different ways. Contribution-based social insurance increasingly focused on the provision of transfer payments for particular, legally defined risks and, by the same token, began to become a privileged system of social security lacking the stigma of poor relief.

Municipal relief, by contrast, developed into a system of personal social services. In the big German cities during the 1890s, as part of a broad contemporary movement of bourgeois social reform, a wealth of innovative institutions and measures for municipal poor relief were realized. These reforms around poor relief can be viewed as a process of distinguishing special risks from a more general risk of impoverishment. Specialized measures and benefits for the unemployed, public health and public housing as well as particular welfare provisions for children and the elderly developed out of the hitherto undifferentiated poor relief system. Aspects of personal advice, instruction and control as well as the claim to a scientific approach to the problems of poverty became the key elements of the new ways in which assistance or welfare were dispensed (Sachße, 1994, pp. 48–89; Sachße and Tennstedt, 1988, pp. 15–45; vom Bruch, 1985).

Modern social services for children and the elderly thus grew out of reforms of the system of municipal poor relief in Wilhelmine Germany, and in some respects they still carry the features of poor relief today. The systems of social insurance established in the 1880s, health, accident and old-age insurance, primarily covered the risks of industrial production. Its constituency, hence, was predominantly male. In contrast, reform of municipal welfare was aimed primarily at problems of reproduction related to the family, the household and local living conditions. Its constituency, therefore, was predominantly female. The formation of social services was also closely linked to women's work within the household (Bischoff, 1994). Social work, the social service profession, consequently emerged as a female profession (Sachße, 1994; Koven and Michel, 1993). The close links to the traditions of municipal poor relief and female family work provide the main reasons for an enduring deficit in the degree of institutionalization, centralization and codification of the social services compared to the systems of social insurance.

The organization of poor relief in nineteenth century Germany was split: alongside public poor relief there was a wide variety of private relief facilities. Across the century civil associations came to play a greater role as an addition to the longer-established charitable foundations. As early as the first half of the century, but to a greater degree between the revolution of 1848 and the founding of the Reich, a local culture of voluntary organizations became established, especially in the cities, which encompassed all areas of civil life. This formed the institutional backbone for private, both confessional and non-confessional, initiatives for the poor and needy (Nipperdey, 1972; Dann, 1984; Sachße, 2000; with particular reference to confessional associations: Kaiser, 1989, pp. 17ff.). The voluntary organizations were private associations, free from state influence. They did not exercise any legal responsibilities, were not subject to any governmental directives and were not dependent on government funding. They were a manifestation of private initiative and private philanthropy, an expression of neighbourly help and control as well as of a sense of solidarity based on the local community.

As a result, in the German cities of the later nineteenth century there was, in addition to public welfare, a colourful multitude of charitable associations, often numbered in the hundreds, active alongside public welfare but in no manner functioning in a coordinated fashion (for Berlin: Fromm, 1894; Die Wohlfahrtseinrichtungen, 1891; for Bremen: Auskunftstelle für Wohltägtigheit, 1899; for Frankfurt: Brückner, 1892 and 1892, Stadtbund, 1901; for Hamburg: Armenkollegium, 1901; for Munich: Die Wohlfahrtseinrichtungen, 1901; for Leipzig: Die Wohlfahrtseinrichtungen, 1905).

Traditional Patterns of Care for Children and Older People

Of course, care for children and for those older people beyond the traditional bonds of the family was not entirely new in late nineteenth century Germany. In the sector of childcare, orphanages and foundling hospitals had been in existence since the late Middle Ages. The early beginnings of industrial capitalism brought about the disintegration and destabilization of traditional social institutions and communities. And with these fundamental social changes the concept of the kindergarten had already begun to take shape by the late eighteenth and early nineteenth centuries: as a concept of an institution of day care for the children of the poor whose families could not provide adequate protection and education (Reyer, 1985; Erning et al., 1987; Mohrmann, 1929). At first there were few kindergartens relative to their cultural impact. It is estimated that about one per cent of all children aged three to six were cared for in kindergarten-like institutions by the middle of the nineteenth century. These kindergartens were provided predominantly by private associations. Only a small minority were organized by (local) public authorities (Reyer, 1987a, p. 50).

In the context of municipal social reform in Wilhelmine Germany, kindergarten care attracted considerable public interest. A high rate of infant mortality and a declining birth rate had alarmed reformers and better provision of health care for infants and children was advocated. Public day care for the children of the poor was understood as another means to limit the perils of disease and immorality. By 1910, kindergartens provided for 13 per cent of children aged three to six in the German Empire in general. A total of 7,259 institutions provided care for 558 610 children. But the South/North divide, which still characterizes public day care for children today in Germany, was then already visible: rates of provision were up to 30 per cent in the southern parts of the Empire but were less than 10 per cent in parts of the North (Erning, 1987, p. 30). In spite of increasing public interest, providers of kindergarten remained predominantly private in the *Kaiserreich* period. In 1912, only 5 per cent of the 4,883 kindergartens in Prussia were run by public authorities (Reyer, 1987b, p. 42).

The tradition of care for the elderly in Germany, too, dates back to the late Middle Ages: to various types of hospitals — public and private, religious and civil (Borscheid,1995; Steinweg, 1929). Better-off elderly, who had no family to care for them, bought themselves places in these hospitals. Poor relief also provided institutional care for the elderly poor. The traditional institution for the elderly, however, was not an old age home in the modern sense. Rather, it was an asylum for a complex mix of inmates: the aged, the poor, the sick, the mad, thieves and vagrants. During the nineteenth century a process of institutional differentiation began: the mad were separated from the sick, and both from the criminal (Borscheid, 1995; Conrad, 1994, pp. 169–195). Bourgeois social reform in Wilhelmine Germany provided the impulse for the intensified differentiation and modernization of institutional care. Progress in scientific medicine, in particular, fuelled a system of separate somatic and psychiatric hospitals. Scientific medicine also claimed responsibility for the invalid and ailing elderly, who were sometimes left out of this institutional specialization. Thus, the early forms of a new type of institution came into existence: the old-age or nursing home (Borscheid, 1995; Irmak, 1998).

The process of institutional differentiation was propelled by competition between the various providers: the churches and religious welfare associations which claimed care of older people as a 'natural' function of Christian charity; the civil associations which wanted to manifest middle-class responsibility for the unity of the nation; and public authorities which struggled to coordinate the variety of institutions and measures for local welfare, both public and private.

FROM WEIMAR TO THE BERLIN REPUBLIC

The Weimar Welfare State

After the First World War, a welfare state was created out of a constitutional compromise between the forces of the left and the right in the new republic.

Confronted with mass poverty on a scale that greatly exceeded that known in the pre-war years, the state took on greater responsibility for the well-being of its citizens. This extension of the state took place in the context of basic economic conditions that were dramatically worse than in pre-war Germany. Consequently, the expansion of the Weimar welfare state did not proceed in a well-planned and continuous manner. Rather, crises continually disrupted it. The mass destitution of the times defined its parameters while its course was attended by discontent and criticism (Böckenförde, 1985; Abelshauser, 1987; Sachße and Tennstedt, 1988, pp. 77–87).

Bureaucratization, centralization, and professionalization are the concepts that perhaps best capture the main trends in Weimar welfare development. The period saw a remarkable expansion not only of social security but also of social welfare at the municipal level. The structures of welfare administration, the fundamental features of which still exist today, clustered around a core structure of social welfare, youth welfare and public health provision. The Weimar Republic was also a period of deep-reaching reorganization in the private welfare sector, which was now called 'independent welfare'. The numerous local associations, which had formed the backbone of private charity in the pre-war period, had been tailored to fit into the milieu of Wilhelmine bourgeois social reform. They now began to lose their core functions. The establishment of a welfare state and the democratization of state and society favoured new forms of organization: local and centralized bureaucracies, political parties, and organized interest groups. Moreover, many of the traditional philanthropic coalitions lost their financial base during the great inflation of the 1920s. In this situation the organizational approach which seemed best equipped for the future was one which the church-based organizations had already developed in the nineteenth century: the creation of central nationwide welfare associations. The Protestant 'Central Committee of the Inner Mission' had been founded as early as 1848. Its Catholic counterpart, the 'Caritas Association', was set up in 1897. The welfare associations found a ready welcome from the Reich's Ministry of Labour. Large, centrally run associations were the forms of interest representation that best fitted the centralized structures of the Weimar state.

Weimar was thus a time of association-building in the realm of welfare. Among them were the Jewish welfare association, the 'Central Welfare Office of German Jews' set up in September 1917, the social democratic 'Workers' Aid' organization (*Arbeiterwohlfahrt*) 1919, and the 'Fifth Welfare Association' 1924. The founding, in December 1924, of a 'German League of Independent Welfare', an umbrella organization of the leading independent welfare associations, constituted the keystone in this process. The Inner Mission, the Caritas Association, the German Red Cross, the German Parity Welfare Association, the Central Welfare Office of German Jews, and the Central Welfare Committee of Christian Workers were members of the League. The socialist 'Workers'

Aid' chose deliberately not to join a predominantly social democratic coalition of associations (Sachße and Tennstedt, 1988, pp. 152–72; Kaiser, 1996; Sachße, 1996).

Care for children and older people in the Weimar Republic

In 1922, the Reichstag passed the new Imperial Youth Welfare Act (*Reichsju-gend-wohlfahrtsgesetz*) which subjected the entire domain of youth welfare services to uniform regulations (Wollasch, 1991, pp. 122–46). The law also provided a new basis for the organization of childcare. Its Section 4 allocated the provision of institutions of day care for children as a responsibility to the municipal *Jugendamt* (Youth Department), the new administrative unit for the organization of youth welfare services. Day care for children was thus legally recognized as a public responsibility. In practice of course, the education of and care for children remained primarily a matter for the family, and public day care was restricted to children whose families could not provide adequate care. Nevertheless, the new law began to shape the outlines of day care for children as a general and public social service.

Due to the inflation of the early 1920s and the financial crisis of the Repub-lic, the quantitative development of childcare stagnated. Only in 1928 was the pre-war level of provision reached (Erning, 1987, p. 33). The structure of pro-viders, however, changed profoundly during the Weimar years. The Imperial Youth Welfare Act strengthened the privileged position of independent welfare providers in childcare. In the terms of its regulations, public authorities were required to restrict their own provision to cases where appropriate private care was not available and at the same time had to subsidize the work of existing, and encourage new, private providers. As a result, and despite a variety of con-flicts at the municipal level, a process began in which public and independent welfare work drew closer together to form a united complex: public authorities depended on the numerous private providers; private institutions depended on public subsidies.

Despite these legal guarantees supporting independent providers, the pro-portion of public provision in childcare did grow. By 1928 approximately 30 per cent of all kindergartens were provided by local public authorities, approxi-mately 70 per cent by independent, in particular religious, welfare associations. This pattern continued, with the exception of the Nazi years, until the German reunification in the early 1990s (Sachße and Tennstedt, 1988, p. 125).

As has been described, the Weimar Republic saw the extension of locally-based social services, financed by municipalities but often run by independent welfare associations. However, it is remarkable how small a part was played by services for older people in this process. One reason was that social reformers of the 1920s were driven by ideas about 'social hygiene' and focused largely on the welfare of young children, mothers and working families who were seen as the 'vulnerable' sections of the productive population. There were limited reviews of provision for older people by municipalities, such as assessments of the numbers involved, but the area remained at the margins of public interest (Irmak, 1998). What public concern there was about the care of older people was of a problematic nature. The 1920s saw the first wave of population debates about the increasing 'demographic burden' of old age. While this gave some legitimacy to local policies planning more homes for older people, the incentive was generated by an utterly negative perception of old age.

There was, however, one factor that provided an incentive for better services for old and frail people. The demarcation line separating social assistance, based on the poor law, from the rather better services based on social insurance, had become blurred in the weakened Germany after the First World War in which many members of both the working classes and the petty bourgeoisie had become deeply impoverished. New types of social assistance benefits and services were developed, without the traditional element of purposeful stigmatization (Sachße and Tennstedt, 1988, pp. 89–99). Old people's homes became separated from institutions housing the destitute. The former were increasingly used by old people with some modest means, a small pension for example (Kondratowitz, 1988), while nursing institutions for the frail and destitute, *Siechenhäuser*, continued to be stigmatized as an underclass asylum even though there were some attempts to remove those seen as unfit for the harsh order of such institutions. The growing medical and hospital sector was also to impact on the care of older people (Steinweg, 1929). Medical institutions developed within the framework of social insurance and central funding. In the 1920s hospital care was increasingly medicalized and professionalized and the merely old were seen to be more appropriately placed in less costly nursing homes. Within nursing homes for the frail and destitute the percentage of older people with mental illness or disabilities rose. The growing 'social hygiene' perspective, with its emphasis on order and discipline and their links to health and poverty, prevented the care of older people becoming a distinct and separate focus (Irmak, 1998).

The economic crises endemic to Weimar and the ever rising cost of social insurance due to the enormous unemployment reinforced the search for economy in welfare. Furthermore the responses to these challenges were shaped by a new preoccupation with 'rationalization', shared by experts and politicians of all sides and leading to a search for scientific classifications of needs and the greater specialization and 'Taylorization' of services and institutions (Conrad, 1994). This resulted in a further incentive to build old people's and nursing homes in order to economize on the hospital system and, it was hoped, to free much needed space within the housing market.

Altogether, this meant that provision for older people was only a very small part of the spread of municipal social services outside the poor law tradition.

Institutional places for older people merely kept pace with the steady growth in numbers, and provision remained below 5 per cent of those over 65 throughout the period from the beginning to the end of the twentieth century (Majce, 1978). Another constant was the important role of the private welfare associations which, as they reorganized into fewer national organizations during the 1920s, became even more powerful actors in local-level policy formulation.

From Social Welfare to Nazi 'People's Welfare'

The Nazi vision of a 'constructive people's welfare' programme took as its starting point a critique of the Weimar welfare state. Nazi polemics suggested that public assistance had always served the weak and the ill, the physically and mentally 'inferior'; it thus fostered a permanent deterioration of the nation's physical constitution. A truly constructive people's welfare programme would, in contrast, hinder the reproduction of these 'inferior' persons and instead promote and build up the valuable, eugenically healthy, elements of the people. Social welfare should be changed from an instrument to integrate the poor and the destitute to an instrument for the improvement of the race. Ideas of racial hygiene became the conceptual backbone of this new welfare. These arguments involved both destructive and 'constructive' components. The negative goal of Nazi welfare was to prevent the reproduction of the 'unproductive', to 'eradicate' the 'inferior'. The positive was conceived as promoting and strengthening those seen as healthy and productive members of the *Volksgemeinschaft* (Sachße and Tennstedt, 1992).

A new party welfare organization, the NSV (*Nationalsozialistische Volkswohlfahrt*), was the main instrument for managing the new direction in welfare. The NSV portrayed itself as the alternative to the overly bureaucratic Weimar welfare state and claimed to represent the true impulses of the German people. Beginning on a modest scale in 1933, it managed to expand into a gigantic mass organization in the years before the war (Hansen, 1991). The NSV concentrated on providing non-institutional services, particularly services for mothers and children. As part of its programme of 'constructive people's welfare' the NSV steadily expanded the kindergarten sector, thereby moving into an arena which denominational welfare organizations had always dominated. Actually, the NSV was the first political organization in Germany to realize the crucial importance of kindergartens as a core element of family policy in modern industrial society. However, all family policy measures were explicitly reserved for eugenically acceptable mothers and children.

The sector of care for older people played a lesser role in Nazi welfare policies. The retired worker may have been due a basic income but provision of care for the sick and the old was not a matter of interest for the Nazi organizations themselves and was left to the denominational welfare associations which suffered various political and financial restrictions during the period. This left little room for extensive and innovative care programmes and, consequently, elderly care generally stagnated during the Nazi years. Under the regime the core belief was that the old and the sick should take second place to those who were biologically more important to the future of the people (Damrau, 1935/36, p. 613).

Social Services in the Post-war Federal Republic

In terms of legislation, organizational architecture, and welfare goals, the emerging welfare state of the Federal Republic was closely linked with the traditions built in the Weimar Republic. A priority was the development of the various systems of social security. The old-age pension system was completely reformed in 1957, health insurance steadily expanded through the post-war decades, unemployment insurance was reformed in 1969. In the sector of social services for children and older people, however, there was little change in the immediate post-war period.

Developments in care for children

By 1950 there were approximately 8,600 kindergartens providing approximately 60,000 places in the Federal Republic. Provision then declined until the mid-1960s when, stimulated by increasing female employment and an overall expansion of the educational system, a period of marked expansion began. In 1965 there were 14,113 kindergartens with 952,875 places in the Federal Republic, which corresponded to a rate of provision of 33 per cent. Provision rose until, by the mid-1980s, kindergarten care had become the norm for almost every child aged 3–6 years. The stigma of poor relief dissipated. In fact, the majority of children came from middle- and higher-income families. Overall, day care provision for children was the responsibility of local authorities but the involvement of private (non-profit) providers also remained high. Until the end of the 1980s almost a third of all kindergarten places were provided by non-profit organizations, namely the religious welfare associations. However, this process of 'normalization' of day care for children, it has to be emphasized, was restricted to kindergartens for children aged 3–6. The rate of provision of care for children aged 0–3 and 6–12, by contrast, remained and still remains well below 10 per cent.

Developments in care for older people

Residential and nursing homes for older people were a rather marginal part of West German post-war welfare state development. While the care of older people was essentially a municipal responsibility, there was initially no public finance available outside social assistance. Municipalities sometimes financed or subsidized the construction of institutional facilities, but the services themselves were mostly run by the big welfare associations. However, in the course of the next decades their share of co-financing, from church taxes, donations or local charitable funds, diminished while the role of municipal social assistance funding increased. While, as described earlier, there had been some changes to the provision of outdoor relief under Weimar in the 1920s, home care remained on a very small scale until the 1970s, often available only within the realm of the local parish or church.

However, as the country prospered, even the social assistance-based system, such as the provision of nursing-home care, grew larger and more generous. The overall physical and staffing standards in old people's and nursing homes improved, especially during the heyday of welfare growth in the 1970s (Kondratowitz and Schmidt, 1986; Irmak, 1998). Costs grew and by the beginning of the 1990s they had reached an average level of 5,000 DM a month per place in nursing homes. Thus access to institutional care meant a person was either already entitled to social assistance or soon would be, once assets had been spent down. Nonetheless, the improvements in standards did not break the cultural association of institutions with a loss of independence. Rather the high costs and the necessity of funding through social assistance strengthened this image. Before the implementation of the new Long Term Care Insurance (LTCI), more than 80 per cent of all people in homes lived there on social assistance, with only some 'pocket money' at their own disposal. All in all, there was little fundamental change in the system of care for older people until the late 1980s. Rather the development was simply in terms of volume; more institutional places, better living conditions in homes, higher staffing levels and improved support for staff. However, alongside this continuity, two distinct shifts in public policy were to change the overall position of dependent older people in the society.

The first of these was the spread of the concept of *Sozialstationen* from the 1970s onwards (Grunow et al., 1979). This became the blueprint for local care centres designed to serve areas of about 50,000 inhabitants. They are usually run by the welfare associations but with financial support from municipalities that have paid for buildings and funded contracts with the provider organizations. Local authorities continued to invest in *Sozialstationen* until the early 1990s, so helping to make home care less marginal and a real growth sector, while the institutional care sector began to stagnate. At the same time, within the public and voluntary sectors, there developed a growing emphasis on social planning for a larger retired population. A range of 'soft services' such as counselling and support for cultural activities helped to define the issue of an ageing society as one of more universal concern and not just a problem for social assistance.

Nonetheless, services for older people were not yet, that is by the 1980s, regarded as a normal part of local authority responsibilities in the same way as provision for children and young people or housing for families. Faced with rapidly rising social assistance expenditures to support the retired population, municipalities joined the chorus of those who argued for a general right to care for those in need and for a new source of funding for such a system.

THE FORMS AND FEATURES OF SOCIAL CARE SERVICES TODAY

The Universalization of Kindergarten Care

On 1 January 1991 the new Federal Child and Youth Act came into effect. It contained a section of detailed regulations for the day care of children. Though it did not provide absolute legal rights, it provided a solid base for provision and further expansion of entitlements. By 1992 further amendments to the new act, won as part of rather separate agreements concerning abortion and the Aid for Pregnant Women and Families Act (*Schwangeren- und Familienhilfegesetz*), produced an explicit right to kindergarten care for every child aged three to six which came into full effect on 1 January 1999. With the establishment of this general entitlement the link between kindergarten and the tradition of poor relief was finally dissolved. Kindergarten care has become a generally accepted personal social service supplementing family care. Kindergarten care remains a devolved responsibility of the local authorities who supervise provision by a complex mix of public and private (non-profit) providers, the Catholic and Protestant welfare associations being the most important though the share of direct state provision has grown, particularly since unification.

Since the 1970s and increasingly since the 1980s, a broad variety of community-based and self-help initiatives have appeared in the day-care arena to organize a great variety of day-care initiatives. The non-profit provision of childcare is no longer the exclusive domain of the big welfare associations. As the plurality of providers has grown, so has the range of ideological and professional forces shaping patterns of day care. However, in contrast to the provision of care for older people, the role of commercial providers has remained slight (see Tables 3.1 and 3.2). However, it is only for children aged between three and six that day care, in the form of kindergarten, has become universal. Of children under three, only 6.3 per cent were in day care in 1994. For them entitlement is restricted to families defined as in social need and who pass a means test. Thus, for the under-threes the traditions of poor relief are still visible. In addition only a minority of places provided in kindergartens are full-time. The backbone of the German system of day care for children, is still part-time kindergarten care.

All other types of day care are of minor relevance. At least in this area, the model of the male breadwinner family still informs the German welfare state.

Current Developments in Services for Older People: From the Margins of Municipal Provision to the Margins of Medical Provision

Given the character of the German welfare state it should be no surprise that an insurance-based model was finally chosen in order to provide more universal access to older people and others with care needs. The Long Term Care Insurance Law (LTCI), implemented in the beginning of 1995, is funded by the contributions of employers and employees which also gives entitlement to spouses and children.

However, the solutions embedded in the LTCI differ in important ways from the norms of the established system of health insurance (for a more detailed analysis see Alber, 1996; Evers, 1998a; Evers and Klie, 1999). In particular, the new system provides substantial contributions to the costs of care in old age but not a commitment to meet all needs. At all the levels of need there remain gaps between what the insurance will cover and what may be required for adequate care. This difference makes itself most felt in the case of nursing-home care where actual costs are often much greater than the 3,300 DM per month maximum support allowed by the LTCI, received by only about a quarter of beneficiaries (Rothgang, 1997, p. 215). The LTCI has, however, extended rights and provisions within the overall sector. It provides protection to informal carers; a yearly holiday and the payment of pension contributions. There is also funding for advice centres and support groups to help people both in coping with informal care and in qualifying as users of services (Evers, 1998b). A result of the new law has been the establishment of a competitive social care market which treats the established voluntary sector and the newer for-profit providers equally (Wissenschaftliches Institut der AOK, 1998). It is no longer possible for municipalities to maintain long-established patterns of payment to particular voluntary sector providers. Contracts are now more formally competed for and negotiated, usually at the regional level of the *Länder* (Evers and Rauch, 1999).

The LTCI has had a number of fairly profound effects upon the ways in which social care is perceived and used, particularly in so far as it affects older people, by far the largest category of beneficiaries. First of all, changing the basis of entitlement from that of social assistance to that of social insurance has encouraged demand. Home care services are now perceived similarly to medical care; neither the basis for their receipt nor the use of the services any longer stigmatizing but rather a function of citizenship and contributions made in employment. However, since the entitlements are not means tested, some of the new money flowing into the care sector is benefiting the better off who previously might have had to pay out of their own resources. Current users cannot claim to have contributed to the scheme for many years in a way that will be possible for future generations.

However, the poor and stigmatizing associations of institutional care will not change in the short term. As has been pointed out, the gap between LTCI payments and the costs of nursing-home care continue to mean that most residents will in addition necessarily have to apply for means-tested social assistance payments. The strict social insurance reimbursement rules and the categories of need which define entitlement are encouraging some providers to meet their obligations in rather literal and technical ways. The home care market that is emerging tends to use price 'menus' of services and standards which differentiate between users mainly in terms of their ability to add to insured services out of private incomes and assets (Schmidt, 1998c).

Although the new system has shifted the balance of care slightly more towards home care and away from institutional solutions, this may have imposed extra burdens on informal carers. The ways in which home care services are reimbursed, through the payment of fixed prices for specified tasks, encourages providers to keep contact time with users to the minimum necessary to enter the home and do whatever is being paid for, to adopt an almost paramedical model of home care (Schmidt, 1998a, b). The more time-consuming, less specifiable but more continuous aspects of caring and tending are left to family and other informal carers (Evers, 1998a). To some extent traditional and female-dominated forms of caring are being sustained and even encouraged by the LTCI and its procedures (Langen and Schlichting, 1990; Jansen, 1999).

On one hand the new LTCI system is dominated by the values and organizational procedures of the longer-established health insurance system. It is the same organizations involved in health insurance that have taken over the provision of care insurance, often using personnel and administrators with a background in health care insurance. The regulations themselves largely mimic those already established in the implementation of health insurance. On the other hand, care insurance is crucially different in that most of the service personnel are relatively unskilled women rather than traditionally male doctors. At the same time the benefits that can be used are effectively cash-limited rather than relatively uncapped as they are in the health insurance sector. Home care providers seek to maximize their role in the provision of rehabilitative and post-hospital, convalescence services for which they are reimbursed according to more generous health insurance rules.

Finally, the assimilation of the care sector into the rules and practices of the health sector entails a process of de-municipalization and de-localization of care. Germany had a strong tradition of local voluntary and charitable activities that were to a significant extent built round the needs of the disabled and elderly. Local healthcare charities ('Fördervereine', 'Krankenpflegevereine') raised money through a variety of social, sporting and recreational activities in ways that both practically and symbolically tied the needs of older people to local responsibility and civic duty. Local care institutions were seen as local assets. Municipalities, reflecting their political base, took responsibility for planning and subsidizing local, charitable sources of care. Now the responsibility has moved to a more distant regional and national level. The perception is that the insurance funds will take responsibility, as in the health sector. While most for-profit home care providers, now about 50 per cent of the market, are still relatively small and local the trend is clearly towards larger more national organizations that benefit from economies of scale and funding. Municipal responsibility is retreating to a stricter implementation of their residual role in applying the rules of social insurance (Evers and Klie, 1999). Formal social care provision is increasingly losing its quality of embeddedness in the local community.

CONCLUSION: A NEW PATTERN OF DEVELOPMENT IN SOCIAL CARE

In Germany social care services have followed a distinct and separate path of development. Both services for children and for older people have features that separate them from other public services. They have until recently been part of the local rather than national welfare state. In this they contrasted with national services like education, employment and health care. They were part of a distinct and long-established mixed economy of local welfare in which significant provider roles have been played by the main, largely denominational, charities, by the parish and its community, labour organizations and other local forms of association and community organization. This made them altogether different from central state-based and highly standardized and uniform service systems. They belonged to a sector which in France is called *services à proximité*, services which are structured in a way that the local public can have a real influence on their organization and activities.

This chapter has also sought to show how in Germany there are significant differences between childcare and elderly care, the two main social services providing for the broad majority of the population. Childcare assumed much earlier the status of a public service meant for all citizens, while elderly care services in Germany have only recently escaped from the margins of welfare, from the separate world of social assistance, and its stigmatizing associations with poverty and loss of individual self-determination. The introduction of social care insurance, LTCI, has marked a major, but still unresolved, shift both practically and culturally. Care services for older people may become de-localized and turn into a subordinate part of the larger system of medical services. Yet at the same time it may tend to reinforce traditional family obligations and roles in social care.

The historical analysis developed in this chapter has sought to highlight some core long-term divisions in welfare provision in Germany:

- universal versus selective and residual provision;
- highly standardized and uniform versus varied and patchy service provision;
- centralized and national versus municipal and local services;
- publicly financed and bureaucratically regulated provision versus mixed economies of funding and management and more varied forms of entitlement based on choice, user fees and membership of local communities.

The question confronting forms of social care now is whether they will be incorporated into the methods and forms of the more impersonal national systems like health care and education services. Predicting the future is a risky venture but a number of observations can be made.

First of all, there is a general point that in historical development nothing ever happens twice the same way. The historical circumstances that determined the development of the dominant national welfare services such as health and education will not return. It is unlikely that the latecomer to this trio, the personal social services, will go through the same stages of development: growing from the private and non-professional into statewide, standardized and fully professional provision. In Germany today it is just those qualities of size, distance from the local and dependence on professional and bureaucratic values that are being questioned. This leads to a second observation. All welfare states have recently experienced debate and change that have destroyed the clear hegemony of any one model of public personal services in health and care. The classical form of welfare provision in industrial society has been characterized by a high degree of public control, professionalization and standardization. These characteristics are now questioned in terms of both their democracy and their effectiveness: in debates about the appropriate mix of public, private and voluntary provision, the balance of professional and lay contributions, the tension between local variety and national standards, and the choice between what is determined by national statute or by individual and collective decisions. In this context the relative variety of provision and organization that still typify childcare and services for older people appear more a positive indication of the future than a negative inheritance of the past.

The development of Germany's social care services may be 'unfinished business', but their future can no longer be determined by reference to the architecture of the established welfare state. Developments in social care are now at the centre rather than at the periphery of change in welfare systems.

REFERENCES

Abelshauser, W. (ed.) (1987), *Die Weimarer Republik als Wohlfahrtsstaat*, Stuttgart: Steiner Verlag.
Alber, J. (1996), 'The debate about long-term care reform in Germany', in Organization for Economic Cooperation and Development, *Caring for Frail Elderly People: Policies in Evolution*, Social Policy Studies No. 19, Paris: OECD Publications.
Alber, J. and Schölkopf, M. (1999), *Seniorenpolitik: Die soziale Lage älterer Menschen in Deutschland und Europa*, Amsterdam: Fakultas Verlag.
Armenkollegium Hamburg (1901), *Handbuch für Wohltäthigkeit in Hamburg: Herausgegeben vom Armenkollegium und in dessen Auftrag bearbeitet von Dr. Hermann Joachim*, Hamburg: Armenkollegium.
Auskunftsstelle für Wohltätigkeit (1899), *Die Wohlfahrtseinrichtungen Bremens: Ein Auskunftsbuch*, Bremen.
BAS (Bundesministerium für Arbeit und Sozialordnung) (1998), *Bericht über die Entwicklung der Pflegeversicherung*, Bonn.
Beher, K. (1998), 'Tageseinrichtungen für Kinder: Perspektiven einer reformierten Statistik', in T. Rauschenbach and M. Schilling (eds), *Die Kinder- und Jugendhilfe und ihre Statistik*, vol. II, Berlin: Luchterhand Verlag, pp. 321–66.
Bischoff, C. (1994), *Frauen in der Krankenpflege: Zur Entwicklung von Frauenrolle und Frauenberufstätigkeit im 19. und 20. Jahrhundert*, Frankfurt am Main: Campus Verlag.
BMG (Bundesministerium für Gesundheit) (2000), *Pressemitteilungen 2000: Dialog Gesundheit: Fünf Jahre Pflegeversicherung, eine Zwischenbilanz*, Bonn.
Böckenförde, E.W. (1985), 'Der Zusammenbruch der Monarchie und die Entstehung der Weimarer Republik', in K. Jeserich (ed.) *Deutsche Verwaltungsgeschichte, Band 4*, Stuttgart: Deutsche Verlagsanstalt, pp. 1–25.
Borscheid, P. (1995), 'Vom Spital zum Altersheim', in J. Reulecke (ed.), *Die Stadt als Dienstleistungszentrum: Beiträge zur Geschichte der 'Sozialstadt' in Deutschland im 19. und 20. Jahrhundert*, St. Katharinen: Scripta-Mercaturae Verlag, pp. 259–79.
Brückner, N. (1892), *Die öffentliche und private Fürsorge: Gemeinnützige Tätigkeit und Armenwesen mit besonderer Berücksichtigung auf Frankfurt am Main*, Frankfurt am Main.
Bundesministerium für Familie, Senioren, Frauen und Jugend (BFSFJ) (1996), *Hilfe und Pflegebedürftige in privaten Haushalten*, Stuttgart.
Bundesministerium für Familie, Senioren, Frauen und Jugend (BFSFJ) (1997), *Hilfe und Pflegebedürftige in Heimen*, Stuttgart.
Bundesministerium für Familie, Senioren, Frauen und Jugend (BFSFJ) (1998), *Zehnter Kinder-und Jugendbericht*, Bonn.
Conrad, Ch. (1994), *Vom Greis zum Rentner: Der Strukturwandel des Alters in Deutschland zwischen 1830 und 1930*, Göttingen: Vandenhoeck & Ruprecht.
Damrau, H. (1935/36), 'Zur Reform des Fürsorgewesens', in *Deutsche Zeitschrift für Wohlfahrtspflege II*, Berlin, pp. 611f.
Dann, O. (ed.) (1984), *Vereinswesen und bürgerliche Gesellschaft in Deutschland*, München: Oldenbourg Verlag.

Deutsches Jugendinstitut (1998), *Tageseinrichtungen für Kinder: Pluralisierung von Angeboten*, München: Zahlenspiegel.

Die Wohlfahrtseinrichtungen Berlins und seiner Vororte (1891), Berlin.

Die Wohlfahrtseinrichtungen in Leipzig (1905), Leipzig.

Die Wohlfahrtseinrichtungen Münchens (1901), München.

Erning, G. (1987), 'Quantitative Angebote öffentlicher Kleinkinderziehung', in G. Erning, K. Neumann and J. Reyer (eds), *Geschichte des Kindergärtens*, vol. 1, pp. 29–39.

Erning, G., Neumann, K. and Reyer, J. (eds) (1987), *Geschichte des Kindergärtens*, 2 volumes, Freiburg im Breisgau: Lambertus Verlag.

Evers, A. (1998a), 'The new long-term care insurance program in Germany', *Journal of Aging and Social Policy*, **10** (1), 77–98.

Evers, A. (1998b), 'Schutz und Aktivierung. Das Beispiel häuslicher Hilfen und Pflegedienste im Rahmen der Pflegeversicherung', in E. Mezger and K.W. West (eds), *Neue Chancen für den Sozialstaat: Soziale Gerechtigkeit, Sozialstaat und Aktivierung*, Marburg: Schüren Verlag, pp. 61–76.

Evers, A. (1999), 'Familienselbsthilfe in Europa', in *Diskurs Heft*, vol. 2, pp. 8–13.

Evers, A. and Klie, Th. (1999), 'Zur Neuausrichtung kommunaler Alterssozialpolitik oder: Nach dem Pflegeversicherungsgesetz — freiwilliges kommunales Engagement?', in R. Schmidt (ed.), *Die Versorgung pflegebedürftiger alter Menschen in der Kommune*, Frankfurt am Main: Mabuse Verlag.

Evers, A. and Rauch, U. (1999), 'Ambulante Altenpflege — Umbau oder Abbau kommunaler Verantwortlichkeiten?', *Zeitschrift für Sozialreform*, **2**, 170–85.

Fromm, B. (1894), *Die Wohltätigkeitsvereine in Berlin*, Berlin:Vereinsbuchandlung.

Grunow, D., Hegner, F. and Lempert, J. (1979), *Sozialstationen. Analysen und Materialien zur Neuorganisation ambulanter Sozial- und Gesundheitsdienste*, Bielefeld: Kleine Verlag.

Hansen, E. (1991), *Wohlfahrtspolitik im NS-Staat*, Augsburg: Mar Verlag.

http://www.bmfsfj.de (1999), *Heimstatistik*. Stand: Juli 1999.

http://www.bmgesundheit.de (1999), *Zahlen und Fakten zur Pflegeversicherung*. Stand: August 1999.

Irmak, K.H. (1998), 'Anstaltsfürsorge für "Alterssieche" von Weimar bis Bonn (1924–1961)', *Zeitschrift für Gerontologie und Geriatrie Bd*, **31** (2), 438–477.

Jansen, B. (1999), 'Informelle Pflege durch Angehörige', in B. Jansen (ed.), *Soziale Gerontologie*, Weinheim: Beltz Verlag.

Kaiser, J.-Ch. (1989), *Sozialer Protestantismus im 20. Jahrhundert*, München: Oldenbourg Verlag.

Kaiser, J.-Ch. (1996), 'Von der christlichen Liebestätigkeit zur freien Wohlfahrtspflege', in Th. Rauschenbach, Ch. Sachße and Th. Olk (eds), *Von der Wertgemeinschaft zum Dienstleistungsunternehmen*, 2nd edn, Frankfurt: Suhrkamp Verlag, pp. 150–74.

Kondratowitz, H.J. (1988), 'Allen zur Last, niemandem zur Freude. Die institutionelle Prägung des Alterserlebens als historischer Prozess', in G. Göckenjahn and H.J. Kondratowitz (eds), *Alter und Alltag*, Frankfurt am Main: Suhrkamp Verlag.

Kondratowitz, H.J. and Schmidt, R. (1986), 'Vorwärts zu den Anfängen: Wohlfahrtsverbandliche Altenarbeit im Spannungsfeld gerontologischer Zielvorstellungen und finanzieller Restriktionen', in D. Tränhardt (ed.), *Wohlfahrtsverbände zwischen Selbsthilfe und Sozialstaat*, Freiburg im Breisgau: Lambertus Verlag.

Koven, S. and Michel, S. (eds) (1993), *Mothers of a New World*, New York and London: Routledge.

Langen, I. and Schlichting, R. (1990), *Altenhilfe auf dem Lande. Erfahrungen eines pra-xisorientierten Forschungsprojekts*, Marburg.

Majce, G. (1978), ' "Geschlossene Altershilfe": Probleme der Heimunterbringung', in L. Rosenmayr and H. Rosenmayr (eds), *Der alte Mensch in der Gesellschaft*, Rein-bek: Rowohlt Verlag.

Mohrmann, A. (1929), 'Stichwort Kindergarten', in J. Dünner (ed.), *Handwörterbuch der Wohlfahrtspflege*, 2nd edn, Berlin: Karl Heymanns Verlag, pp. 387–89.

Nipperdey, Th. (1972), 'Verein als soziale Struktur im späten 18. und frühen 19. Jahr-hundert', in H. Boockmann (ed.), *Geschichtswissenschaft und Vereinswesen im 19. Jahrhundert: Beiträge zur Geschichte historischer Forschung in Deutschland*, Göt-tingen: Vandenhoeck & Ruprecht Verlag, pp. 1–44.

Reyer, J. (1985), *Wenn die Mütter arbeiten gingen ... Eine sozialhistorische Studie zur Entstehung der öffentlichen Kleinkinderziehung im 19. Jahrhundert in Deutschland*, 2nd edn, Köln: Pahl-Rugenstein Verlag.

Reyer, J. (1987a), 'Entwicklung der Trägerstruktur in der öffentlichen Kleinkinderzie-hung', in G. Erning, K. Neumann and J. Reyer (eds), *Geschichte des Kindergärtens*, vol. 1, pp. 40–66.

Reyer, J. (1987b), 'Geschichte der öffentlichen Kleinkinderziehung im deutschen Kai-serreich, in der Weimarer Republik und in der Zeit des Nationalsozialismus', in G. Erning, K. Neumann and J. Reyer (eds), *Geschichte des Kindergärtens*, vol. 2, pp. 43–82.

Rothgang, H. (1997), *Ziele und Wirkungen der Pflegeversicherung: Eine ökonomische Analyse*, Frankfurt am Main: Campus Verlag.

Rothgang, H. and Schmähl, W. (1996), 'The long term costs of public long-term care in-surance in Germany. Some guesstimates', in R. Eisen and F.A. Sloane (eds), *Alterna-tives for Ensuring Long-Term Care: Economic Issues and Policy Solutions*. Amsterdam: Kluwer Academic Verlag, pp. 181–222.

Sachße, Ch. (1994), *Mütterlichkeit als Beruf*, 2nd edn, Opladen: Westdeutscher Verlag.

Sachße, Ch. (1996), 'Verein, Verband und Wohlfahrtsstaat: Entstehung und Entwick-lung der "dualen" Wohlfahrtspflege', in Th. Rauschenbach, Ch. Sachße and Th. Olk (eds), *Von der Wertgemeinschaft zum Dienstleistungsunternehmen*, 2nd edn, Frank-furt: Suhrkamp Verlag, pp. 123–49.

Sachße, Ch. (2000), 'Freiwilligenarbeit und private Wohlfahrtskultur in historischer Perspektive', in St. Nährlich and A. Zimmer (eds), *Engagierte Bürgerschaft*, Opla-den: Leske und Budrich, pp. 75–88.

Sachße, Ch. and Tennstedt, F. (1988), 'Geschichte der Armenfürsorge in Deutschland', *Fürsorge und Wohlfahrtspflege 1871–1929*, Band 2, Stuttgart: Kohlhammer.

Sachße, Ch. and Tennstedt, F. (1992), 'Der Wohlfahrtsstaat im Nationalsozialismus', *Geschichte der Armenfürsorge in Deutschland*, Band 3, Stuttgart: Kohlhammer.

Schmidt, R. (1998a), 'Neupositionierung im Konkurrenzgeflecht: Optionen und Ge-fährdungen ambulanter Pflegedienste im Spektrum von SGB V und SGB XI', in R. Schmidt (ed.), *Neue Steuerungen in Pflege und Sozialer Altenarbeit*, Regensburg: Transfer Verlag.

Schmidt, R. (1998b), *Neupositionierung im Konkurrenzgeflecht. Optionen und Gefähr-dungen ambulanter Pflegedienste*, Diskussionspapier Nr. 18 des Deutschen Zen-trums für Altersfragen, Berlin.

Schmidt, R. (1998c), *Leistungsdifferenzierung in der vollstationären pflege*, Diskus-sionspapier Nr. 21 des Deutschen Zentrums für Altersfragen, Berlin.

Stadtbund der Vereine für Armenpflege und Wohltätigkeit (1901), *Die private Fürsorge in Frankfurt am Main*, Frankfurt am Main.

Statistisches Bundesamt (1996a), *Fachserie 13: Sozialleistungen. Reihe 6.3: Einrichtungen und tätige Personen in der Jugendhilfe (1994)*, Stuttgart: Verlag Metzler-Poeschel.

Statistisches Bundesamt (1996b), *Fachserie 13. Sozialleistungen: Reihe 6.3.1: Tageseinrichtungen für Kinder 1994*, Stuttgart: Verlag Metzler-Poeschel.

Statistisches Bundesamt (1996c), *Fachserie 13. Sozialleistungen: Reihe 6.4: Ausgaben und Einnahmen der öffentlichen Jugendhilfe 1994*, Stuttgart: Verlag Metzler-Poeschel.

Steinweg, D.J. (1929), 'Stichwort Altersfürsorge', in J. Dünner (ed.), *Handwörterbuch der Wohlfahrtspflege*, 2nd edn, Berlin: Carl Heymanns Verlag.

vom Bruch, R.(1985), 'Bürgerliche Sozialreform im Deutschen Kaiserreich', in R. vom Bruch (ed.), *Weder Kommunismus noch Kapitalismus. Bürgerliche Sozialreform vom Vormärz bis zur Ära Adenauer.* München: Beck Verlag, pp. 61–179.

Wissenschaftliches Institut der AOK (1998), *Der Pflegemarkt in Deutschland*, Bonn.

Wollasch, A. (1991), *Der Katholische Fürsorgeverein für Mädchen, Frauen und Kinder 1899–1945*, Freiburg im Breisgau: Lambertus Verlag.

4. Care for Children and Older People in Japan: Modernizing the Traditional

Mutsuko Takahashi

INTRODUCTION

This chapter explores patterns of social care in contemporary Japan and their context of growing and increasingly diverse social needs. It will also analyse discrepancies between welfare policies and their implementation and review debates about what should be done about these failings. Recently, the main focus of political discussion about the future of Japanese welfare has been the ageing of the society. The share of the population aged 65 or more in 1970 was 7.1 per cent, growing to 14.5 per cent in 1995. By 1998, 16.2 per cent (20,508,000) of the whole population (126,486,000) were 65 and over. It is estimated that in 2025 the ratio of older people will reach 27.4 per cent (Kôseishô, 1999, p. 338). At the same time the fertility rate, 1.39 per 1000 in 1997 (ibid., p. 337), is likely to remain very low. The Japanese government has not been successful in convincing people to have more children. Japan shares the concerns about 'the future of low-birthrate populations' that are found in Europe (Day, 1992).

Continuing industrialization and urbanization have led to imbalances at the regional and local levels. It is rural rather than urban areas that face the more rapidly accelerating ageing of population as younger people move to cities. The proportion of those 65 and over varies greatly between prefectures, ranging from a high of 21.1 per cent in the Shimane prefecture to a low of 9.7 per cent in the Saitama prefecture in 1994 (Sômuchô, 1995, pp. 8–9). These regional disparities are expected to grow, causing tensions in the debate about appropriate national care policies. The structure of Japanese politics means that social care strategies need to be locally based in order to win effective support.

Recent welfare developments in Japan are closely linked to a pattern of administrative reform that emphasizes decentralization and deregulation. Since the early 1980s central government has taken the initiative in decentralizing public sector administration by relocating tasks and duties to local government.

In Japan deregulation is understood as the devolution of central government control, *kisei kanwa* in Japanese, rather than *kisei teppai*, abolishing regulation and control altogether. For example, the new public care insurance system for older people that came into effect in April 2000 incorporates administrative reforms that clarify the responsibilities of the local municipalities for the provision of care to local residents and seek to increase the variety of care services through deregulation.

THE PATTERN OF SOCIAL CARE PROVISION IN CONTEMPORARY JAPAN

Japan is a welfare state in that it has comprehensive social security and welfare systems that cover the whole population. However, direct subsidies to incomes are usually limited to the poorest. One of the distinctive features of the Japanese pattern is that care services have been given only a small part of public expenditure and the main emphasis has been on pensions and health care. In 1996 pensions took 51.8 per cent of total social expenditure, health care 37.3 per cent, while forms of social care consumed only 4.2 per cent. In the same year social expenditure as a whole took 17.21 per cent of the national income and the average expenditure per household was ¥1,528,300 (£8,600, €12,300). The social welfare services received barely 4.2 per cent of social security expenditure in 1996 (National Institute of Population and Social Security Research, 2000a, 2000b).

In a report entitled 'A Vision of the Welfare in the 21st Century' submitted by an advisory committee to the Minister of Health and Welfare in March 1994, it was suggested that welfare services should be given more emphasis. The distribution of pensions, medical care and welfare services in the social security budget was 5:4:1 in the early 1990s, and the report proposed to change it to 5:3:2 in the near future (Fukushi seisaku kenkyû-kai, 1996, p. 12). Since the mid-1980s the Japanese government has been holding back overall social security expenditure, but not that on social welfare services. In this way the state has admitted the need for more developed social welfare services to cope with the increasing care needs of an ageing society.

A characteristic of existing social care services is that the state prefers to provide them directly rather than allow individuals to choose more freely and purchase the services for themselves. Whenever local authorities attempt to offer a cash benefit for any welfare purpose, it tends to be labelled as a 'purposeless waste of public money on welfare' (*baramaki*). This is mainly because of the influence of the right wing in political debates since the mid-1970s in which some left-wing local governments have been criticized for expanding welfare expenditure (see, for example, Yokoyama, 1992, pp. 58–9). This question of the appropriate role of cash benefits in social care will be discussed later in relation to the public care insurance system for elderly care.

While there are many welfare organizations outside the public sector, they are often characterized as 'semi-public' because they operate in very close collaboration with government and provide welfare services under the supervision and with the financial support of the public sector. In fact these 'independent' welfare organizations could not exist without their public funding (Arizuka, 1998, p. 9). For instance, when independent social welfare organizations set up new services, 75 per cent of the cost of construction of buildings and purchase of property is paid by central government (50 per cent) and the prefecture (25 per cent) (Kôseishô, 1999, p. 412). One may wonder in what sense these non-statutory organizations can really be outside the public sector if they so heavily depend on government money (Sanada, 1996). In theory, only 'non-profit-making' independent welfare organizations are given official permission to function as providers of welfare services. This is mainly a product of the history of Japanese care provision: due to the late start of the public sector in welfare, historically the non-profit organizations have played an essential role in providing social welfare services. However, the more 'deregulation' is pursued, the more opportunities are given to 'profit-making' private companies in the market for welfare services. The deregulation policy is impacting not only on the care of older people, through the public care insurance system launched in April 2000, but also on childcare services.

Currently, the search for a proper balance between social care and family care usually ends in controversy and uncertainty in contemporary Japan. Contrary to the idealized image of the traditional Japanese family, family care cannot always be realized in a harmonious manner and without causing trouble and conflict among those involved. The care-giving functions of the Japanese family could not be entirely relied on during the rapid modernization and urbanization of the post-1945 era that greatly changed people's ways of living. It is no longer realistic to expect the family alone to take care of older people and children. But, at the same time, social care has not entirely been freed from stigma and social welfare tends to be associated in the minds of many citizens with means-tested benefits for the poor.

Childcare

In the search for a policy response to the declining birth rate, the Japanese government published the so-called *Angel Plan* (*Enzeru puran* in Japanese) in December 1994 to promote social support for childcare. It mainly proposed to help working mothers by improving day care, and it is indeed important to increase the flexibility of day-care arrangements. However, the *Angel Plan* seems to have had little impact on the current situation because it took too little

account of labour market changes. It is not only because more women work outside the home that the birth rate has been declining. Rather, the dominant practice in Japanese working life has been to keep working days so long that both
women and men who are in paid work have little time for childcare. The society
has been preoccupied with 'production' for economic growth while 'reproduction' has been undermined. The issue of the declining birth rate tends to be
reduced to 'the women's question', or the 'crisis of motherhood', and fails to
include a comprehensive approach to parenthood which includes fatherhood
and the realities of working lives for both men and women.

In Japan children start elementary school in April of the year in which they
reach the age of six. Generally children under six years old are taken care of
either by their own family (by parents, especially mothers) or in day-care centres and kindergartens. The day-care centres (*hoikusho*), supervised by the Ministry of Health and Welfare, play an essential role in looking after children,
especially those under three years old. Day care for children between three and
five years old is available not only from the day-care centres but also from kindergartens (*yôchien*) supervised by the Ministry of Education. The public and
private sectors co-exist in the provision of day care and pre-school education.
Moreover, recently day care for school-age children has been given more attention as some day-care centres, often in collaboration with elementary schools,
take care of children under ten after school for a couple of hours in the late after-
noon. In what follows, the current framework of the Japanese childcare system
is examined by discussing major controversies about childcare provision.

Day-care centres
The public sector, especially municipalities (cities, towns and villages), provides childcare by financing and regulating day-care centres in local communities. The public sector plays an important role in ensuring that childcare is of
standardized quality and in keeping the price as low as possible. The Ministry
of Health and Welfare determines basic standards for day-care centres. By
meeting the official standards, the centres can identify themselves as *ninka
hoikusho* (officially authorized day-care centres). They are run either by municipalities or by independent social welfare organizations. (See Tables 4.1 and
4.2.) The municipalities control admissions to day-care centres on the basis of
an annual round of applications from parents. The fees are based on the parents'
annual income and range from ¥1,000 (£5.50, €8) to ¥41,800 (£240, €337) per
month in the case of the Adachi ward in Tokyo in 1998 (Zenkoku and Hoiku,
1998, p. 302). The social security system provides a child allowance to households with children under three years old and an annual income less than
¥2,840,000 (£16,000, €23,000). The monthly child allowance (*jidô teate*) is
¥5,000 (£30, €43) for the first child, ¥5,000 for the second, and ¥10,000 for the

Table 4.1 Authorized children's day-care centres, 1997

	Number	Capacity (persons)	Enrolment
Public	13,074	1,113,540	894,334
Private	9,327	801,686	753,552
Total	22,401	1,915,226	1,647,886

Source: Almanac of Data on Japanese Children, vol. 6, p. 406.

Table 4.2 The age distribution of children in authorized day-care centres, 1998

	Number	Per cent
Under 1 year	59,064	3.5
1 and 2 years	421,433	24.9
3 years	403,098	23.8
4 and over	807,533	47.8

Source: Kôseishô, 1999, p. 428.

third and subsequent children. In 1998, 1,928,553 households containing 2,157,668 children received this allowance (Kôseishô, 1999, p. 430).

There are also *muninka hoikusho*, day-care centres that are not officially authorized (Table 4.3). Because they do not meet the official standard for authorization, they are not provided with financial support by municipalities. These unauthorized day-care centres are run by private, for-profit organizations. It is mainly their flexibility that allows them to compete with the authorized centres. The quality of care by the unauthorized day-care centres varies considerably. Some are said to focus on profit rather than on quality to the extent that the children's well-being may be endangered. Such problematic cases are mostly found in large cities where not a few working parents have difficulty in arranging proper childcare in authorized day-care centres. Although the officially authorized day-care centres had an enrolment capacity of 1,920,000 children in April 1998, only 88.3 per cent of the capacity was used for 1,690,000 children in total (Kôseisho, 1999, p. 249). Despite this nominal excess capacity, there are waiting lists. In April 1999, 32,225 children were waiting for vacancies in authorized day-care centres mainly in large cities (*Asahi Shinbun*, 19 November 1999, p. 3). The inflexibility of the operating hours of authorized day-care centres causes inconvenience for parents who have to commute between home and the workplace. Employment also often means a long working day for the

Table 4.3 Unauthorized day-care centres, 1998

Type	Number	Children enrolled
Workplace	3,561	52,909
Remote places	1,382	24,461
'Baby hotels'	649	16,958
Others	4,052	131,970
Total	9,644	226,298

Source: Zenkoku and Hoiku, 1998, p. 284.

parents. The *raison d'être* of 'unauthorized' day care is that it is the individual household's solution to the deficiencies of family and employment policies. In short, the co-existence of authorized and unauthorized day-care centres reveals the gap between policy and the real needs of childcare.

There is a statutory requirement that municipalities provide childcare for 'children in need of care' (*hoiku ni kakeru mono*) such as in dual-career and lone-parent families and where parents are sick or disabled. In this sense authorized day-care centres constitute a welfare service for families with care needs. However, this is an example of an area where there is a gap between policy and implementation. In practice the policy is interpreted as applying only where mothers are able neither to take care of their children nor to arrange childcare informally by using grandmothers, neighbours or friends. Thus, in Japan, childcare has not essentially been seen as a citizen's right. Rather the historical origins of authorized childcare are rooted in a role as an emergency welfare response of municipalities in the 1940s and, until very recently, little change to the system itself means it fails to endorse a right to childcare. The Law on the Welfare of Children (*Jidōfukushi-hō*) was revised with effect from April 1998. The revision was mainly intended to increase choice for users of childcare, by offering longer operating hours at the officially authorized day-care centres, and by expanding provision, especially for infants under one year old. The required ratio of childcare staff to infants under one year old was increased from 1:6 to 1:3. In addition, the revised law changed the job title of staff in the centres from *hobo* (day-care mother) to the gender-neutral *hoikushi* (day-care worker).

Until recently, in order to be recognized and regulated as an authorized 'social welfare organization' (*shakai fukushi hōjin*), independent providers could not be overtly profit-oriented. However, as of April 2000 the 'deregulation policy' has been extended to childcare provision, and ordinary 'profit-making' enterprises can now become officially authorized providers (*Asashi Shinbun*, 21 February 2000, p. 10). The main aim of this deregulation is to allow for more varied and flexible childcare, responsive to demand from parents but within national standards. There will now be more choice among the officially authorized day-care centres. On the other hand, those who cannot afford the more expensive childcare that this liberalization is likely to bring forth may be disadvantaged. The deregulation policy suggests a new division of labour between the public and the private providers of childcare. For example, the public sector may focus more on social need, targeting children with disabilities or social disadvantages. It may also concentrate more on research and development within the sector and on the education and training of professional childcare workers.

Kindergartens and day-care centres
Kindergartens are run both by local authorities and by independent educational organizations, including some with a religious orientation. In Japan it is not unusual for religious organizations to be involved in educational provision. Even before Japanese modernization began in the mid-nineteenth century, Buddhist temples, for example, played a central role in primary education, running schools at the local level called *terakoya*. The education system in modern Japan since the second half of the nineteenth century has developed through a co-existence of public and private schools. In particular, private schools and colleges, again often established by religious organizations, some of which were Christian, contributed much to the development of the higher education.

The original aim of kindergartens was to provide children aged between three and five with pre-school education rather than with an alternative to family care. From the administrative point of view, the difference between kindergartens and day centres is the difference between education and welfare, corresponding to the division of labour between the two relevant government departments, the Ministry of Education and Ministry of Health and Welfare. Despite these differences, however, their functions overlap considerably. From the point of view of children and their parents, both kindergartens and day centres are the places for children to go to, and be with other children, while their parents do something other than childcare. Currently nearly two-thirds of primary school children have had some experience of a kindergarten. It is a significant source of pre-school care and education.

Traditionally, the basic operating hours of kindergartens are four hours a day, which is fewer than those in day-care centres. However, as the proportion of working mothers has increased, so today's parents often expect kindergartens to take care of children for as long as day-care centres. The decline in the number of small children has also led to competition between kindergartens and day-care centres. Consequently the functions of kindergartens have tended to become similar to those of day-care centres. Not a few kindergartens offer day care in addition to the educational provision so that children can stay longer while their parents/mothers are working. The Ministry of Education now provides funding for the extra day-care services in kindergartens (*azukari hoiku*)

(Zenkoku and Hoiku, 1998, p. 62). Users of day-care services in kindergartens are usually charged additional fees of about ¥1,000 (£5.50, €8) per day (ibid., p. 66). In this sense, the differences between kindergartens and day-care centres have become ambiguous despite the distinction between the two responsible government departments.

In 1997 there were nearly 15,000 kindergartens in Japan, 45.8 per cent were in the public sector and 58.2 per cent provided by the independent sector. Tables 4.4 and 4.5 show the distribution of children by age in kindergartens and the overall distribution of children up to the age of six in different forms of day care in 1997.

Table 4.4 The age distribution of children in kindergartens, 1997

	Number	Per cent
3 years old	350,401	19.6
4 years old	682,115	38.1
5 years old	757,007	42.3
Total	1,789,523	100.0

Source: Kôseishô, 1998, p. 155.

Table 4.5 Distribution of children among different forms of day care in 1997
        (thousands)

	Family care only		Kindergartens		Day-centres	
Under 1	1,145	(95.3%)	na		56	(4.7%)
Aged 1 & 2	1,966	(82.9%)	na		406	(17.1%)
3 year olds	468	(39.0%)	350	(29.2%)	381	(31.8%)
Aged 4,5 & 6	758	(25.3%)	1,439	(48.0%)	800	(26.7%)

Source: Kôseishô, 1998, p. 155.

The Care of Older People

The care of older people is currently the subject of ongoing welfare reforms and often reveals core ideological conflicts and ambivalences between family care and social care. While the care-giving functions of the Japanese family have declined in recent decades, the need for elderly care has been increasing and diversifying. An idealistic image of the traditional Japanese family still persists but in fact it is no longer possible for many families to provide adequate care for their older relatives without outside help. In 1999 an opinion poll for the national daily newspaper, *Asahi Shinbun*, found that 61 per cent of interviewed people do not want to rely on the family when they grow old whereas 36 per cent still wished to do so (*Asahi Shinbun*, 29 March 1999, p. 2). A survey conducted by the Japanese government in 1998 showed that 73 per cent of interviewed citizens over twenty years old had specific concerns about their welfare in old age (Kôseishô, 1999, p. 162). Clearly a substantial number of people do not want to burden their families in later life.

Thanks to the progress of medical care and improved living standards, average life expectancy in Japan is the highest in the world: 77.19 years for men and 83.82 for women in 1997 (ibid., p. 197). Such long life expectancy is not only good news but also a source of worry. The number of older people with physical and mental disabilities is rising (Table 4.6).

Table 4.6 An estimate of the number of older people who will need care (millions)

	Frail elderly	Confused	Confused and bed-bound	Total
1993	1.0	0.1	0.9	2.0
2000	1.3	0.2	1.2	2.8
2010	1.7	0.3	1.7	3.9
2025	2.6	0.4	2.3	5.2

Source: Kôseishô, 1999, p. 197.

Welfare services for older people

The Japanese government has been seeking to reform care provision systems by reintegrating them with medical care. We will focus here on the ten-year project, *The Golden Plan 1990–99*, and on the new public care insurance system that came into operation in April 2000. The current Japanese welfare system for the care of older people offers a variety of services such as: (a) home help services (home helpers providing housework services), (b) respite care (institutional care of bed-ridden people for a short duration), and (c) day-care services (day-centres providing services such as bathing, meals, medical checkups, rehabilitation and so on) (Kôseishô, 1998, p. 243). In addition, outside urban areas there are centres providing home-based advice and guidance (*zaitaku kaigo shien sentâ*). The use of all these care services has been rising, and the Ministry of Health and Welfare now admits that there is a shortage in the supply of care services. Regional disparities have also grown, mainly because some municipalities have not yet sufficiently adjusted their care provision (see Table 4.7).

Table 4.7 Use of services for older people and regional variations

	1989 national median provision[a]	1989 regional variation[b]	1996 national median provision[a]	1996 regional variation[b]
Home help	41.5	66.5	119.4	150.3
Day care	15.8	36.5	142.8	251.8
Respite care	6.1	14.0	36.8	56.7

Note
a Days on which service used per 100 people over 65.
b Difference between highest and lowest region.

Source: Kôseishô, 1998, p. 244.

It is more widely recognized in Japan today that home care, or community care (*zaitaku kea*), needs to be developed in order to reduce the institution-alization of older people. On the other hand, researchers point out differences in the understanding of 'home care' between Japan and the West. Many Japanese older people live at home cared for by their families, whereas for example in Sweden older people often opt to live 'at home' by making full use of the social care services available (Yamanoi, 1996, pp. 80–82). Within the Japanese mean-ing of home care, social care by outsiders remains secondary and additional to family care. This is an example of the difficulties that are encountered in com-parative studies where one seeks to compare similar forms across different cul-tures. Home care remains a less practicable choice for many Japanese because it is taken to mean 'family care' and thus likely to require that a member of the family gives up a working life in the midst of the development of her/his career. The idea of home care supported by non-family help is still hard to grasp in a society in which the ideal of the family remains strong even if the reality is rather different.

Institutional care of older people
In Japan, other than care in medical hospitals, the following main sources of care are in principle available:

- Nursing homes for disabled older people (*tokubetsu yôgo rôjin hômu*, often called '*tokuyô*' in Japanese). These institutions care for people who need regular long-term care.
- Rehabilitation centres (*rôjin hoken shisetsu*). These are facilities that offer rehabilitation to people who are not ill but who still have some level of dependency or need for convalescence. They provide both residential and day care.
- Residential homes (*kea hausu*). These are institutions that care for people with slight disabilities and which seek to sustain as much personal independence as possible.
- Welfare centres. These are multipurpose centres providing support to older people living in sparsely populated areas.
- Health centres. From these doctors and nurses visit frail older people living at home to provide medical services.

Institutional care still has a negative image for many. It is as if the old person has been abandoned by their family and relatives. To avoid the stigma that may attach to the family, older people may be sent to hospital instead of a residential welfare institution even though they are not greatly in need of medical care. An excessive reliance on medical hospitals for elderly care has long been discussed as a manifestation of the contradictory relations between medical care and social welfare in Japan. This phenomenon is also called 'hospitalization of the elderly for social reasons' (*shakaiteki nyûin*) and refers to situations where hospitals function as *de facto* care homes for older people rather than as purely medical institutions. This practice also reflects a shortage of care homes and consequently some hospitals accept elderly people as long-term patients when they can no longer continue their lives at home. This is socially constructed hospitalization and not medical care. Recent revisions to regulations governing hospitals discourage stays of over three months. Beyond that point the economic compensation that the hospital gains through the medical insurance of the patient is reduced. This rule was intended to promote cheaper and more medically efficient use of hospitals. In 1997 the average duration of a hospital stay per patient in Japan was 42.5 days, far longer than in any other industrialized country (Kôseishô, 1999, p. 377). Now hospitals are reluctant to allow older people to stay more than three months, with the result that some may find themselves transported from one hospital to another. Pressure has recently been exerted to extend the three-month rule to six months because of the inconvenience caused to many older people and their families.

In a related revision of regulations, hospitals are no longer allowed to hire care assistants (*tsukisoi*) to provide non-medical support for patients. These helpers were not qualified nurses but defined as nursing staff more broadly. With this revision the Ministry of Health and Welfare intended hospitals to improve the quality of care by increasing the employment of qualified nurses in place of the care assistants. However, contrary to the intention of officialdom, the reform has not had the desired effect. Hospitals have not compensated for the reduction in the numbers of assistants and consequently relatives of older hospital patients may have to come in to do some of the more minor care tasks themselves.

The Golden Plan of the 1990s

The *Golden Plan* was an ambitious national programme intended to substantially increase provision in the community for older people with care needs. For the period 1990 to 1999 the plan set targets for the volume of services and combined this with a policy of decentralization of responsibility, largely to the level of the municipality. The plan set targets for the volume of provision of community services such as home helps, respite care, day care, welfare centres, health centres, residential homes and nursing homes. In many cases the bulk of the planned provision was to be met by the independent sector. Initially, relatively little information was available on the pattern of need. The Ministry of Health and Welfare was slow to complete a national assessment of need and municipalities had to rely on their own local surveys. After additional data became available, the plan was revised in 1994 and became known as the *New Golden Plan*. By 1999 the key constraints had become clearer. A major problem had been the recruitment of the necessary labour such as qualified home-helpers. Although money was available and allocated in national budgets, the labour was often not available at the local level (*Asahi Shinbun*, 29 March 1999, p. 1). Overall there were considerable gaps between the initial plans and what was realized in terms of both provision and improvements in indicators of well-being among older people. To some extent the Golden Plan had been a paper tiger.

The new care insurance system

From April 2000 a new national system of care insurance was added to the existing system of health insurance. All people over forty years old are required to join the scheme. For those in employment the cost is added to their health insurance deductions. For those in retirement a charge is made on their pension payments. The deductions are graduated and the monthly contributions paid by pensioners vary between about ¥1,400 (£8, €11) and ¥6,250 (£35, €50) per person with an average of about ¥2,900 (£16, €23). There is a substantial subsidy from the taxpayer; half of all costs are effectively paid by the state. The system is managed by the municipalities, but with practical and financial support from central government.

Under the care insurance scheme older people who believe they need assistance can ask their municipality to carry out a needs assessment. These are conducted by qualified social work staff in the older person's home using a standardized and computerized questionnaire of some 80 questions about the physical and mental condition of the applicant. In addition to the personal interview, the assessment requires a medical statement from a general practitioner. As a result of the assessment the older person is allocated to one of seven degrees of need: 'independent' (*jiritsu*), 'needs minimal social support' (*yô-shien*), and five levels of 'need for social and nursing care' (*yô-kaigo*). The applicant has a right of appeal.

Once need has been identified, an individual 'care plan' (*kea puran*) is prepared with advice and help from welfare experts called 'care managers' (*kea manêjâ*, or *kaigo shien senmon'in* in Japanese). The user can choose to combine various services within the budget allowed for a level of assessed need. The care insurance covers 90 per cent of the cost of the services while the user pays 10 per cent in addition to the basic monthly insurance fees already mentioned. However, the total individual charge is capped and varies according to household income with a minimum of about ¥15,000 (£90, €130) per month payable by people in receipt of the state old-age pension (*Asahi Shinbun*, 5 February 2000, p. 4). There are maximum costs that can be covered under the insurance for each category. Most importantly, the care insurance system provides no cash benefits but only services.

The Ministry of Health and Welfare encourages independent providers to contract to supply care services. This has led to the creation of what is called the 'silver industry', referring to the service industry that has entered the market for care services to older people. Competition is therefore possible but only within the constraints set by the state in terms of service standards and prices and by the minimum wage legislation which plays an important role in this labour intensive market. Overall the arrangements reveal the ambivalence of the state to opening up provision of care to the private sector. While competition, variety and flexibility are sought, this 'deregulation' takes place in the framework of considerable 're-regulation' in terms of prices and quality. A complex set of maximum prices have been set for personal care and home help services, graduated according to the length of time involved. A falling rate of payment per hour discourages providers from oversupplying care. Residential homes, nursing homes and hospitals face a similar schedule of maximum daily charges that can be levied varying according to five levels of need for care.

Debate and uncertainty in the new social care insurance system

At the time of writing (2002) there was little evidence available on the working of the new social care insurance system since its start in April 2000. However, considerable reservations have been expressed by welfare experts and by the municipalities that are required to finance and operate the new system. The main concerns expressed have been: (1) the lack of adequate local infrastructures to supply the services, (2) the continuing reliance on hospital care implied by the new arrangements, (3) the limits set to services per person, (4) the financial risks to municipalities, and (5) uncertainty about how the needs assessment process is working (Satô et al., 1997, p. 112). Municipalities in particular have been concerned about the lack of detail in the legislation about the financial implications for local authorities and about their position where they are unable to provide the services which assessments indicate people should receive and for which they have paid their contributions. These concerns reveal the top-down nature of the reform process and the degree to which it was based on broad estimates of likely demand for, and supply of, social care services. The Ministry of Health and Welfare is reported to have designed the care insurance system on the basis of an estimate that only about 40 per cent of older people in need of social care would actually make use of the new insurance entitlements in 2000, the first year of operation (ibid.).

For political reasons some changes to the system were made even before implementation in April 2000. Politicians became anxious about the electoral consequences once older voters became aware of the social insurance contributions they would have to pay out of their wages or pensions. As a result payments by retired people were postponed to September 2000, and until September 2001 they will be charged only half of the planned rates, the difference being made up by the state and younger taxpayers (*Asahi Shinbun*, 24 November 1999, p. 3).

More significantly perhaps, a change has been made allowing the municipalities to make cash payments to those who take care of an older person at home instead of using the services of the care insurance system. The maximum amount payable is ¥100,000 (£600, €850) per year, households are means tested and the older person must have been assessed as being in the two highest levels of need. This alternative of payment for care was won by the politician, Kamei Shizuka, who argued that family care was being ignored in the design of the new system. However, the real outcome of this essentially political and ideological compromise remains unclear. Older people who are assessed as being in one of the two highest dependency levels of the new system are likely to be very frail indeed.

The restructuring of long-term care facilities for older people
The 1990s saw very rapid expansion of facilities for older people that provide both medical and social care, particularly the rehabilitation centres (*rôjin hoken shisetsu*) and a new type of hospital unit specializing in longer-term care of older people (*ryôyô-gata byôshô-gun*) (see Table 4.8). Between 1989 and 1998 the number of places in rehabilitation centres rose from 13,000 to almost 200,000. These centres are mainly run by independent health providers (1,692 centres) or more rarely by independent social welfare organizations (357). Only 110 are run directly by municipalities (Kôseishô, 1999, p. 426). They provide

Table 4.8 Forms of long-term institutional care for older people, 1996

	Approximate monthly cost per person ¥	Approximate user monthly fees ¥	Space per person (minimum, m^2)
General hospitals	500,000	39,000	4.3
Long-term care units	400,000	39,000	6.4
Rehabilitation centres	330,000	60,000	8.0
Nursing homes	271,000	45,000	10.0

Source: Kôseishô (web-site), http://www.mhw.go.jp/topics/kaigo99_4/kaigo5.html.

various services including residential care and day care. The Japanese word *hoken* refers to the assistance that straddles the boundary between medical and social care and the rehabilitation centres are expected to integrate the two forms of care.

Special hospital units for the care of older people (*ryôyô-gata byôshô-gun*) were first established in 1993 and are increasing rapidly in number. They provide the hospital system with a new role in the care of the frail elderly. In these units the residential function is more explicitly recognized. Patients' rooms are slightly larger than in ordinary hospitals and there is greater provision of rehabilitation treatments and services. The maximum number of beds in one room is limited to four. The doctor–patient ratio is 1:48 compared with 1:16 in general hospitals. The capacity of these specialized hospital units has increased from 2,823 beds in 1993 to about 187,000 beds in 1999 (*Asahi Shinbun*, 31 January 2000, p. 9). While remaining attached to hospitals, the care units emphasize the residential care function by employing more care assistants and fewer doctors and nurses. While hospitals are normally required to provide one nurse for every three patients, the new care units have one nurse for every six patients and one welfare worker for every four patients (*Asahi Shinbun*, 5 February 2000, p. 4).

The Ministry of Health and Welfare created the new care units for older people as a response to the failings of geriatric hospitals. Since the 1970s there had been reports of very poor care in long-term geriatric hospitals: patients were left untended for long periods in poor conditions, they were likely to become bedbound and were given too many drugs and too little rehabilitation (*Asahi Shinbun*, 31 January 2000, p. 9). The newer care units for older people (*ryôyô-gata byôshô-gun*) have been developed within general rather than geriatric hospitals. Funding can be obtained from both the health care and the social care insurance systems. This is a source of both opportunity and risk for older patients. By using health insurance funds the units can avoid the need for assessments by municipal social workers as required by the social care insurance rules. The medical professions continue to dominate the new units and social care professionals have relatively little influence despite the fact that the units are intended and funded to bridge the gap between medical care and social care. The new units have ensured that the hospital system continues to play a major role in the care of older people.

THE HISTORICAL BACKGROUND TO JAPANESE SOCIAL CARE PROVISION

The early roots of Japanese social care lie in a history of voluntary and charit-able work by individuals and groups with a religious motivation. From as far back as the seventh century, in pre-modern Japan, Buddhist temples typically did much pioneering welfare work (see for example Ikeda, 1994). Later, as in Western societies, Christian churches often played an important role in poor relief. After the ban on Christianity, which lasted from the seventeenth to the mid-nineteenth century, came to an end, some Christian voluntary activity appeared. One example was the Okayama orphanage (*Okayama koji'in*). Ishi'i Jûji (1865–1914), a Japanese Christian, established it in 1887 as one of the first private welfare institutions for children. In this sense not only Buddhism but also Christianity is to be acknowledged for a contribution to the early develop-ment of welfare in Japan.

It was only from the Meiji period (1868–1912) that central government seri-ously attempted to pursue nationwide forms of administrative integration. Ear-lier, for example in the Tokugawa period (1603–1868), there was no nationwide administration that could support welfare activities, and only a few of the local hereditary clans paid any attention to the well-being of their subjects. From the latter half of the nineteenth century Japanese society entered an era of modern-ization initiated by the Meiji government and its construction of the nation state. The 1874 Ordinance (*Jukkyû kisoku*) is one of the key events in the history of Japanese social welfare as it demonstrated a formal commitment of the state to social welfare. It was the first official attempt to establish a nationwide prin-ciple of assistance to the poor. Still, the 1874 Ordinance merely declared how important it was for the subjects of the Japanese emperor – not the govern-ment – to help each other. The basic principle the 1874 Ordinance was self-help and family care rather than any state responsibility. In very limited cases the state provided small amounts of poor relief. In addition, imperial social funds were used to assist individuals and groups in organizing care for the poor, sick or abandoned. The Okayama orphanage was one of the institutions supported by imperial funds (Takahashi, 1997). The imperial social funds were based on the good will and charity of the emperor and given as an act of imperial mercy to his subjects. The emperor was seen as the father figure of the whole nation but any state welfare role remained minimal.

By the end of the nineteenth century industrialization had begun to generate urban poverty and it became an issue central government could no longer ignore. The living conditions of the urban poor were much discussed as a 'social problem'. In April 1896, a group of officials and scholars established the Society for Social Policy, a Japanese version of the German *Verein für Sozialpolitik*. Initially it influenced debates about the protection of factory workers and on poor relief. Still, decades passed before any amendment was made to the 1874 Ordinance. The Poor Relief Law (*Kyûgohô*), which was passed in 1929 and came into force in 1932, finally replaced the 1874 Ordinance. The Poor Relief Law offered a minimum income to some of those unable to earn a livelihood by themselves. The main group of recipients were lone elderly, orphan children, poor women in pregnancy, and those with physical and mental disabilities. This law allowed local municipalities to provide such forms of protection as a minimum income, medical care, health care for new mothers, and assistance with funeral expenses (Okamoto, 1991, p. 33).

In the 1930s and early 1940s the Japanese government introduced a limited range of pension schemes and passed laws related to public health. Such social policies as there were usually had a militaristic element which aimed to protect the human resources necessary to Japanese expansionism in Asia and the Pacific. Social welfare in pre-1945 Japan was known as *shakai jigyô* and it targeted specific groups of people living in particularly poor conditions and suffering from various social problems. In short, Japanese welfare provision made little progress in the pre-1945 period, and there remained much room for private sector initiatives on the part of both individuals and welfare organizations. The government gave some financial support to private social welfare organizations on the basis of the 1938 Social Welfare Law. This law did not define what social welfare was but rather made a concrete list of those social welfare services worthy of public subsidy (Kitamura, 1991, p. 97). It remained the case that those to whom help was provided by the formal sector were stigmatized as second-class citizens, lacking a will to work or a proper self-help network of family and relatives.

In the early twentieth century a system of welfare commissioners (*minsei i'in seido*) developed. It is an interesting example of how local initiatives could eventually extend nationwide. The Governor of the Okayama prefecture, Kasai Shin'ichi, was inspired by a Prussian system practised in the city of Elberfelt and launched a similar system of district welfare commissioners in April 1917. They were known as *saisei komon* (rescue commissioners) and they were voluntary and honorary positions without financial compensation (Ikeda, 1994, p. 125). Similar developments followed in the Tôkyô prefecture in 1917 and the Ôsaka prefecture in 1918 for handling social problems related to urban poverty (Ikeda, 1986, p. 512). By the 1930s the welfare commissioners system became more widespread and was integrated into the implementation of the 1932 Poor

Relief Law. The system was further formalized in the 1936 Law on Local Commissioners (*Hômen i'inhô*).

These welfare arrangements were criticized during the post-war occupation
mainly because of uncertainties about the social and legal identity and compe-
tence of those who functioned as commissioners. The commissioners were volunteers but they had considerable powers over who received public assistance
and their behaviour was often arbitrary (Ishida, 1983, pp. 194–7). This, neither
entirely public nor private, system was also strongly associated with the legacy
of pre-1945 militarism and imperialism and appeared to exercise unaccount-
able authority. The system of welfare commissioners was amended and they
became known as *minsei i'in*.

Welfare Developments in Post-1945 Japan

The key starting point for post-war development is the occupation period. The
Law for the Welfare of Children (1947), the Law for the Welfare of the
Physically Handicapped (1949), and the revised Life Protection Law (*Shin
seikatsu hogohô*) of 1950 form the basis of social welfare policy in post-1945
Japan. These laws addressed the most urgent social problems then facing the
country: orphans wandering the streets, the disabled returning from the front,
and the impoverished lives of a people dependent on the black market. Emergency administrative measures (*sochi* in Japanese) were required but these took
very little account of citizens' social rights and wishes. Emergency measures
created a top-down approach to administration that persisted until the early
1990s and induced a passive attitude to welfare reform on the part of citizens.
For example, municipalities provided child day care to remedy perceived inadequacies in the care provided by parents, and not because the parents have a
right to alternative childcare while they go to work. The motive was to protect
or rescue children rather than to help parents.

As outside researchers and experts tend to point out, a welfare society in the
Nordic sense has not emerged in Japan. There are historical reasons for this. In
the occupation period three factors were significant: the severe economic problems the Japanese government faced, the cultural differences between Japanese
and Western interpretations of social rights, and the contradictions and inconsistencies in the occupying authority's policies for 'reforming' Japanese society. The economic crisis meant that the government was simply unable to carry
out all the social reforms demanded by the occupation authorities. The demands
that Western notions of rights be translated into laws and constitutional revisions confronted the Japanese government with considerable cultural and lin-
guistic difficulties. The concept of human rights was known and acknowledged
in Japan and there was a tradition of protest and social movements dating back
to the mid-nineteenth century. What was special were the ways in which the

occupying authority pressured the government to produce social reforms. It required the Japanese government to clarify the division between the public and private sectors and to make clear a public responsibility for social welfare and particularly for the development of a system of social security. A range of social welfare laws was passed in the late 1940s under pressure from the occupation administration but they remained an uncompleted project. The emergence of the cold war changed United States policy towards Japan and under the US–Japan Security Treaty the country was remilitarized through the creation of a 'Self-Defence Force' despite the commitments of the 1947 constitution. The American priority changed to seeing Japan as a bulwark against the expansion of communism in Asia rather than as a demilitarized welfare society (Takashima, 1995, pp. 206–9).

In 1951 the Law on Social Welfare Services (*Shakai fukushi jigyôhô*) was passed and created a comprehensive legal basis for the social administration of post-war Japan. According to Arizuka (1998, p. 61), the 1951 law was a hybrid produced by Japanese officials who were attempting to integrate various rather contradictory elements: the existing 1938 Social Welfare Law, the demands and directions of the American high command and the realities of life in Japan so soon after the Second World War. Before the war social welfare had largely been the domain of some 6,700 private welfare organizations. By the late 1940s their number had fallen to some 3,000 but they remained the main sources of welfare assistance. In contrast the American authorities emphasized the responsibility of the state for people's welfare: it was the state that should explicitly guarantee citizens' rights to life, liberty and well-being. At the same time the severe financial weakness of the defeated Japanese state meant it could not meaningfully take on this responsibility. In searching for a compromise solution to these various demands and constraints, and recognizing that private welfare providers would need to remain a significant source, one of the key solutions was to introduce community charity funds (*kyôdô bokin*). These were set up in 1947 to provide financial support to the private welfare organizations (Kitamura, 1991, p. 96).

Japan regained complete sovereignty in 1952 and more coherent welfare reform became possible. In 1961 universal state social security provision was effectively obtained by extending pensions and unemployment insurance to all categories of workers. Among social welfare measures passed during the 1960s were the Law for the Mentally Retarded (1960), the Law for Welfare of the Aged (1963) and the Law for Welfare of Mothers and Children (1964) (Yokoyama, 1991). With this new legislation, in addition to the three basic welfare laws of the late 1940s, Japanese social welfare reached a second stage of post-war development which extended provision from relief-oriented policies targeting the completely impoverished to the support of the socially disadvantaged including the handicapped, the aged, lone mothers and their children

(Murakami, 1991, p. 252). The third stage in the development of Japanese social welfare has consisted of several waves of administrative reform since the 1980s. These, with their emphasis on minimal government and on deregulation and decentralization, provided a structural basis for the welfare reforms of the 1990s. Responsibility for welfare policies was shifted from central government to local administration at the municipal level in cities, towns and villages.

The crest of this wave was represented by the revision of the 'eight basic welfare laws' in August 1990. For example, the revised Law for Social Welfare Services (*Shakai fukushi jigyôhô*) contrasts with the original 1951 law in the way in which it widens the permissible target group. Earlier, the eligible were defined as 'those who need help, guidance and support' but provision was limited by requiring that help be given 'without damaging a sense of independence'. This limitation was designed to exclude those who could be defined as feckless or lazy. The revised 1990 law simply speaks of 'those who need welfare services'. In addition, the revised version explicitly includes key concepts such as deinstitutionalization, community care (*zaitaku fukushi*), integration, normalization, decentralization and deregulation (Furukawa, 1993, pp. 131–2).

THE IDEOLOGICAL AND POLITICAL CONTEXT OF JAPANESE CARE PATTERNS

Patterns of care provision are the products of social tradition mediated by ideology and the politics of welfare. In Japan the family has long served as the main source of care and conservative interpretations of family obligations remain influential, particularly where the care of older people is concerned. The family is the expression of mutual support and the preferred source of general well-being. It serves well as the ideal mode of care. However, problems occur once the ideal of family care constrains individuals; for example, where there is a fixed view of gendered responsibility. Once the ideal of family care becomes institutionalized as the social norm, individuals face great social pressure forcing self-sacrifice in order to meet family obligations. Traditional and institutionalized rules of obligation cast a shadow over family care in contemporary Japan. At the same time structural changes in the form and activities of the Japanese family are crucially altering its capacity to care for children and older people. The Japanese nuclear family is now generally smaller in size and capacity, and the possibility of relying on it to provide all care is an illusion (see Table 4.9). The male breadwinner/female housewife model is increasingly less relevant, as more women are in paid work. Social change is forcing the public and governments in Japan to reformulate the ideology of care. However, the ideal of the family still needs to be demystified before the reality of care and its future prospects can be seen clearly.

Table 4.9 The household circumstances of older people (65 and over) in Japan, 1975 to 1996

	Per cent		
	1975	1985	1996
One-person households	8.6	12.0	17.4
Older couples	13.1	19.1	25.0
Parent(s) & unmarried children	9.6	10.8	13.6
Three-generation households	54.4	45.9	31.8
Other forms	14.4	12.2	12.2

Source: Sômuchô, 1998, pp. 28–9.

Table 4.10 Main providers of care to dependent older people (65 and over), 1996

	Per cent	
Family (living in the same household)	66.8	
Other relatives	5.5	
Of which		
Wives		31.6
Wives of eldest sons		27.6
Eldest daughters		15.5
Other daughters		4.5
Husbands		5.0
Eldest sons		4.4
Other sons		1.2
Others		11.1
Hospitals and clinics	16.4	
Others	5.6	
Unknown	5.7	

Source: Sômuchô, 1998, p. 61.

Gender Relations as an Ideological Aspect of Childcare

Nowadays it is no longer accurate to make a clear-cut distinction in classifying women in Japan either as housewives or as working women. Some mothers opt to stay at home as housewives, particularly while their children are small, others continue in paid work by making use of day care for their children. Even among 'housewives' there is a range of solutions to childcare; many women combine part-time work with different forms of childcare. The term 'house-wife' (*shufu*) often simply means to be a married woman regardless of the degree of commitment to a working life outside the home. In other words, the conception of a working mother has a large spectrum of meaning in the Japanese social context. Working mothers are not only those women who are career-oriented but also those who primarily identify themselves as housewives while spending considerable lengths of time working outside the home.

Nonetheless, most women with a child under three years old will stop paid work either because support is available from their spouse or possibly because of social pressure based on certain beliefs about child development. It is widely accepted that unless mothers stay at home while their children are infants under three years old the personal development of the children may be severely damaged. Forms of social care by others outside the family still generate prejudice and stigmatization in Japan, and some working mothers feel guilty about not being able to spend much time with their children. On the other hand, those mothers who stay at home with their small children may not be perfectly happy either, because devotion to childcare can severely limit contact with the world outside the home, particularly in the Japanese context. It is questionable whether it is good for women or their children to be trapped within a nuclear family where, because the husband spends a great deal of time at work, the mother passes much of her time isolated from adult contact. There is a degree of silence about the key issues in dealing with what is best for children and what role fathers should play in the rearing of their children. In Japanese discourses on childcare little is said in terms of 'social rights', such as a woman's right to work or a child's right to social care. Childcare in Japan has long been discussed simply in terms of what is best for small children and who are the people most appropriate to provide it.

The Japanese social security system provides for maternity leave of six weeks before and eight weeks after childbirth. In addition, since April 1991, the Act on Childcare Leave (*Ikuji kyûgyôhô*) makes it possible for either of the parents of a child under one year old to take a year's unpaid leave. Initially no economic support was offered to employees who wished to take advantage of this entitlement and few did so. In 1995 the Employment Insurance Law (*Koyô hokenhô*) was amended and, as a consequence, those who take childcare leave are now paid by the employer 25 per cent of her/his basic monthly salary during the leave. Although the opportunity for childcare leave is offered gender-equally, the great majority who make use of it are women whose working careers tend to be regarded as secondary to their husbands. At the same time, as Muriel Jolivet points out, there remains strong social pressure in the workplace which means that many working women, though entitled to childcare leave, dare not take it (Jolivet, 1997, p. 46). Indeed, although Japan has had an Equal Employment Opportunity Law since 1986, it has had little effect on this problem. In brief, gender equality is still not taken very seriously in Japanese working life.

The Japanese government has encouraged the 'housewife institution' through taxation and social security policies (Ôsawa, 1996, pp. 46–52). When a woman earns only a small amount, that income is not taxed and the breadwinner spouse is given the tax allowance of the dependent spouse. The basic pension offers a spouse pension, the so-called 'housewife pension', to the wives of full-time employees so long as the 'housewife' stays mostly at home and does not earn beyond a specified minimum. Nonetheless, the female labour market participation rate was 49.1 per cent in 1995 (men 78.8 per cent), which is a more or less similar level to that in other industrialized societies: 46.8 per cent in France, 47.2 per cent in Germany, 50.6 per cent in the UK, 56.6 per cent in Sweden and 58.9 per cent in the USA (Keizaikikakuchô, 1997, pp. 297, 305). The Japanese female participation rate has been rising and is often linked to the declining fertility rate.

Debates About Welfare in the Political Arena

Japanese political parties have been in a process of restructuring since 1993 when the Liberal Democratic Party (LDP) could no longer maintain its dominant position in the Diet as the *de facto* single party of government. This change is regarded as the end of the 1955 political system in which the LDP had had a monopoly on government for several decades. The effects of the change have however been limited by the inability of the other parties to sustain cooperation. The LDP has continued to dominate the cabinet but in coalition with others, including the Social Democrats, and excluding the communists. A change in people's attitudes to politics is reflected in a decline in voter turnout. In recent years only about half of the electorate has voted. Despite this lack of voter interest, it is within party politics that the debate on welfare takes place. In this sense Japanese democracy is in crisis.

Twenty years ago the discourse on welfare was dominated by a critique of Western models of welfare such as those found in the British and Swedish welfare states. The debate tended to emphasize Japanese economic achievements in contrast to most other industrialized societies. Japanese social traditions, in particular family care, were often portrayed as a strength. Employers were seen as providing adequate incomes and pensions for the welfare of their workers and their families. A belief in 'groupism' underpinned an optimistic faith in the Japanese family and workplace. This was a philosophy of welfare that appealed to politicians and business leaders who saw a bright future for a Japanese society and economy that minimized social expenditure. At the end of the 1970s the

Japanese economy was overcoming recession while in the West several welfare
states were in fiscal crisis. These opinions appeared to be confirmed by the economic boom from the late 1980s to the early 1990s, now called the 'bubble
economy'. The successful performance of the economy also encouraged a form
of nationalism in the 1980s that perceived the Japanese system as unique and
better than the Western models. However, the term the 'Japanese model' is not
particularly helpful in understanding the realities of Japanese welfare.

CONCLUSION: CURRENT DEBATES AND THE FUTURE OF SOCIAL CARE

Participatory Welfare?

In the 1990s the Japanese government has been actively encouraging citizens to
participate in voluntary work in the context of a discourse about a welfare society based on participation. To some extent these exhortations are a recognition
that local communities, undermined by industrialization and urbanization, need
to be reconstructed. In the cities there are few signs of 'community spirit' when
residents have little to share in daily life and are often unintegrated and fully
occupied by work and commuting.

Paradoxically, in this context the old system of welfare commissioners
(*minsei i'in*) has found a new relevance in social welfare through its distinctive
double identity, being both semi-private and semi-public. The essence of this
system is to let a selected group of citizens function as a 'go between', linking
municipal officialdom with the problems of local residents such as children's
welfare, the care of older people, lone parenthood and other forms of social
exclusion. As discussed earlier, there is an ambivalent form of voluntariness
involved here. The commissioners, *minsei i'in*, are indeed unpaid volunteers
from their communities. However, it is the public authorities that accept and
confirm these volunteers in their roles. Although in principle the role of the
commissioners is to communicate the wishes of the public to the authorities,
much of their time is taken up with charitable work, a form of poor relief, with
different groups in need. The average age of these voluntary commissioners is
over sixty, they are almost evenly divided between men and women and of the
200,000 or so who have this status about 15,000, three-quarters of them
women, are primarily involved in aspects of children's welfare (Kôseishô,
1998, p. 430).

The National Council for Social Welfare (*Zenkoku shakai fukushi kyôgikai*)
organizes voluntary activity at the local level and in particular promotes work
with children and older people. The council is a semi-public organization under
the Ministry of Health and Welfare and had a nationwide network at the

municipal level of more than 3,370 local organizations in 1998. According to available statistics (Tables 4.11 and 4.12), 79,025 groups involving about 5,460,000 citizens were engaged in community activities in 1997. Some groups

Table 4.11 Types of voluntary activity, 1996

	Welfare groups %	Community groups %
Welfare of older people	57.7	58.7
Welfare of disabled people	48.7	38.5
Welfare of children	13.6	20.2
Recreation and sport	0.6	2.6
Cultural activities	1.7	4.8
Environmental issues	8.6	20.7
International cooperation	1.5	2.5
Community action	2.9	9.2
Others	14.8	20.0

Source: Kôseishô, 1998, p. 430.

Table 4.12 The socio-economic background of volunteers, 1996

	Welfare groups %	Community groups %
In paid employment		
self-employed	8.1	10.0
full-time employees	12.1	13.1
part-time employees	8.2	8.3
others	1.7	3.8
Out of the labour market		
housewives	47.5	34.0
school students	2.6	4.8
college students	1.9	1.3
retired/pensioners	7.1	6.2
others	2.5	11.4
No answer	8.0	7.1

Source: Kôseishô, 1998, p. 430.

focus primarily on welfare needs such as those of older people and the disabled, other voluntary associations, such as societies and clubs, have a more general community focus which may or may not involve welfare work.

In 1998 the Diet passed a new law governing non-profit organizations (NPOs) designed to encourage greater voluntary activity on the part of citizens. The profile of non-profit welfare organizations has risen since the great Kôbe earthquake in January 1995 revealed how dysfunctional and inefficient some local government had become, particularly when faced with an emergency. Local bureaucracy was unable to offer flexible help to local residents in crisis because of rigid divisions of labour. In contrast, it was revealed that there were many citizens ready and willing to assist without the prospect of reward or status. The new NPO law will make it easier for non-profit organizations to set themselves up on a proper legal and financial basis and to operate in a variety of settings including welfare services.

However, this more enlightened approach to volunteerism on the part of the Japanese government has not entirely removed the scepticism of some welfare experts. They question the efficacy of a government-regulated voluntary sector, whether voluntary work always needs to be authorized by the governments, and whose goals and priorities are represented by the sector. They argue that 'citizens' obligations' should not become an excuse to avoid greater clarification of government responsibilities.

Another example of government complacency of this sort is its view of the much higher rate of labour market participation by older Japanese compared with most other industrialized countries (Table 4.13). The government takes the view that older people are keen to keep working in later life and it is suggested that the vitality of Japanese society is related to this willingness to continue

Table 4.13 The labour market participation rates of older people

	All %	Women %	Men %
65 and over			
Japan 1997	24.2	15.4	36.7
US 1997	12.2	8.6	17.1
UK 1993	5.1	3.5	7.4
Germany 1996	2.7	1.6	4.4
60 and over			
Japan 1997	33.3	21.7	48.6

Source: Kôseishô, 1999, p. 176.

contributing to the society. In short, it is one of the reasons one does not have to worry too much about the future of an ageing Japan (Kôseishô, 1999, p. 176) This 'official view' is a reflection of the enormous value still placed on paid work in Japanese culture. It is perceived as the ultimate form of self-help and the answer to most welfare needs. The ideological message is clear: that individuals are expected to contribute to society through work and voluntary activities and that this implies no specific counterbalancing obligations on the part of the state.

REFERENCES

Arizuka, Masakatsu (1998), *Shakai fukushi gyôseiron. Kiso kôzô no kaimei to kaikaku no kadai*, Tôkyô: Chûô hôki shuppan.
Campbell, J.C. (1984), 'Problems, solutions, non-solutions, and free medical care for the elderly in Japan', *Pacific Affairs*, **57** (1), Spring, 53–64.
Day, L.H. (1992), *The Future of Low-Birthrate Populations*, London and New York: Routledge.
Fukushi seisaku kenkyû-kai (1996), *Kônaru shin-fukushi seisaku. 'Shin-gôrudo puran' 'Enzeru puran' no yôten kaisetsu*, Tôkyô: Ministry of Health and Welfare, Taisei shuppansha.
Furukawa, Kôjun (1993), 'Sengo Nihon no shakai fukushi to fukushi kaikaku', in Furukawa Kôjun et al. (eds), *Shakai fukushi ron*, Tôkyô: Yûhikaku, pp. 97–135.
Ichibangase, Yasuko (1971), *Gendai shakai fukushi-ron*, Tôkyô: Jichôsha.
Ikeda, Yoshimasa (1986), *Nihon shakai fukushi shi*, Kyôto: Hôritsu bunkasha.
Ikeda, Yoshimasa (1994), *Nihon ni okeru shakai fukushi no ayumi*, Kyôto: Hôritsu bunkasha.
Ishida, Takeshi (1983), *Kindai Nihon no seiji bunka to gengo shôchô*, Tôkyô: Tôkyô daigaku shuppankai.
Itô, Shûhei (1994), *Shakai hoshô-shi. Onkei kara kenri e. Igirisu to Nihon no hikaku kenky*, Tôkyô: Aoki shoten.
Jolivet, M. (1997), *Japan: The Childless Society?*, translated by Anne-Marie Glasheen, London and New York: Routledge.
Keizaikikakuchô (Economic Planning Agency) (1997), *Heisei 9-nen ban kokumin seikatsu hakusho: hataraku josei — atarashi'i shakai shisutemu o motomete*, Tôkyô: Ôkurashô insatsukyoku.
Kitamura, Yoshiko (1991), 'Shakai fukushi seido no kakuritsu', in Yokoyama, Kazuhiko and Tada, Hidenori (eds), *Nihon shakai hoshô no rekishi*, Tôkyô: Gakubunsha, pp. 85–104.
Kôseishô (Ministry of Health and Welfare) (1998), *Heisei 10-nen ban kôsei hakusho*, Tôkyô: Ôkurashô insatsukyoku.
Kôseishô (Ministry of Health and Welfare) (1999), *Heisei 11-nen ban kôsei hakusho. Shakai hoshô to kokumin seikatsu*, Tôkyô: Ôkurashô insatsukyoku.
Miyata, Kazuaki (1981), 'Shin seisaku-ron ronsô', in Sanada, Naoshi (ed.), *Sengo Nihon shakai fukushi rons*, Kyôto: Hôritsu bunkasha, pp. 179–219.
Murakami, Kimiko (1991), 'Shakai fukushi jigyô no kakujû, tenkai', in Yokoyama, Kazuhiko and Tada, Hidenori (eds), *Nihon shakai hoshô seido no rekishi*, Tôkyô: Gakubunsha, pp. 252–269.

National Institute of Population and Social Security Research (2000a), *Kokuritsu shakaihoshô jinkômondai kenkyûjo*. At http://www.ipss.go.jp/English/IPSS/P2-4_e.html.

National Institute of Population and Social Security Research (2000b), *Kokuritsu shakaihoshô jinkômondai kenkyûjo*. At http://www.jpss.go.jp/Japanese/kyuhuhi-h9/4/d6.html.

Okamoto, Takiko (1991), 'Kyûgohô no jidai', in Yokoyama, Kazuhiko and Tata, Hidenori (eds), *Nihon shakai hoshô no rekishi*, Tôkyô: Gakubunsha, pp. 30–41.

Ôsawa, Mari (1996), 'Shakai seisaku no jendâ baiasu', in Hara, Hiroko; Maeda Mizue and Ôsawa, Mari (eds), *Ajia taiheiyô chi'iki no josei seisaku to joseigaku*, Tôkyô: Shin'yôsha.

Sanada, Naoshi (1996), *Minkan shakai fukshi ron. Shakai fukushi ni okeru kô to min*, Kyôto: Kamogawa shuppan.

Satô, Yoshio, Mizumaki, Nakamasa and Kobata, Yôichi (1997), *Kaigo hokenhô no zen'yô to jitsumu taisaku*, Tôkyô: Nihon hôrei.

Soeda, Yoshiya (1992), 'Seikatsu hogo seido no tenkai', in Tôkyô daigaku shakai kagaku kenkyûsho (Research Institute of Social Sciences, University of Tokyo), *Tenkanki no fukushi kokka, Ge*, Tôkyô: Tôkyô daigaku shuppankai, pp. 171–247.

Sômuchô, (Coordination and Management Agency) (1995), *Chôju shakai taisaku no dôkô to tenbô*, Tôkyô: Ôkurashô insatsukyoku.

Sômuchô, (Coordination and Management Agency) (1997), *Sûji de miru kôreishakai 1997*, Tôkyô: Ôkurashô insatsukyoku.

Sômuchô (Coordination and Management Agency) (1998), *Kôrei shakai hakusho, heisei 10-nenban* (1998 White Paper on an ageing society), Tôkyô: Ôkurashô insatsukyoku.

Takahashi, Mutsuko (1997), 'Ishi'i Jûji in search of Utopia through Okayama orphanage in Meiji Japan', a paper presented at the 8th International Conference of the European Association for Japanese Studies, 27–30 August, Budapest, Hungary.

Takashima, Susumu (1973), *Gendai no shakai fukushi riron*, Kyôto: Mineruba shobô.

Takashima, Susumu (1995), *Shakai fukushi no rekishi. Jizen jigyô kyûhinhô kara gendai made*, Kyôto: Mineruba shobô.

Yamanoi, Kazunori (1996), 'Suêden no kôreisha seisaku o rikaisuru nanatsu no kagi', in Seikatsu fukusi kenkyû kikô, *Suêden ni okeru kôreisha kea no kaikaku to jissen*, Tôkyô: Chûô hôki shuppan, pp. 72–112.

Yokoyama, Kazuhiko (1991), 'Bunritsu gata kokumin kai hoken taisei no kakuritsu', in Yokoyama, Kazuhiko and Tada, Hidenori (eds), *Nihon shakaihoshô seido no rekishi*, Tôkyô: Gakubunsha, pp. 123–39.

Yokoyama, Kazuhiko (1992), 'Fukushi gannen' igo no shakai hoshô', in Tôkyô daigaku shakai kagaku kenkyûsho (Research Institute of Social Sciences, University of Tokyo), *Tenkanki no fukushi kokka, ge*, Tôkyô: Tôkyô daigaku shuppankai, pp. 3–78.

Zenkoku hoiku dantai renrakukai and Hoiku kenkyûsho (eds) (1998), *Hoiku hakusho 1998-nen ban* (1998 White Paper on child care), Tôkyô: Sôdo bunka.

5. Social Care in the United Kingdom: A Pattern of Discretionary Social Administration

John Baldock

INTRODUCTION: BRITISH EXCEPTIONALISM IN SOCIAL CARE

The main intention of this chapter is to describe and explain the nature of British 'exceptionalism' in the provision of public support for childcare and the care of older people. It will be argued that in the United Kingdom, until recently, the public contribution to the provision of childcare has been selective, and even arbitrary in its coverage of needs, and limited and uneven compared with that in many other industrial, and particularly European, nations. The role of the state in the care of older people is similarly distinct: inconsistently selective in terms of needs, socially and geographically inequitable, administratively disorganized and subject to chronic crisis and failure. In both the cases of childcare and care for older people it will be suggested that the roots of these exceptionally British qualities lie in a history of class-based social administration and in values inseparable from Britain's political and cultural history.

The Continuity of a Subject Political Culture

In the accounts of social care development in the other four countries described in this book a central focus is on political processes and the ways in which politics have determined the state's contribution to the supply of care and hence the very nature of social care systems. The emphasis in these accounts is both on how policy making has been structured, for example by constitutional arrangements and political parties, and also on the political histories of these nations. Economic and demographic changes, such as women's changing roles in the labour market, as well as more violent historical events, such as war and civil war, revolution and constitutional reform, have eventually worked through democratic processes to produce social policy settlements and reforms. Under-standing social care in these countries is largely a matter of understanding their politics and its historical and cultural contexts.

However, British political history, including the period most relevant here, that since the Second World War, has been qualitatively different from that of the other nations described in this volume, with the partial exception of the United States. Three substantial differences are particularly relevant:

- The second half of the twentieth century was dominated by Britain's rela-tive economic decline; this was the central concern of party politics and left less room for social policy expenditure compared with faster-growing economies.
- Britain continued to seek a role as a world power alongside the United States and this too deflected both resources and political focus from inter-nal social provision.
- Political and administrative continuity over a very long period has left the relationship between citizen and state largely unchanged, unquestioned and outside the realm of politics.

These points need some brief elaboration so that their implications for social care policy can be drawn out in the rest of the chapter.

First, British economic growth, at an average of 2 per cent a year over the whole of the post-war period, has been markedly lower than in Finland, Ger-many and Japan though not so far off that seen in the United States. However, unlike the United States, Britain was subject to chronic balance of payments problems and threats to the value of the pound. Regular sterling crises, such as those in 1947, 1956, 1967, 1976 and 1992, meant 'stop–go' fiscal policies and abrupt and unplanned reductions in public and particularly social expenditure (Owen, 2000). Consequently substantial extensions of public social policy commitments were rarely initiated after the initial legislation between 1944 and 1948 had set up the 'Beveridge welfare state'. Indeed, for much of the post-war period, social policy reform has meant finding ways to constrain and make more efficient existing social programmes. Plans to extend social rights, for example to create a comprehensive system of pensions above the state mini-mum, something the United Kingdom still lacks, were regularly nipped in the bud by economic crises (Barr, 1991, pp. 155–8). The effects on the develop-ment of social care policies were particularly profound because these had not been part of the Beveridge reforms and therefore had no secure legislative foun-dations from which to grow. As the rest of this chapter seeks to show, there was little political incentive for political parties and governments to compete over social care services. Occasionally the management of the National Health Ser-vice and the direction of education policy have featured in electoral politics.

But social care issues were left out of the democratic process and became the preserve of bureaucratic politics within the worlds of Whitehall civil servants and local government officialdom.

Second, the effects of modest economic growth were exacerbated by the continuing preoccupation of British governments with the nation's supposed 'big power' status. This meant high levels of military spending as Britain sought to remain a significant nuclear power and to keep its place at the 'top table' in the cold war and its aftermath: participation in the Korean war; maintaining military forces in Germany and elsewhere round the globe; and engaging in various world policeman roles from Suez, to the Arabian Gulf, the Falklands and most recently in Afghanistan. At the same time the slow disengagement from the former British empire occupied much political and administrative energy. British citizens paid a high price for these priorities, as food rationing and very high tax rates continued for as long after the war as it had lasted. The cross-party acceptance of the Beveridge welfare state has been described as the 'post-war settlement', and in a fundamental sense it was understood by many in the political and administrative classes as quite literally that; arrangements that were settled and done after which the political élite returned to their former and rather grandiose preoccupations (Barnett, 2001).

Third, and most important, has been long-term continuity in political institutions and administrative traditions. Unlike the experience of most western European nations and Japan, the end of the Second World War was not accompanied by constitutional reform and new patterns of politics. On the contrary, the British experience of war reinforced wide public trust in the institutions of the state. Admittedly 1945 saw the election of a reforming Labour government but this was the culmination of a long process of political realignment that had been building for many years before the war. It brought to government a generation of politicians who had shared power in the wartime coalition with the Conservatives. The Labour party was not a social democratic party in the European mould and its influence over the next 55 years of the century was in any case to be modest: 20 years of government compared with 35 years of Conservative rule. As a result there has been less expectation of significant social policy initiatives on the part of the electorate. Based on surveys carried out in 1959, Almond and Verba in their classic study, *The Civic Culture*, characterized the attitudes of British citizens towards government as deferential and trusting:

> In Britain strong subject orientations have persisted despite the development of more active participant orientations. The British citizen...did not lose respect for the independent authority of government...The kind of balance between active and passive orientations is in turn reflected in the way in which the political system balances governmental power and governmental responsiveness. In Britain the persisting deferential and subject orientations foster the development of strong and effective governments and maintenance of an efficient and independent administrative struc-

ture...It is possible that deference to political elites can go too far, and that the strongly hierarchical patterns in British politics — patterns that have often been criticized as limiting the extent of democracy in that nation — result from a balance weighted too heavily in the direction of the subject and deferential roles. (Almond and Verba, 1965, p. 361)

While this image of British politics has been modified by later research and subtly amended by the course of time (see for example Kavanagh,1989), there is little disagreement, in fact there has been relatively little academic discussion, about its implications for the development of social policies generally and social care policies in particular. The nature of British political culture has meant that social policy development has not taken place within popular electoral politics but largely behind closed doors among administrators and their attendant experts. The continuity of British politics and government has sustained fundamental assumptions about the role of the state and the limits to the policy agenda, which are widely agreed by those who matter and go largely unquestioned by the rest, that is to say the public. Among these assumptions are trust in the civil service, the 'subject civic culture' that Almond and Verba described, which allows the bureaucracy to dominate social policy change. This role is itself played out in the context of shared values about the forms and limits of state action, particularly within a senior civil service class largely recruited from limited and similar social and educational backgrounds. The most comprehensive study of social policy making in post-war Britain (Hall et al., 1975) is entirely a study of how policies are initiated and either survive or perish in the bureaucratic world of Whitehall. This substantial book barely considers parties and electoral politics but examines the characteristics that allow a policy idea to attain legitimacy, feasibility and support among the 'authorities having power to settle its priority' (ibid., p. 507). It is clear from the case studies used to construct the account that social care issues were especially vulnerable to failure in this contest. They would be least likely to win legitimacy and support in competition with other priorities. As Dennis Kavanagh puts it in his reappraisal of the civic culture thesis:

> The British have traditionally emphasized a negative view toward liberty, one that left the citizen free to do as he wished, unless the activity was formally proscribed. There are still few positive legislative guarantees of personal liberties and no bill of rights. There is [only] a general agreement that the state should intervene to promote such collective goals as full employment, maintenance of law and order, and the setting of safety standards. (Kavanagh, 1989, p. 158)

In the late 1990s these expectations and the trust in government began to be undermined essentially because of failures in just these areas. In particular, the crises of 'mad cow disease' and the foot and mouth epidemic, as well as a growing realization that British public services, particularly health care, do not match the best in Europe, began to test the core traditional assumption that government bureaucracies can be relied on to behave impartially and protect the public from harm. However, as this chapter seeks to show, for much of the last 55 years social care policy making was left to the bureaucracies of central and local government, informed to a degree by academic and professional experts. This was indeed 'social administration' rather than social politics and it generated a particular formation of social care provision, limited by the Treasury's definitions of what could be afforded and managed in such a way that no categorical citizenship rights to care were established. Two recent accounts of social care in Britain demonstrate the outcomes of these patterns of governance.

Disorganized Childcare Policies

A recent study of pre-school provision for children in the United Kingdom compared it with that available in the other European community nations and particularly that available in France and Sweden (Moss, 2001). It concluded that there is no clear policy for children under three years old, no general entitlement to public funding of pre-school care or any clear and universal entitlements to provision. For those aged three to six, increased provision is now being developed but it is towards predominantly part-time care while many European nations provide full-time care. In Britain most pre-school care is privately provided at cost levels to parents that are the highest in Europe and which are linked to increased part-time working by mothers and overtime working by fathers As a result access is both socially and geographically unequal. These failings occur in the context of a nation that has the highest level of child poverty in Europe. Policy has changed since the election of 'New Labour' in 1997. Over the last four years the British government has been pursuing a 'National Childcare Strategy', described later in this chapter, but this, Moss argues, has led to a 'frenetic stream of government initiatives' but little progress towards the standards of universal access and provision more commonly found in Europe. The focus on childcare by the current government is historically unique and novel but Britain remains exceptional in that access is unpredictable and use is socially differentiated. British families cannot take for granted a basic infrastructure of entitlement that is available in most other European nations.

Incoherent Care Policies for Older People

In a similar way the bald national statistical data on social care for older people hides a social reality that is quite different to that found in many other industrial nations. One of the strengths of the Royal Commission on Long Term Care, reporting in 1999 after two years work (Sutherland, 1999a), is that it sought not merely to record the costs and volume of provision but also to capture the social reality of the world of care faced by older people in Britain. It concluded that within the current system

> there are too many flows of funds which have been designed for different purposes and what the individual does or does not get out of it depends on a number of complex decisions which are out of their control. People have no idea what to expect. The tendency of the system to require impoverishment — and its proof — before it will help leads to despair which in our judgement is unacceptable. Modestly prudent people risk losing their dignity, partly as a result of their condition and partly because of how the system deals with it. People have no choice but to receive services for which all but the poorest have no further choice but to pay. (Sutherland, 1999a, para. 4.50)

The commission documented the ways in which the organization and funding of social care in Britain is divided between the National Health Service (NHS) and the local authorities and between the public and private sectors. The result may be a mixed economy of care, but it is also one in which access and use is structured by income, social class, and place of residence in ways that bear little relation to need. Since the publication of the Royal Commission's report these financial and administrative divisions have not improved but lie behind the return of the core problem of 'bed-blocking'. Because of constraints on local government spending and restrictions on the payments to the private nursing homes which care for publicly funded old people, more beds in NHS acute wards are blocked by older people ready for discharge to 'community care' than at any time in the last twenty years (Carvel, 2001). The paradox as well as the wastefulness of this outcome is that much of the reform of social care over the last decade was intended to resolve just this core problem of bed-blocking and all the consequences that attend it.

The thesis in this chapter is that these deficiencies in social care in contemporary Britain, both those in childcare and the care of older people, reflect organizational arrangements, administrative procedures and social values that are embedded in the history of services since the Second World War. After a brief outline of current patterns of provision, we seek to develop this explanation.

CURRENT PATTERNS OF CHILDCARE PROVISION

Provision and Funding

British parents face a complex and rapidly changing mixed economy of childcare. Until very recently the dominating idea driving all childcare policy in Britain had long been that mothers should not go out to work, except on a very part-time basis, before their children began full-time school. This fundamental policy assumption was in part sustained by the relatively early age that British children begin school. Since the Elementary Education Act 1880 all children in the United Kingdom have normally begun school during the year in which they have their fifth birthday. This means that a considerable proportion of children start school when they are four. In 2000, 97 per cent of four year olds were attending school (ONS, 2001, p. 59). Inconveniently for working parents, the hours of full-time school are essentially part-time: 9.00 a.m. to 3.00 p.m. or 3.30 p.m. Many working parents therefore need some form of childcare outside normal school hours. In addition, at least for the first three months or so, a child's attendance at school is likely to be even more part-time, in a reception class for only some of the days of the week and some of the hours of full-time school. If the parents of four-year-olds are in work outside these hours they will need to find day care for at least some days of the week. In 2000, 16 per cent of four-year-olds attended some form of pre-school care (ibid., p. 59).

Childcare outside standard school places is the product of a complex mix of voluntary, private and state provision. Because oversight of childcare provision is the responsibility of local and regional authorities, it is difficult to obtain good figures for the whole of the United Kingdom. However, the coverage is relatively similar across England, Wales, Scotland and Northern Ireland. In England, for example, in 1998 there were 830,000 registered childcare places available to 5.1 million children under the age of eight (Cm 3959, 1998, para. 1.22). Provision varied considerably between local authority areas: the borough of Walsall had available only 66 day-nursery places per 10,000 children under eight compared with 1,186 places in Calderdale (ibid.).

The types of provision vary greatly too. The dominant form of non-parental childcare is informal provision by family and friends. Beyond that, mainly voluntary groupings of parents supply several hours a week at toddler groups for those under two, at playgroups for those under four, and at before-school and after-school clubs for school children whose parents are not at home at those times. Childminders are mostly private, self-employed and working from their own homes. Nurseries, mainly private-for-profit but to a lesser extent provided by local authorities and the voluntary sector, also supply care for children whose parents are at work. Local authority nursery places are mainly allocated to children who are defined as being in some type of social or special educational need.

The system is almost entirely funded privately by parents. The state pays only for the few local authority nursery places and subsidizes low-income working parents through tax credits. Access to formal childcare is therefore largely income dependent. As Wasoff and Dey (2000, p. 116) put it: 'Users of formal care are more likely to be in full-time work with higher incomes, higher status work and dual income households. Lone parents face the greatest

obstacles in obtaining affordable care, which is the major barrier to their seeking employment'. The Daycare Trust has found that the cost of a nursery place
in 2001 was between £135 (€203) a week in inner London and £91 (€137) a
week in the northeast of the country for a place five days a week 8 a.m.–6 p.m.
The weekly cost of a childminder is €165 per week (London average) and €133
per week (national average). Before- and after-school places must also be paid
for by parents. However, since 1999 it has been possible to assist parents with
these costs with money from the National Lottery Fund which can be bid for by
'Local Care Partnerships', bodies representing local authorities, private and
voluntary providers, employers and parents. While this is in principle a feasible
way of helping poorer parents, it is just one example of what Peter Moss (2001,
p. 4) has called the 'frenetic stream of government initiatives' which results in
few parents, or even professionals, being aware of all the potential sources of
subsidy and which leads to great variety in costs and access.

It is difficult to assess the size of the gap between the number of children
who might use day-care places, were they available and affordable, and the
number that are actually available. However, given that in at least one of the
countries examined in this volume there are indeed places or home care allowances available on demand, that is in Finland, it is worth making an estimate
(see Table 5.1). In 1999 there were some 631,000 places in day nurseries or with
registered childminders in England, Wales and Northern Ireland (ONS 2001,
table 8.23). This works out at roughly one place for every nine children under
eight years old, or one for every six children under five. In the same year, 1999,
55 per cent of mothers with children under five were in employment and 28 per
cent were working full-time (ibid., table 4.7). While it is often the case that one
childcare place can be used by two or more children at different times of the
week there remains a substantial shortfall.

Clearly, the demand for childcare is a function of its supply. Parents adjust to
what is available and order their lives in terms of what they find possible. In a
study conducted for the Department of Education and Employment in 1996
only 19 per cent of working married mothers with children under five and 15
per cent of working single mothers used any form of formal child care other
than school (Ward et al., 1996). Forty per cent of the mothers said that they had
no need for care other than themselves because they only worked in school
hours, worked at home or took their children to work with them. As pointed out
earlier, because once children reach four a substantial proportion of them will
be attending reception classes in primary schools, it is parents of those aged
three or less who bare the brunt of the scarcity of childcare. The Family Policy
Studies Centre (1998) estimated that in the mid-1990s only 5 per cent of children under three attended any form of nursery care.

Overall this is a supply of childcare provision that is low compared with Finland and Germany but more similar to that available in Japan and the United

Table 5.1 Day-care places for children in England, Wales and Northern Ireland

	1987	1999	1987–1999 % change
Public sector			
Day nurseries	29,000	16,000	–45
Play groups	4,000	3,000	–25
Childminders	2,000	9,000	+350
Private/voluntary			
Day nurseries	33,000	247,000	+648
Playgroups	441,000	386,000	–12
Childminders	159,000	360,000	+126
Out of school clubs	na	119,000	

Source: Adapted from ONS, 2001, table 8.23.

States. British parents, particularly mothers of young children, are caught between the reality of an economy in which the male breadwinner wage no longer exists but in which childcare policy has remained rooted in a past where it was expected that mothers of young children would wish to stay at home. As two commentators aptly point out:

> In Britain we neither assume one thing nor the other. We do not assume mothers will work — so there is little formal childcare provision. We do not assume mothers will not work — so there is little support for a family wage. (Wasoff and Dey, 2000, p. 119)

Working parents have to operate in a context where there are no clear universal principles of support and entitlement that lead to predictable, established forms of childcare. Rather, parents have to discover as best they can what is available in their neighbourhood and to put together relatively ad hoc packages for the provision and financing of the childcare they need.

The New National Childcare Strategy

There has recently been what is effectively a reversal of public policy on pre-school care. The government has recognized the deficiencies outlined above and is committed to providing sufficient day care to enable all parents to go out to work if they wish. The National Childcare Strategy (Cm 3959, 1998) was launched in May 1998 and aims to ensure the availability of childcare outside the home for all children aged 0–14 where it is needed. Although this new policy is consistent with small changes in practice that had begun to take place through the 1990s, as governments began to respond to the demands of working parents, it marks a dramatic shift in assumptions from the established policies of at least the last century. Policy now points in only one direction and assumes that all parents of young children should be enabled to work if they choose to.

The new strategy has two parts. First it aims to increase the supply of childcare places. Second it uses tax credits to help low- to middle- income parents pay for the places. More childcare is planned and will be provided mainly through the private sector (Cm 3959, 1998). Beginning in 1999 the main aims have been to:

- double the number of out-of-school places for school-age children;
- provide universal nursery education for all four-year-olds;
- double the number of nursery places for three-year-olds; and
- improve the regulation and training of staff in childcare.

Parents' ability to pay for the increased supply of places is being assisted in two ways. First by subsidizing the incomes of working parents generally and second by paying special 'credits' to assist with the specific cost of a childcare place.

The *Working Families Tax Credit* (WFTC) is a central instrument in the current Labour government's policy to encourage more parents to take paid jobs. It uses the tax system to subsidize the incomes of the relatively low paid. WFTC is payable to all those working 16 hours a week or more. In 2001 it pays a minimum of approximately €350 a month with additions for dependent children depending on their ages (€100 for child 0–11; €145 for 11–16; €180 for 16–18). The benefit is taken away by stages once the wage earner is being paid €650 a month.

Childcare Tax Credits for Working Families (CCTC) are also available to parents who work 16 hours a week. The money can be used to pay for registered (that is inspected and approved by the local authority) childminders, nurseries and play schemes, but not for non-registered childcare by relatives and neighbours. However, only parents whose incomes are relatively low can benefit (up to €2,750 per month with one child; up to €3,750 per month with two children). The maximum that can be paid is 70 per cent of actual childcare costs. The money is also paid in arrears so parents have to find the money before they receive it from the state. These payments do not amount to universal support for childcare. Because they largely assist those on lower incomes it is middle-income families who are above the CCTC thresholds that may now be most disadvantaged. Very highly paid people can afford to buy full-day, full-week nursery care.

It is not yet clear how successful these changes in policy have been. They are certainly ambitious. The plan is to create an extra 600,000 childcare places between 1998 and 2004 (Cm 3959, 1998). By the end of March 2000, 140,000 new places had been created within England alone. However, because of turn-over in the market of largely private provision, 66,000 places had been lost during the same period leaving a net gain of 74,000 places (Department of Health, 2000). Relying on largely private provision appears to mean relying on a high turnover of suppliers. Day-care pressure groups continue to report difficulties in turning a very significant policy shift into a reality for parents and their children.

CURRENT PATTERNS OF CARE FOR OLDER PEOPLE

The Balance of Institutional and Home Care

Public funding and provision for older people is a complex interaction of institutional and home care services. Put simply, a society with a relatively high level of institutionalization, assuming it is focused on the more disabled, will require proportionately less provision of home care services than a society where institutional care is lower. In Britain the proportion of people aged 65 and over in institutional care is approximately 5.5 per cent. This is rather less than in Finland, slightly less than in Japan, and at similar levels to Germany and the United States (Sutherland, 1999b, p. 161). The proportion of older people in the United Kingdom receiving home care services is nonetheless lower than in Finland but above that in Germany, Japan and the United States (ibid.). This comparison does not, however, take account of the intensity (number of hours) of home care received. Indeed, it is very difficult to attach much meaning to international comparisons of social care provision because the patterns and efficiency of allocations to both institutional and home care services vary considerably between countries.

In Britain, while the levels of dependency of older people in institutions are generally higher on average than those in the community, there is considerable overlap. Research for the Royal Commission on Long Term Care shows that, broadly speaking, nearly 50 per cent of those in care homes have low or no dependency compared with about 80 per cent of those over 65 in the whole population. Conversely some 28 per cent of those in the community were unable to perform two or more activities of daily living compared with about 40 per cent of those in care homes (ibid., p. 6). In short, dependency is only one of the factors determining the balance of care between institutions and community.

NORTHBROOK COLLEGE LIBRARY

Levels of informal care, individual preferences and the funding arrangements for institutional care are the main determinants. The last factor is particularly important in the United Kingdom because only those with limited assets and incomes are eligible for state social care support in residential or nursing homes.

Restricted Public Expenditure on Home Care

Home care services in England and Wales, whether from public or private sources, are rationed according to income and only those living at the minimum income guarantee level are usually eligible for free services, that is about a half of all dependent older people. The exception is Scotland, where from July 2002 personal care services are to be provided free of charge to all people who need them both in the community and in institutions. This is a major policy development initiated by the new Scottish parliament in response to the main recommendation of the Royal Commission on Long Term Care.

There are a number of means- and needs-tested social security benefits that add slightly to the incomes of people in the community with dependencies but these are generally set against charges and rapidly eroded if the recipients choose to use home care services. The volume of publicly provided home care services in the United Kingdom has remained relatively stable in relation to population since the mid-1970s. This is because of deliberate restrictions on public social care expenditure, including that of local authorities, designed to ensure that overall expenditure rose only in line with the growth of the economy. By lucky accident economic growth of about 2 per cent a year has just matched the rise in the number of older people. Policy debate about social care has therefore been almost entirely limited to issues to do with the distribution of publicly funded home care services and not their volume.

The fundamental assumption that total provision could not become more generous than the levels achieved by the mid-1970s was a product of the absolute primacy given to the goal of reducing the size of the public sector that has been shared by all governments and significant political parties for the last quarter of a century. It is a constraint set by the political and financial establishment and it effectively defines the limits of the legitimate democratic agenda. It is a position that contrasts sharply with the political debate in Germany that preceded the legislation for social care insurance. That was a debate about how much larger a share of national product should go to social care. Similarly, in Japan in the 1990s, the Golden Plan became a democratic issue. But in Britain social care has always remained a matter of social administration and not of representative politics. Growth in provision has been left to the private market. The fact that successive governments have been able to subjugate policy on social care for older people to the objectives of public expenditure management is a demonstration of the degree to which social care policy is determined out-side the arena of representative party politics. The distinctively 'non-political' nature of social care issues is discussed in more detail later in this chapter.

Targeting Services on the Poorest and the Most Needy

Three aspects of contemporary home care services are particularly relevant to understanding their contribution to the welfare of older people. First, a key aim of substantial reforms of the social care system initiated in 1994, to increase the concentration or targeting of services on those with the highest needs, appears to have succeeded. As a result many older people with minor or no dependencies no longer get services. Second, there remain substantial numbers of older people with significant care needs who receive neither formal nor informal family care. Third, the availability of services varies greatly from area to area meaning that any national generalizations say very little about the chances of an older person in a particular area actually using help. It is therefore not possible to talk of clear rights or entitlements to social care among older people in the United Kingdom. All that can be said is that an older person with some degree of limitation in activities of daily living and an income at the level of social assistance is in principle eligible to apply for state-funded services. However, many who fulfil these criteria do not use services.

Table 5.2 sets out the pattern of distribution of the main social care services in 1994. It shows that only a fifth of those with some degree of dependency were in receipt of home care. The main reasons why many dependent people were not receiving services are likely to have been: they received all the help they want from informal carers; they did not recognize a need for services; they did not know of the availability of services; they may not have qualified for services under local authority assessment criteria; they perceived services to be lacking in some aspect of quality. We do not know the relative importance of these possible explanations. As the Royal Commission on Long Term Care concluded, 'there is little available research evidence on this very important area' (Sutherland, 1999b, p. 15).

From April 1994 the NHS and Community Care Act came into force. This was a major piece of legislation designed, among other things, to align the targeting of home care services more precisely with need and to support informal carers. More recent data from the General Household Survey (Table 5.3) shows that the first of these objectives has been achieved but probably at the expense of the second.

The policies pursued since 1994 have resulted in a sharp shift of public provision to those without informal care support. The policy of supporting informal carers has not been delivered. The same research (Pickard et al., 2001) demonstrates a concentration of publicly funded home care hours on those with

Table 5.2 Percentage of those 65+ in receipt of service in last month, UK,
*   1994*

	Home help	Nurse	Day centre	Meals on wheels	Lunch club	Private help
No dependency	2	2	1	1	1	6
At least one IADL or ADL	20	17	8	8	6	13
All	7	6	3	3	3	8
Total number	610,000	530,000	260,000	240,000	290,000	670,000

Note: IADL = instrumental activity of daily living; ADL = activity of daily living.

Source: Wittenberg et al., 1998.

Table 5.3 Receipt of home care by dependent* older people 65+ by
*   household type*

	% public home help/care		Average hours home help/care		% total hours of home care	
	1994/5	1998/9	1994/5	1998/9	1994/5	1998/9
Alone, no informal care	41	31	3.0	6.0	18	42
Alone, with informal care	28	17	3.4	4.8	36	39
Living with others	12	8	2.6	4.7	5	6
Married	11	6	7.4	3.9	41	13
All dependent people	21	13	4.1	5.0	100	100

Note: * Unable to perform at least one IADL.

Source: Pickard et al., 2001, table 4.

the highest levels of disability. As a result those with less severe needs have had
services taken from them. Overall the result has been a polarization of service
use. Those with low incomes and higher needs are more likely to obtain public
assistance or subsidies. At the same time research shows that higher-income
elderly, or 'self-funders' as they are now called, are accessing both institutional
care and social care at lower levels of dependency than the average through the
private care market (Netten and Darton, 2001). Those of moderate incomes are

caught in between, less able to obtain state support and less able to afford private care. This is the classic outcome of selective means-tested state provision. It is the modern, though certainly less harsh, equivalent of the poor law. It is a very different model of social care provision from the more universalistic forms found in the cases of Finland and Germany in this book, and also more selective than allocations under Medicare in the United States.

The two reforms that have emerged, after a long gestation period, in response to the Royal Commission on Long Term Care, both reveal how levels of provision have been cut off from any real measures of need. In deciding how much to spend on the new funding of free nursing services for self-funders in nursing homes in England between from 1 October 2001 to the end of the financial year, the Department of Health, after some research, has fixed provision at exactly £100 million (Pearce, 2001). In Scotland, where both free nursing and personal care is to be available to all, whether in institutions or at home, the Scottish Executive has set aside exactly £125 million for each of the next two years (Bauld, 2001). It remains to be seen whether the new 'entitlements' will be genuinely demand-determined or simply bureaucratically rationed provision within pre-determined cash limits. The latter is the more likely. Britain has long been wedded to its deeply embedded traditions of administratively determined, selective social care.

THE HISTORICAL EVOLUTION OF CARE FOR OLDER PEOPLE

The Limited Role of the State until the Second World War

Up to the beginning of the Second World War the evolution of the state's role in the care of older people is a story that is simply told. It is not unlike those found in the other chapters in this book except, because of Britain's more stable political and constitutional history, it is generally a less eventful story. Until about the middle of the twentieth century, in all industrial societies some version of the poor law and the logic of means-tested public assistance dominated the state's treatment of dependent old people. In Britain, poverty rather than physical dependency was perceived as the chief problem of old age. Continuity in social order and in political and administrative development meant that, from the passing of the Poor Law Amendment Act in 1834 to its abolition in May 1948 and replacement by the National Assistance Act, there was little change in the principles that determined the role of the state in the lives of older people. This is where the experience of the United Kingdom differs from that of the other countries in this volume. In none of the other accounts is there so little disruption to the organization of political life and the structure of public administration over so long a period of time. By 1834 Britain was already an industrialized and urbanized society. The right to vote may have been limited to men of property but the core system of parliamentary, representative government would continue to evolve rather that change dramatically. The economy was subject to cycles of growth and recession but the longer term was one of sustained economic improvement. In contrast, the other summaries of national history in this book describe transformations from autocracy to democracy, violent civil wars, profound shifts in economic structure, these sometimes accompanied by revolution and followed by dictatorship. Only in the case of the United States is there an approximately similar continuity of political life but accompanied by a civil war, much more dramatic economic change and the very different context of a growing, frontier society.

In the first half of the twentieth century the demographic insignificance of old age, in 1931 average life expectancy was 58 for men and 62 for women (ONS, 2001, table 7.1), and the exceptional continuity in the organization of the state and society combined to ensure that issues to do with care of older people had little political salience. They were not the stuff of political conflict and compromise. Nor were they much influenced by older people or knowledge of their wishes. Rather issues to do with the welfare of older people were decided by administrators acting in accordance with long-established statute and procedure. Within the poor law since Elizabethan times a core principle was the responsibility of families to care for or to pay for the care of their relatives. The last reformulation of the poor laws, the Poor Law Act 1930, restated this quite clearly:

> It should be the duty of the father, grandfather, mother, grandmother, husband or child, of a poor, old, blind, lame or impotent person, or other poor person, not able to work, if possessed of sufficient means, to relieve and maintain that person. (cited in Means and Smith, 1998, p. 18)

Where families could not or would not support and care for older people they could either buy the care they needed out of their own resources or they could apply to enter the poorhouse run by the parish. Old people with financial means generally used domestic servants as sources of care. Servants were readily available in the urbanized Britain of the nineteenth century and they continued to be a key source of help for the better-off elderly until the beginning of the Second World War. Means and Smith (1998), in their important account of the history of social care for older people, upon which much of this section depends, quote a 1945 report from the Ministry of Labour that characterizes well the expectations of the governing classes of mid-twentieth century Britain:

> Family life among the middle and upper classes in this country has for generations rested largely on the assumption of domestic help of some kind being available...The

single handed care of an old-fashioned house with stone passages, coal fires, and an antiquated range has proved a heavy task during the war for a mistress bereft of her maids. There is much evidence of strain and consequent ill-health. (Cmd 6650, 1945, p. 4)

The 1931 census showed that almost 5 per cent of households in Britain employed at least one domestic servant. In England and Wales there were still almost 1.2 million domestic servants in a population of just under 40 million and many of these were involved in the care of children or of older people (Marsh, 1965). Even so, by the 1930s, the availability of domestic servants had in fact declined substantially from its peak in the late nineteenth century and an alternative for the better-off older person was to live permanently in a small hotel. This must have appeared an ideal solution to many for, when Nye Bevan, the socialist minister of health, introduced the National Assistance Bill to parliament in 1947, he optimistically spoke of it creating publicly managed and funded 'new hotels for old people' which would be used 'in exactly the same way as many well-to-do people have been accustomed to go into residential hotels'. The image was picked up by the popular press which spoke of 'hotels for old folks' (cited in Means and Smith, 1998, p. 139). This did not happen. For at least two decades after 1948, many local authority old people's homes were in fact no more than renamed public assistance institutions or former workhouses. Despite Bevan's egalitarian hopes, the public role continued to be defined and understood within the culture, as it had been for hundreds of years, as the older person's source of help of last resort.

The Consequences for Older People of the Beveridge Welfare State

The Second World War marked a turning point in the development of social policy and social services generally but had least impact on provision for older people. Muriel Brown, in her history of local authority welfare services for older people, describes the reorganizations after the war as 'not the product of clear thinking on the needs of groups they were to serve so much as the almost casual outcome of the tidying-up of the social service scene' (Brown, 1972, cited in Means and Smith, 1998, p. 111).

Three elements of the post-war welfare state were particularly significant for older people; the extension of state pensions, the establishment of the National Health Service and the organization and funding of local authority institutional and domiciliary services. Yet in all three areas the needs of older people were not the paramount object of the reforms. The consequences for older people were mainly the result of hurried and hidden decisions, made by ministers or often civil servants beyond public scrutiny.

All three elements of reform place took place in a post-war context in which frail older people had come to be seen as a problem. The treatment of older people in the Second World War is important because it highlighted attitudes prevalent in government and the civil service and revealed a pattern of policy making that survives to this day. At the beginning of the war the government expected huge casualties and so took emergency control of many hospitals. In 1939 thousands of frail older people were abruptly discharged from hospital beds including 140,000 in just two days (Titmuss, 1976, p. 193). Many of the beds thus cleared then remained empty. Most of these old people returned to families often unprepared to care for them, others ended up in poorhouses and the few remaining hospitals not included in the emergency arrangements. Some were simply left to their own devices and a later inquiry headed by Seebohm Rowntree concluded there were cases of 'aged persons dying in circumstances of great squalor and loneliness because local authorities have been unable to fulfil their legal obligations to receive them into an institution' (Rowntree, 1947). Once bombing began in 1940, millions of people were made homeless in a matter of months. 'Large numbers of frail elderly people...began to gather in public air raid shelters' and were seen by the authorities as a danger to the health and particularly to the morale of the wider population (Means and Smith, 1998, p. 23). Schemes were set up with a purpose that a London County Council Report described as 'clearing aged persons from air raid shelters' (ibid., p. 25). By the end of the war tens of thousands of vulnerable older people had been evacuated from their home towns and had found themselves crowded into public assistance hospitals and in special hostels set up by voluntary organizations, particularly the Quakers, and later by local authorities. There followed considerable negotiation between local authorities and central government as to the meeting of the costs of these displaced people (Titmuss, 1976, pp. 448–51; Means and Smith, 1998, pp. 21–52).

It was in this context that the arrangements for the new National Health Service were negotiated and planned. There was considerable concern in the Ministry of Health and among professionals over the possibility of older people 'blocking' beds and the whole design of the new system contained a bias against the old, the dependent and the frail. The NHS was divided into three sectors: the hospitals dominated by consultants concerned to practise acute medicine, the family practitioner service and the local health authorities 'who were left with a residual collection of environmental health services, midwives, health visitors, home helps and district nurses' (Doyal and Pennell, 1979, p. 182). This was the point at which care services for older people became cut off from the mainstream of the post-war welfare settlement and relegated to a relatively underfunded and lower status, local government backwater. Children's services escaped this fate through the creation of a new, more professional local department directly linked to the Home Office and with protected funding from central government (Packman, 1975, pp. 5–19). It is a central argument of this chapter that policy development in the British care services has been an administrative rather than a democratic process. It is doubly damaging to a set of services when they are allocated to a less powerful part of the administrative system. This is what happened to social care services. The problems that arise from the separation of social care from health services is a persistent theme of policy analysis in many countries, but it was made particularly acute in Britain by the way in which care services for adults were left to a local government world that was distinct from the central civil service in terms of prestige and even the social class of those who worked in it. The separation of local social care from a national health service run from London became deeply entrenched in administrative and budgetary processes (Lewis, 2001).

Quite why the post-war reforms took place in the ways and at the times they did is still debated by historians. The initial view was that the Beveridge Report of 1942 (Cmd 6404) and the legislation that followed it between 1944 and 1948 were the political expression of major shifts in attitudes and expectations born out of the depression of the 1930s and the sacrifices of the 1940s. A return to the widespread poverty of the recession years was unacceptable to the electorate after the sacrifices of war. The consequences of war itself had been collectively endured by the whole population and there was support for public solutions to social problems. This image of a solidaristic British society has been revised by later work (summarized in Page, 1996, pp. 60–94). It is clear that Britain remained a class society. Certainly a key and necessary basis for social reform was the election of the first majority Labour government in 1945. However, the degree to which that government's legislation marked a radical break with the social policies of the past soon began to be questioned. Richard Titmuss wrote of the development of the welfare state as 'part of a broad, ascending road of social betterment provided for the working class since the nineteenth century and achieving its goal in our time' (1961, p. 34). Later accounts (Brown, 1982; Fraser, 1973; Glennerster, 2000) have confirmed this more evolutionary perspective, showing how many of the post-war policies were logical extensions of past practice and were designed to minimize social and administrative upheaval. The Beveridge Report both reflected and helped construct the spirit of the times. Certainly the idea of the universalist Beveridge welfare state was more coherent as ideology than in practice. Viewed from outside the country it came to be endowed with radical qualities that were not always found in the social reality of post-war Britain.

Older People as 'Obstacles' to Social Reform

It is now generally agreed that Beveridge's vision of post-war reconstruction was a gendered one and particularly dependent on male-breadwinner, family-

wage assumptions in its plans for a social security system. What is less appreci-
ated is that the report and the conventional wisdoms of the time were also ageist
by today's standards. Beveridge described his plan as:

> based upon a diagnosis of want. It takes account of two other facts about the British
> community...The first of these two facts is the age constitution of the population,
> making it certain that persons past the age that is now regarded as the end of working
> life will be a much larger proportion of the whole community than at any time in the
> past. The second fact is the low reproduction rate of the British community today...
> The first fact makes it necessary to seek ways of postponing the age of retirement
> from work...The second fact makes it imperative to give first place in social expendi-
> ture to the care of childhood and to the safeguarding of maternity. (Cmd 6404, 1942,
> para. 15)

While Beveridge's wish to delay retirement may now appear prescient, his
concerns to privilege the family and childhood and to limit the costs of an ageing population were in tune with governing opinion and ultimately of greater
significance. Later in his report he argued that 'it is dangerous to be in any way
lavish to old age, until adequate provision has been assured for all other vital
needs' (ibid., para. 236). The late 1940s and the early 1950s were quietly but
significantly ageist and pro-natalist. The 1949 Royal Commission on Population warned of 'steady increases in the number of older people over the coming
decades' but did not suggest that this required better benefits and services but
rather that society should protect itself against those who 'consume without
producing...[which] makes them a factor reducing the average standard of
living of the community' (Cmd 7695, 1949, p. 113). While the Treasury
acceded to children's services being subsidized by central government to the
extent of 50 per cent of costs, the Chancellor of the Exchequer drew the line at
providing similar assistance for the care of older people.

Combined with these fears about the costs of older people was a limited
understanding of old age itself. Contemporary views about the nature and needs
of old age now appear limiting and discriminatory. There was little understanding that older people with disabilities could be helped to stay at home or any
awareness that this might be their preference. Seebohm Rowntree's 1947 survey, *The Problems of Ageing and the Care of Old People*, while having a significant influence on future policy by drawing attention to the condition of public
assistance institutions, the renamed poorhouses, remained sure that the answer
was better institutional care. It argued that more old people's homes would

> lessen the need for extensive plans of home help, home nursing, visiting, and home
> meals services for old people who would be better off in a Home or Institution. The
> right sphere for such domiciliary services is in helping able-bodied old people in
> cases of temporary illness or during convalescence. (Rowntree, 1947)

These were the assumptions that informed the negotiations within government over the future financing of local authority provision, which it was agreed would be almost entirely concerned with residential care. Support for people in their own homes would be best left to voluntary societies and good neighbourliness (Parker, 1965). Means and Smith (1998) provide a fascinating account of negotiations among civil servants over the scope and financing of the National Assistance Act 1948, the legislation that still mainly governs provision for dependent older people, and show how they were informed by values and assumptions that were to constrain social care services for older people and probably still do.

Among those assumptions was a clear but rarely elaborated view that different social classes of old people could not be mixed. Before the Second World War voluntary organizations (Rotary, the Red Cross Society), professional organizations (the National Union of Teachers, the Musicians Union) and church societies (the Methodists, the Free Churches) ran homes for 'those who would never feel at home in a state institution' (British Red Cross Society quoted in Means and Smith, 1998, p. 104) but who could not afford entirely private nursing homes or to enter residential hotels. During the war voluntary agencies, particularly the Old People's Welfare Council, the Women's Voluntary Service and the British Red Cross Society expanded their residential provision for people they described as 'those with an income of up to £200–£250' and 'residents of approximately the same educational standard' (ibid.). After the war, when it was increasingly impressed on government by campaigners and the voluntary sector that the large-scale housing of old people in public assistance institutions should no longer be continued, there nonetheless remained a whole tone that suggested that this was a debate about housing the working-class older person (Means and Smith, 1998, pp. 70–80). It is hard to imagine that many of the senior civil servants who guided the reforms ever considered themselves to be the likely users of the services they were reforming.

This separation within the world of social care of those services that better-off and professional people are likely to use, and those that cater for more ordinary or working-class people is a particularly British characteristic that is almost invisible but remains very real. One of the key achievements of the new post-war Labour government was that it had resisted civil service plans to pay retired people a universal pension that was less than that paid to the unemployed or the sick, an arrangement that Beveridge had accepted as inevitable. Instead the 1946 National Insurance Act set a universal retirement pension of 26 shillings a week for single people and 42 shillings a week for couples. For older people with no other income, 21 shillings could then be taken to pay for a place in a local authority old people's home. Those with additional resources could add to the money and go into a better class of home or use it to pay for private help. In this way the universal welfare state helped to sustain class differentials in social care which survive today in patterns of use of both domiciliary services and institutional care. Much of the residential sector is socially and ethnically differentiated. Some nursing homes still discreetly point out that they do not accept 'social security residents', signalling to the middle-class customer that they will be among their own kind. Means and Smith go further and link the class nature of social care in Britain to the reluctance to develop domiciliary rather than institutional services which characterized the National Assistance Act 1948 and which then determined development over the next forty years, until the NHS and Community Care Act 1990. They quote Peter Townsend:

> The failure to shift the balance of health and welfare policy towards community care also has to be explained in relation to the function of institutions to regulate and confirm inequality in society, and indeed to regulate deviation from the central social values of self-help, domestic independence, personal thrift, willingness to work, productive effort and family care. (Townsend, 1981, p. 22)

Domiciliary Services for Older People

The post-war construction of the 'Beveridge' welfare state did not explicitly address the needs of older people living in their own homes. It certainly did not offer entitlements to home care. The 1948 National Assistance Act was mainly concerned with the provision and funding of residential care. This preoccupation is summed up by Julia Parker: '[The Act] made no attempt to provide any sort of substitute family life for old people who could no longer be supported by their own relatives. Institutional provision was accepted without question' (Parker, 1965, p. 106). The 1946 National Health Service Act permitted the local authorities to develop some services in the community, notably the provision of home helps. This service had initially been created to assist nursing mothers and there was some opposition among officials in the Ministry of Health to the powers being used to assist older people. It was felt they would absorb resources better used to support the pro-natalist objectives of post-war Britain.

However, during the forty years after the implementation of the 1948 Act a range of non-institutional domiciliary services for older people did develop, among which the home help service became the largest. In addition, community nursing services were financed and provided by the NHS and meals on wheels and day centres were largely managed and delivered by voluntary organizations that received their funding from local authorities. This pattern of development was recognized in the 1968 Health Services and Public Health Act which gave local authorities general, but largely discretionary powers to promote the welfare of older people in the community. The services that developed, mainly home helps, were to be subject to substantial reform following the NHS and Community Care Act 1990 which contracted out most public provision to voluntary and for-profit providers. That act would also specifically recognize a reality that had developed over the previous decades: that state support for older people living in institutions and in their own homes was limited and, in principle, rationed to those with the highest needs and lowest incomes; that the majority of older people living at home must seek and fund their own support using what the 1990 reforms called the 'mixed economy of care'.

Where public providers did provide services it was almost always under legislation that permitted rather than required them to do so. Consequently there were and remain substantial territorial inequalities, or 'injustices' (Davies, 1968), between local authorities in the availability of services. As one observer put it, 'there are many services for old age, there is no policy for old age' (Ruck, 1960, p. 131). Where local and health authorities did not have powers to help, much home care provision necessarily developed within the voluntary sector, among them day centres, lunch clubs, meals on wheels, visiting schemes and social work advice. Although these services were often mainly funded by the public sector they too inevitably developed in a variable, almost ad hoc, way across the country, available in some places and not others and rationed differently depending on the balance of supply and demand and the provider concerned. Again Ruck comments on the lack of a rationale to the rationing by pointing out that voluntary sector provision often reached the 'hale and hearty' rather than the 'frail and solitary' (1963, p. 35). The vibrancy of the voluntary sector is often seen as a British strength by European observers. What they perhaps miss is that it is often an inegalitarian vibrancy and one that has evolved in response to a long history of partial, even accidental increments to public provision. This pattern and tradition of social care did not allow the accumulation of any sense of citizen entitlement to services. British old people cannot know what they are entitled to, only discover what happens to be available. From the point of view of the user this is disordered welfare and access becomes a sort of gift or stroke of luck.

The Persistent Undersupply of Services

A strong but not always explicit feature of British home care services has been a concern that 'too generous' services would undermine family and individual responsibility. Means and Smith cite many examples from the 1950s and 1960s of experts and politicians warning of the need to encourage, even enforce, the obligations of family and particularly of women (1998, pp. 223–6). In fact there was no evidence at all that informal care was in retreat. A paucity of services of all sorts relative to need has been discovered by numerous studies throughout the decades since the Second World War (Townsend and Wedderburn, 1965;

Hunt, 1970; Cmnd 3703, 1968; Audit Commission, 1986). Often there was evidence that, taking account of the growing proportion of older people in the population, the family was doing more not less. For much of this period, in order to meet all recognized needs adequately, and particularly to match the best found in other European nations, British provision of services such as home help and personal care would have needed to increase by a factor of two or three in many local authorities (Hunt, 1970; Kraan et al., 1991). An important milestone in understanding of the degree of unmet need for care was the massive survey of disability carried out by the Office of Population, Censuses and Surveys (OPCS) in 1986. For the first time the intensity of need in a random sample of the population could be calibrated against the level of provision they received. Often a rule of inverse provision appeared to operate; the more difficult the condition, the less public support could be relied on. For example, the OPCS study showed that many families caring for older people suffering from dementia received very little public help (Table 5.4).

It does not seem unreasonable to draw the conclusion that there are large numbers of carers supporting severely ill older people in the community at any one time and that a substantial proportion do so unaided by social or health services to any significant degree. Family care, particularly intensive personal care, has usually meant care by women (Green, 1988; Rowlands, 1998). Feminist scholars did a great deal to reveal women's roles as carers (see Chapter 1) and from 1990 the need to support carers was increasingly recognized in

Table 5.4 Percentage of older people 65+ with advanced cognitive
impairment in private households receiving services in the past
year, Great Britain, 1986

Service	Received service %
Psychiatrist	12
Community nurse	36
Health visitor	12
Meals on wheels	8
Home help	24
Social worker	14
GP	91
Respite care	11

Source: Martin et al., 1989.

legislation. The NHS and Community Care Act 1990 required local authorities to consider the needs of family carers and the Carers (Recognition and Services) Act 1995 gave them an entitlement to have their needs assessed. Yet, as pointed out above, much recent evidence points to their receiving less not more help. The rhetoric of 'support' for carers is capable of various interpretations. A real, if not always an intended outcome, of carer-friendly policies is to reinforce rather than ease women's informal care work.

Social Care Without Social Entitlements

A key difference between the evolution of social care services for older people in Britain and that in most other industrial nations is that the important decisions have rarely been the product of public debate of the issues followed by democratic political choices and compromises. Rather they have resulted from settlements between different sections within the public bureaucracy: trade-offs between the Treasury and the spending ministries; battles over territory between civil servants; administrative allocations of responsibility between central and local government. In the other chapters of this book are to be found accounts of deals made between elected politicians or between political parties representing different interests but which then lead to new social entitlements. In Britain the House of Commons rarely debates social care issues and when they do interest and attendance is low. Means and Smith (1998, pp. 267–8) report a rare debate on 'care of the elderly' in the House of Commons in 1967 at which speakers complained of 'the sparseness of our numbers' and that the 'the subject has no glamour'. Phoebe Hall, in her account of the debates on the very important Social Services Act 1970, reports that the numbers of Members of Parliament who attended the debates were very low, the legislation was rushed and the Minister of Health responsible, Richard Crossman, thought the subject 'boring' and left decisions to his officials (Hall, 1976). The main role that MPs play in the development of social care policies is through the House of Commons committee system. The Health Committee fairly regularly investigates areas of provision and policy largely by calling ministers and civil servants before it and questioning them about what they are doing. These inquiries and the reports that follow them reveal very clearly that elected politicians do not make social care policy but merely follow and occasionally question it. Bureaucratic policy making does not extend social rights. Civil servants are usually more concerned to defend their powers and limit the demands that the public might make. The evolution of social care has been a bureaucratic rather than a democratic process. It has provided services on a discretionary basis and not in response to citizenship entitlements.

THE HISTORICAL EVOLUTION OF CHILDCARE SERVICES

This section is much shorter than the account of the evolution of care services for older people. The reason is simple: much of what is meant by the term 'childcare' in the Britain is simply not very relevant to the issues dealt with in this volume. This book is concerned with a conception of 'childcare' rooted in meanings of the term that are more current in mainland western Europe than they are in Britain or the United States. Childcare in this sense refers to forms of communal provision for the routine care of young children at times when their parents are not available to do so, generally because the parents are at work in the formal labour market. It is essentially about day-care services for pre-school children. In Britain this is a relatively new meaning of the word 'childcare'. This is not merely a semantic issue; it reflects the fact that until recently pre-school day care was not an object of public policy except where other childcare and family policies were involved. A search through the literature on the history of public policy and 'childcare' in Britain (and the United States, as for many authors the two histories are much the same) reveals one that treats issues to do with nurseries, early education and day care as of minor significance or mentions them not at all. Rather childcare has meant: saving children from cruel and abusive families (Behlmer, 1982; Gordon, 1989); protecting children from exploitation as workers (Hopkins, 1994); managing the behaviour of parents (Donzelot, 1980); a preoccupation with the home as the incubator of crime and delinquency (Platt, 1969); using families to promote children's health (Dwork, 1987; Klaus, 1993); extolling the virtues of motherhood above employment (Fildes et al., 1992); raising the incomes of non-working mothers and those on low incomes (Macnicol, 1980); influencing childrearing practices within the family to support of the strength of the nation and its international, even imperial role (Skocpol, 1992), or all of these together (Meyer, 1983). That these have been the foci of the state's concerns for childhood and families reflects fundamental historical and cultural priorities that continue to influence the role of the state in the lives of families, women and children, and which sharply distinguishes the Anglo-Saxon countries from others.

> Until the nineteenth century policies had been drawn up with a concern either for the child's soul or for the future manpower needs of the state. Both of these concerns remained in place in the nineteenth and early twentieth centuries, but they were joined by a new one, a concern to save children for the enjoyment of childhood...Philanthropy was central to this child-saving activity. Philanthropists opened and ran homes for orphans and other neglected children, they organized schemes of emigration, they set up kindergartens and schools, they founded societies for the prevention of cruelty to children and they had numerous programmes for visiting the poor. (Cunningham, 1995, p. 134)

In twentieth century Britain the history of childcare policies is the incremental transfer of most of these functions to the state. Today the term 'childcare' in public policy documents still largely means protecting deprived or abused children (Pringle, 1998, p. 33). These are assumed to be a tiny minority of all children. In the terms of the three key pieces of legislation since the Second World War, the Children's Acts of 1948, 1963 and 1989, they are children 'in need of care and protection', that is to say those at risk of harm or who are without parents (Canaan, 1992). These statutory limitations were accentuated by the creation of the new local authority Children's Departments in 1948. This was to become a dynamic service but one of limited focus.

> Instead of involving Health, Education and Public Assistance Committees at local government level, new ad hoc Children's Committees were to be set up, with responsibility for most groups of deprived children... Nor were they to be responsible for anyone *other* than deprived children, for the Curtis Committee was anxious that all their energies should be concentrated upon this neglected group, and it was for this reason that alternative solutions, such as making Education Committees responsible, were rejected. In other words, it was to be a truly specialist service. (Packman, 1975, p. 6)

These administrative arrangements were consistent with policy and ideology. In Britain, until recently, the idea that the state should organize and subsidize the care of children merely so that their mothers might go out to work was simply not part of the normal agenda of public policy. The process by which the idea has slowly been incorporated into social welfare goals has not constituted a revolution, rather it has been part of a slow acceptance of the economic, and to a lesser extent moral, imperative of equal opportunities for women. Universal nursery provision has never been a high-profile public issue in Britain. It is an objective that has simply crept into public policy discourse and its presence is probably still not fully apparent to many in politics and government administration.

The high point of public provision for children under school age still remains the emergency nurseries of the Second World War (Wilson, 1977, pp. 134, 154). However, these were rapidly closed down after 1945 when it was assumed that women would return home to the protection of the new Beveridge welfare state of family allowances, full employment and the family wage for men. Local authorities continued to run some day nurseries (see Table 5.1) but only for those children defined as being in social need. This provision was available very unequally across the country, often seen as stigmatizing and provided for a tiny fraction of families in severe social and economic difficulty. Pre-school care returned briefly to the political agenda in the 1967 with the publication of the Plowden Report, *Children and their Primary Schools*, produced by the independent but government-funded Central Advisory Council for Education

(Department of Education and Science, 1967). The team that produced the report had visited the United States and observed programmes of compensatory education in deprived areas designed to help children from poorer families take better advantage or education ('Headstart' programmes). The committee particularly recommended pre-school education in areas of social deprivation. A sterling crisis followed soon after and the idea was dropped until, in 1972, it was taken up by the then Minister of Education, Margaret Thatcher, whose department produced a white paper recommending pre-school provision for all parents who wanted it. While the idea was again justified in terms of equality of opportunity for children, there is little doubt that Mrs Thatcher's own experience of combining a career and motherhood played a part. However, this time the idea was once again undermined by economic problems: the oil price rise in 1974 and the sterling crisis of 1976. These are just further examples of the tension between economic and social goals that has particularly characterized British history.

In the end, pressure for change was to come not in terms of children's educational opportunities but from a realization in the Treasury that the economic benefits of women's participation in the labour market required accessible pre-school childcare. But it had required twenty years of rather ineffectual social rights legislation first. The Equal Pay Act of 1970 and the Sex Discrimination Act of 1975, both vigorously supported by women's pressure groups at time, had a limited impact on pay differentials or on the concentration of women in less-skilled and part-time jobs. The legislation was passed without sufficient recognition of the practical difficulties faced by women in the labour market. The 1975 Employment Protection Act which introduced, for the first time, limited rights to maternity leave and pay (forty weeks leave but pay for only six weeks and available mainly to women who had been working full-time) was a further example of the gap between a slowly growing commitment to gender equality and an understanding of its practical realities. By the 1990s it was becoming increasingly clear to the policy establishment that the absence of childcare facilities was an obstacle to economic efficiency. In 1996, a year before losing power, John Major's government had begun to introduce a system of nursery school vouchers which parents could use to buy care for children aged three and four. With the election of New Labour in 1997 this was replaced by the National Child Care Strategy described earlier in this chapter. While this programme has yet to generate substantial improvements in pre-school childcare provision, it marks a crucial policy shift. Combined with the Working Families Tax Credit, which adds substantially to the incomes of lower-paid parents, it promises to provide parents with a genuine choice between state-subsidized childcare or caring for children at home. A key element in the development of the new direction in policy is its support by the Chancellor of the Exchequer, Gordon Brown, as a mechanism for reducing family poverty and securing the supply of female labour. While economic considerations remain paramount, as they always have in British social policy, the new direction in childcare support may turn out to mark, in terms of Anne Helene Gauthier's typology (1996), the long awaited shift of the United Kingdom from the category 'pro-family but non-interventionist' to 'pro-family and pro-egalitarian'.

In short the history of day care for children under five whose mothers go out to work is also very simply told. Since the industrial revolution, and until very recently, it was a need left to relatives, friends and private nannies. When the proportion of mothers working began to rise rapidly after about 1980, market provision in return for private payments began to feature significantly. It was only in the very last years of the twentieth century that the state began to accept a significant degree of financial and practical responsibility for universal childcare needs. As the study by Peter Moss, summarized at the beginning of this chapter, shows, the acceptance of responsibility by the state has not yet led to universal and accessible pre-school childcare.

CONCLUSION

This chapter has sought to explain how and why public social care in the United Kingdom is different from that provided in other industrial countries. The core point is that while both childcare and care services for older people are available in forms and quantities that appear similar to those elsewhere they do not amount to social entitlements in ways that might be assumed or that can be found in some of the other countries described in this book. Over the last sixty years, the British people and those who govern them have come to accept that they have rights to health care and education and at least entitlements to national insurance benefits. In contrast, childcare and services for older people have not entirely thrown off their poor law inheritance and access to them remains, and is largely accepted as, unequal and contingent upon administrative discretion, geography and even social class.

There are three main reasons for this. First, these services were largely excluded from the post-war welfare settlement and relegated to less well-funded and less prestigious parts of the system of public administration. Second, social care issues have rarely been significant in party politics and electoral competition. The key pieces of legislation have almost always been non-controversial and simply empowered the state to provide services but have not given citizens entitlements. As a result, the services have been managed and developed beyond the public gaze in the relatively private worlds of central and local government administration. Third, the long-term continuity of British political history has meant that cultural and ideological expectations of public provision in these areas of social care have not been stimulated. Social care has continued to be seen as largely a private, domestic issue to be dealt with by the family or through the market. All of these reasons have, however, become less significant as economic and social change has undermined the core assumptions on which they were founded. The policies of New Labour appear to recognize this. The National Childcare Strategy, and different policy responses to the Royal Commission on Long Term Care currently appearing in England, Wales and Scotland may mark a new beginning. There is now a chance that British people will come to perceive that, as citizens, they have rights to pre-school care for their children and to care at home when they are old.

REFERENCES

Almond, G.A. and Verba, S. (1965), *The Civic Culture, Political Attitudes and Democracy in Five Nations*, Boston and Toronto: Little, Brown & Company.

Audit Commission (1986), *Making a Reality of Community Care*, London: HMSO.

Barnett, C. (2001), *The Verdict of Peace: Britain between her Yesterday and the Future*, London: Macmillan.

Barr, N. (1991), 'The Objectives and Attainments of Pension Schemes', in T. Wilson and D. Wilson (eds), *The State and Social Welfare*, London and New York: Longman.

Bauld, L. (2001), 'Scotland Makes it Happen', *Community Care*, **1395**, 36–7.

Behlmer, G.K. (1982), *Child Abuse and Moral Reform in England 1870–1908*, Stanford: Stanford University Press.

Brown, M. (1972), 'The Development of Local Authority Welfare Services from 1948–1965 under Part III of the National Assistance Act, 1948', PhD Thesis, University of Manchester.

Brown, M. (1982), *Introduction to Social Administration in Britain*, 5th edition, London: Hutchinson University Press.

Bryson, C., Budd, T., Lewis, J. and Elam, J. (1999) *Women's Attitudes to Combining Paid Work and Family Life*, The Women's Unit, London: Cabinet Office.

Canaan, C. (1992), *Changing Families, Changing Welfare: Family Centres and the Welfare State*, Hemel Hempstead: Harvester Wheatsheaf.

Carvel, J. (2001) 'Care Crisis Keeps Elderly Patients in Hospital', London: *The Guardian*, 15 June.

Cm 3959 (1998), *Meeting the Childcare Challenge: A Framework and Consultation Document*, Department for Education and Employment, London: Stationery Office.

Cm 4579 (2000), *The Children Act Report 1995–1999*, Department of Health, London: Stationery Office.

Cmd 6404 (1942), *Social Insurance and Allied Services*, London: HMSO.

Cmd 6650 (1945), *Markham/Hancock Report Report on the Post-war Organisation of Private Domestic Employment*, London: HMSO.

Cmd 7695 (1949), *The Report of the Royal Commission on Population*, London: HMSO.

Cmnd 3703 (1968), *Report of the Committee on Local Authority and Allied Personal Social Services* (Seebohm Report), London: HMSO.

Cunningham, H. (1995), *Children and Childhood in Western Society since 1500*, London and New York: Longman.

Davies, B.P. (1968), *Social Needs and Resources in Local Services*, London: Michael Joseph.

Department of Education and Science (1967), *Children and their Primary Schools* (The Plowden Committee Report), London: HMSO.

Department of Health (2000), *Supplement to Cm 4579: The Children Act Report 1995–1999*, London: Stationery Office.

Department of Social Security (1998), *Households Below Average Income 1979 to 1996/7*, London: Stationery Office.

Donzelot, J. (1980), *The Policing of Families*, London: Hutchinson.

Doyal, L. and Pennell, I. (1979), *The Political Economy of Health*, London: Pluto Press.

Dwork, D. (1987), *War is Good for Babies and other Young Children: A History of the Infant and Child Welfare Movement in England 1898–1918*, London: Tavistock Publications.

European Commission (1999), *Social Protection for Dependency in Old Age in the 15 EU Member States*, Directorate General for Employment, Industrial Relations and Social Affairs, Unit v/E.2, Luxembourg: Office of Publications for the European Communities.

Family Policy Studies Centre (1998), *Families and Child Care*, Briefing Paper 6, London: FPSC.

Fildes, V., Marks, L. and Marland, H. (eds) (1992), *Women and Children First, International Maternal and Infant Welfare, 1870–1945*, London and New York: Routledge.

Fraser, D. (1973), *The Evolution of the British Welfare State*, London: Macmillan.

Gauthier, A.H.(1996), *The State and the Family: A Comparative Analysis of Family Policies in Industrialized Countries*, Oxford: Clarendon Press.

Glennerster, H. (2000), *British Social Policy since 1945*, 2nd edition, Oxford: Blackwell.

Gordon, L. (1989), *Heroes of Their Own Lives, the Politics and History of Family Violence, 1880–1960*, London: Virago.

Green, H. (1988), *General Household Survey 1985: Informal Carers*, London: HMSO.

Hall, P. (1976), *Reforming the Welfare: The Politics of Change in the Personal Social Services*, London: Heinemann Educational.

Hall, P., Land, H., Parker, R.A. and Webb, A. (1975), *Change, Choice and Conflict in Social Policy*, London: Heinemann.

Harding, L.F. (1996), *Family, State and Social Policy*, Basingstoke: Macmillan.

Hunt, A. (1970), *The Home Help Service in England and Wales*, London: HMSO.

Hopkins, E. (1994), *Childhood Transformed, Working-class Children in Nineteenth-century England*, Manchester: Manchester University Press.

Kamerman, S.B. and Kahn, A.J. (eds) (1997), *Family Change and Family Policies in Great Britain, Canada, New Zealand and the United States*, Oxford: Clarendon Press.

Kavanagh, D. (1989), 'Political Culture in Great Britain: The Decline of the Civic Culture', in G.A. Almond and S. Verba (eds), *The Civic Culture Revisited*, London: Sage Publications, pp. 140–52.

Klaus, A. (1993), *Every Child a Lion: The Origins of Maternal and Infant Health Policy in the United States and France, 1890–1920*, Ithaca: Cornell University Press.

Kraan, R., Baldock, J., Bavies, B.P., Evers, A., Johansson, L., Knapen, M., Thorslund, M. and Tunissen, C. (1991), *Care for the Elderly: Significant Innovations in Three European Countries*, Boulder, CO and Frankfurt am Main: Westview Press and Campus Verlag.

Lewis, J. (2001), 'Older people and the health-social care boundary in the uk: half a century of hidden policy conflict', *Social Policy and Administration*, **35** (4), 343–59.

Macnicol, J. (1980), *The Movement for Family Allowances, 1918–45, A Study in Social Policy Development*, London: Heinemann.

Marsh, D. (1965), *The Changing Social Structure of England and Wales, 1971–1961*, London: Routledge & Kegan Paul.

Martin, J., White, A. and Maltzer, H. (1989), *Disabled Adults: Services, Transport and Employment*, OPCS Surveys of Disability in Great Britain, Report No. 4, London: HMSO.

Means, R. and Smith, R. (1998), *From Poor Law to Community Care: The Development of Services for Elderly People*, 2nd edition, Bristol: Policy Press.

Meyer, P. (1983), *The Child and the State: The Intervention of the State in Family Life*, Cambridge: Cambridge University Press.

Moss, P. (2001), *The UK at the Crossroads: Towards an Early Years European Partnership*, Facing the Future Policy Paper No. 2, London: The Daycare Trust.

Netten, A. and Darton, R. (2001), 'Formal and Informal Support Prior to Admission: Are Self-funders being Admitted to Care Homes Unnecessarily?', in S. Tester, C. Archibald, C. Rowlings and S. Turner (eds), *Quality in Later Life: Rights, Rhetoric and Reality*, Proceedings of the British Society of Gerontology, Stirling: University of Stirling, pp. 60–64.

Office for National Statistics (ONS) (2001), *Social Trends No. 31*, London: Stationery Office.

Oldfield, N. and Autumn, C.S.Y. (1993), *The Cost of a Child: Living Standards for the 1990s*, London: Child Poverty Action Group.

Oppenheim, C. and Harker, L. (1996), *Poverty: The Facts*, 3rd edition, London: Child Poverty Action Group.

Owen, G. (2000), *From Empire to Europe*, London and New York: Harper Collins.

Packman, J. (1975), *The Child's Generation: Child Care Policy from Curtis to Houghton*, London and Oxford: Martin Robertson and Basil Blackwell,

Page, R.M. (1996), *Altruism and the British Welfare State*, Aldershot: Avebury

Parker, J. (1965), *Local Health and Welfare Services*, London: Allen & Unwin.

Pearce, J. (2001), 'Free nursing care: do the sums add up?', *Community Care*, **1393** (20), 10–11.

Pickard, L., Wittenberg, R., Comas-Herrera, A., Darton, R. and Davies, B. (2001) 'Community Care for Frail Older People: Analysis using the 1998/9 General Household Survey', in S. Tester, C. Archibald, C. Rowlings and S. Turner (eds), *Quality in Later Life: Rights, Rhetoric and Reality*, Proceedings of the British Society of Gerontology, Stirling: University of Stirling, pp. 201–6.

Platt, A.M. (1969), *The Child Savers: The Invention of Delinquency*, Chicago: Chicago University Press.

Pringle, K. (1998), *Children and Social Welfare in Europe*, Buckingham and Philadelphia: Open University Press.

Rowlands, O. (1998), *Informal Carers, An independent study carried out by the Office of National Statistics on behalf of the Department of Health as part of the 1995 General Household Survey*, London: Stationery Office.

Rowntree, B.S. (1947), *Old People: Report of a Survey Committee on the Problems of Ageing and the Care of Old People*, Oxford: Oxford University Press.

Ruck, S. (1960), 'A policy for old age', *Political Quarterly*, **31** (2), 120–31.

Ruck, S. (1963), *Local Government and Welfare Services*, London: Routledge & Kegan Paul.

Skocpol, T. (1992), *Protecting Soldiers and Mothers, the Political Origins of Social Policy in the United States*, Cambridge, MA and London: Belknap Press of Harvard University Press.

Sutherland, Sir Stewart (1999a), *With Respect to Old Age: Long Term Care — Rights and Responsibilities, A Report by The Royal Commission on Long Term Care*, Cm 4192-I, London: Stationery Office.

Sutherland, Sir Stewart (1999b), *With Respect to Old Age: Long Term Care — Rights and Responsibilities, The Context of Long Term Care Policy*, Research Volume I, Cm 4192-II/I, London: Stationery Office.

Tinker, A. (1992), *Elderly People in Modern Society*, 3rd edition, London and New York: Longman.

Titmuss, R.M. (1961), *Essays on the Welfare State*, London: Unwin University Books.

Titmuss, R.M. (1974), *Social Policy: An Introduction*, London: Allen & Unwin.

Titmuss, R.M. (1976), *Problems of Social Policy*, re-issued edition, London: HMSO.

Townsend, P. (1981), 'The structural dependency of the elderly: the creation of social policy in the twentieth century', *Ageing and Society*, **1** (1), 5–28.

Townsend, P. and Wedderburn, D. (1965), *The Aged in the Welfare State*, London: Bell & Sons.

Ward, C., Dale, A. and Joshi, H. (1996), 'Combining employment with childcare: an escape from dependence', *Journal of Social Policy*, **25** (2), 223–247.

Wasoff, F. and Dey, I. (2000), *Family Policy*, Eastbourne: Gildredge Press.

Wilson, E. (1977), *Women and the Welfare State*, London: Tavistock Publications.

Wittenberg, R., Pickard, L., Comas-Herrera, A., Davies, B. and Darton, R. (1998), *Demand for Long-Term Care: Projections of Long-Term Care Finance for Elderly People*, Canterbury: Personal Social Services Research Unit, University of Kent.

6. Care for Children and Older People in the United States: Laggard or Merely Different?

Joseph Heffernan

INTRODUCTION

The established view is that the United States is a 'laggard welfare state'. This means that it was slow to set up publicly funded programmes such as old-age insurance, worker's compensation and unemployment insurance. Even now the United States has not introduced a children's allowance or comprehensive public health insurance. As a consequence, public spending on 'social welfare' lags rather far behind other affluent nations, but with Japan as a notable exception. In the main, however, US citizens wear this badge of low public spending on social welfare as one of honour rather than approbation.

Why does one country spend more public money on welfare than another? (See Table 6.1.) In part the explanation depends on the kind of answer sought. In the comparative literature a great deal of ink has been spilled trying to explain the size of public sector spending. The question this literature asks is:

Table 6.1 *Public spending on social welfare functions as a share of GDP 1996 (per cent)*

	Pensions	Health	Unemploy-ment	Family support	Social care	Total %
Finland	9.9	7.9	7.5	4.6	3.1	34.0
Germany	11.2	8.6	4.4	2.2	3.4	29.8
Japan	5.9	5.6	0.4	0.4	0.7	13.0
UK	7.2	6.6	1.8	2.4	5.8	23.7
US	6.5	6.6	2.1	0.6	2.0	16.4

Source: OECD.

what explains the growth of public spending for social welfare ends? Does the explanation lie with a 'logic of industrialization' as argued by Harold Wilensky (1975)? Or is public spending on welfare a reflection of particular constitutional structures, political party organization, unique historical circumstance or, lastly, are other more general conditions such as culture, ideology or religion the crucial determining factors? In addition, there are outcomes and qualities of social services other than the volume of expenditure to be explained. For Gøsta Esping-Andersen (1990) a more relevant question is what are the implications of a welfare system's origins in terms of the satisfaction of the citizen-client with the arrangements and choices available? From a more normative perspective, a political scientist might ask 'do the social welfare options available reflect the current majority preference but with due respect for the right of the minority?'. Economists are more likely to focus on the efficiency consequences of any nation state's particular allocation of social welfare responsibilities, while students of public policy pay more attention to the equity consequences. Social workers and other professionals may rather concern themselves with the consequences for the lives and opportunities for women, children, or the least privileged citizens.

However, public spending alone is not a measure of social welfare provision in a country. The comparative literature clearly demonstrates that needs for income security, occupational security, health care, adequate affordable housing and personal social services are met through a complex interaction of four linked sectors; the public, market, non-profit, and the informal, and, in the case of the last, particularly by the family. Should one sector in one nation state respond with remarkable levels of both efficiency and equity then there is less need for other sectors to respond. Thus, without looking at sector responsibility and function, it is meaningless to call one nation advanced and another laggard simply because of the level of public spending. This book, and the project on which it is based, study social care arrangements in five affluent democratic nations. The driving assumption is that these are five affluent democracies where deficiencies in social care are not explicable by either oppression or scarcity. There must therefore be other more subtle and elusive reasons. A further assumption is that these five countries fit five well-accepted models of welfare response.

In this chapter the intention is first to discern the degree to which in the United States social care arrangements reflect the model ascribed to it and, second, to provide a brief historical explication of how the model developed for both childcare and care of the frail elderly.

In the United States there is a high level of cynicism about how well the political system allows public policy to reflect public preferences (Dionne, 1991). During the Clinton years both health and welfare policies held a central position in domestic policy debates and substantial reforms were proposed, only some of which succeeded. The US Congress decisively rejected a public expansion of the health care system sought by the Clinton administration. Just prior to that the Congress had first adopted and then quickly diluted a comprehensive programme of public protection against catastrophic health care costs, including those of long-term care (Holstein and Minkler, 1991). In 1996 the system of income security for single-parent households was radically reconstructed when the infamous AFDC (Aid for Families with Dependent Children) was replaced by a 'more geographically diverse, more stringent and more punitive program', Temporary Assistance for Needy Families (TANF) (Kamerman and Kahn, 2001). In all of these developments, there is evidence of a clear preference for market mechanisms and market incentives to deal with the problems at hand. Most academic and journalistic commentary asserts that these outcomes of the policy-making process were largely in accord with overwhelming public preference (see, for example, Hacker, 1997; Skocpol, 1996; Johnson and Broder, 1996). As the Clinton administration reached its conclusion, the welfare debate faded away, the market model having largely won the day (see, for example, Drew, 1996, Weaver, 1998). However, all of the policy histories have something of the quality of Longfellow's 'but for the want of a horseshoe nail [the war could have gone the other way]'. Moreover they all suggest that, in the battle of grand ideas, social policy shifts depend on the way ideas are transmitted from the élite to citizens; they are top-down accounts. Social care policy does not appear to be driven by groundswells of public pressure. They also highlight the tendency to inaction built into American national political institutions; a product of the separation of powers, federalism and conflicts between contending élites. Further, the US courts have ruled that no fundamental constitutional rights have been violated by these choices of policy.

The US system of social care is indeed market driven. When you or I become more elderly and less able to meet our daily activity needs unassisted, to whom should we turn? Should we rely on a spouse, if we have one, should we rely on our children, if they give a damn? Perhaps we would rather rely on our parish, church or synagogue. Maybe we would like to use cash and buy care from some ready and willing open market providers? Or would we rather go and knock on the door of the local poorhouse? The same range of choice applies to finding care for our very young children. What we would prefer to do and what we are forced to accept by existing arrangements are not necessarily the same. It is certainly true that only government can establish a legal right to social care. But that is true of all legal rights, for that is what government does. Because government does it, that does not mean they do it well, efficiently, effectively, or even equitably. The recent health care debates reflect the objective reality that many people in the United States, when the real options are before them, want their health care arrangements to remain mostly in the market sector. So it is too, apparently, with social care. But once again, the lack of public systems, like those found in European countries, does not mean there are no systems at all.

However, few would disagree that the least privileged citizen in any state would prefer a public system because no matter how bad it is, it is probably better than what the market, voluntary or informal systems would offer such a least privileged citizen. The same is clearly not true for the more privileged. The most frequently cited comparative work is Gøsta Esping-Andersen's *The Three Worlds of Welfare Capitalism* (1990). He points out that for the social democrat the provision of welfare by market mechanisms is problematic because markets fail to establish rights to welfare and because the market mechanism, to accomplish other ends, is intentionally structured to be inequitable. On the other hand, the market-oriented liberals bash the traditional welfare state arrangements because of their perceived efficiency costs. They frequently argue that these costs produce the very problems that welfare is structured to combat (Mead, 1997). They argue further that the traditional welfare state fails to establish a balance between the rights and obligations of the citizen. Esping-Andersen concludes, along with Theda Skocpol (1996), that it is not market forces or citizens' preferences that decide the relative balance of responsibility between sectors. Instead the key factors are state constitutions, the political institutional structure and political parties.

BROAD CHANGES IN PROVISION FOR YOUNG AND OLD SINCE THE 1960S

Since 1960 American society has undergone a number of major transformations. Residential mobility has contributed to the demise of the extended family and paradoxically to a dramatic change in the labour force participation of married women. Life expectancy has increased but so also has the need for assistance in the activities of daily life. Married mothers raised their labour force participation from less than 20 per cent to more than 60 per cent. The shifts reduced the supply of home care-givers and increased the demand for various forms of institutional childcare and institutional eldercare, particularly for the frail elderly. The number of childcare 'slots' and the number of nursing-home care beds grew but not sufficiently to meet the new demand. Among the 7.3 million elderly in need of long-term care in 1994, 5.7 million received it at home or in a community setting (Binstock, 1996, p. 6). Among children under five in need of day care while their mothers worked, only 38 per cent received care from formal sources, either for-profit or voluntary. An additional 20 per cent went to the homes of care givers (childminders) and 33 per cent were cared for at home by relatives and other unregulated care givers (Michel, 1999, p. 236). It is important to point out that the family and other informal systems remain the norm in giving social care in the United States. For the growing share that does receive care outside the family, the norm is market care.

In the United States formal care arrangements at the beginning and the end of life are market-reliant systems. Payments for care come from the earnings of mothers and the improved economic circumstance of America's aged. This pattern dominates both our pattern of direct spending and our agency structures. The child day-care system has essentially developed since the 1960s. During this time the number of children in need of some form of substitute care has grown at a prodigious rate. The share of children in care in market-oriented care centres has grown more than twice as fast as any other source. While there is some agitation for public provision of child day care, it is for the most part a subtitle in how to move single mothers off welfare rather than a debate over how to provide a more substantive, adequate and affordable child day care to everyone (Michel, 1999). Over the last forty years there has been a dramatic change in the patterns of labour force participation which has taken care-givers, particularly married women, out of the home and out of home care-giving. These new populations of wage earners expected, and were expected, to pay for care for their children with their new wages. There has also been a new source of spending power available to older people occasioned by the growth of public transfers and larger and better-protected pensions programmes in the United States. Yet, of course, there remains the problem with the 'market success' of the US model that not all citizens, particularly the least privileged, share the benefits of these market solutions.

For both childcare and eldercare in the last quarter of the twentieth century either money found a market or the market found the money. For most children their mother's new income from paid work provided an income stream to pay for child day care. For older people greater federal financial participation in old-age assistance and old-age insurance provided an income stream to purchase care for the frail elderly in an open market. These solutions occurred in a nation where, in comparison with other affluent democracies, there was a historic distrust of government. The amount of money spent indirectly by the state in the form of cash transfers to pay for, or to subsidize, people's use of privately provided health and long-term care has completely dwarfed the money spent directly on publicly provided social care programmes.

Nonetheless, the improved economic condition of the aged is directly attributable to public sector actions. Increased social insurance benefits, particularly for lower-income aged, the adoption of a federal social security programme to replace state old-age assistance programmes, and an improved pension protection programme all contributed to the better economic condition of all aged, but particularly of the poor aged. With the adoption of Medicaid[1] the economic capacity of America's frail and poor elderly to pay for care was further enhanced. As phrased by Holstein and Cole, 'In this manner, a particularly

American solution to long term care needs emerged. It rested on the traditional distrust of a large and activist government, interest group politics (of the aged as consumers and the nursing care industry as providers) and the expanded need for care otherwise unavailable' (Holstein and Cole, 1996). Paradoxically very similar explanations may account for the failure to develop a universal public child day-care system:

> Although childcare policy received considerable attention at the federal level for nearly four decades, little progress was made toward developing a system of universal care. Rifts between public and private provision, and among the clients and advocates of different types of care, created a divided constituency that was, in turn, perpetuated by congressional vacillation between targeted and universal policies. (Michel, 1999, p. 278)

The consequences of the divided constituency were particularly evident in the Comprehensive Child Development Act of 1971, which began as a bipartisan effort but ended with a stinging veto from President Richard Nixon. From that point forward public child day care, except for the poor, was a highly partisan issue and no real progress could be made.

THE CARE SERVICES IN THEIR SYSTEM CONTEXTS

The Policy Context of Care of Older People

For dependent older people the policy issues have been constrained by the confluence of three circumstances. First, within the national political system there has been a reluctance to accept new federal responsibilities at a time when there is electoral pressure to cut the federal government's activities and expenditures. Second, the need for social care is eclipsed in public debate by the need for medical care. Third, there has been considerable confusion over whether the long-term care policy debate is part of health reform or welfare reform or a free-standing issue of its own. In a political system dominated by the legislature, the House of Representatives and the Senate, this constrained public construction of the debate decides which politicians and interests will dominate policy far more than it does in parliamentary systems, where the executive or cabinet is more likely to control the agenda (Harrington, 1991).

The history of care for the frail elderly who are both poor and without family support has been largely intertwined with the policy history of support for the poor. The poorhouse, the main expression of public responsibility well into the twentieth century, was to be the domicile of those who were old, sick and poor as well as those simply old and poor. The heavy hand of history now shapes and constrains the perceptions of public policy options with regard to long-term care. Partly as a result, the organization of long-term care in the United States is rather complex. Although many people in the US think of long-term care as synonymous with a public, private or voluntary nursing-home, the predominant provider is still the family. Some 22 per cent of the disabled elderly were in nursing home of some kind in 1990 (OECD, 1996, p. 280). As the degree of the disability becomes more severe, the share seeking nursing-home care goes up. Although at any moment in time nursing homes serve less than a quarter of the frail elderly, more than half of the aged are projected to spend some time in one in the course of their old age. Projections of the size of the future nursing-home population are difficult. The proportion of all Americans over 65 in a nursing home is now 7.3 per cent. This proportion is expected to increase to 14 per cent by 2020 and to one-quarter in 2060, as the elderly population becomes older and thus more disabled (Darney, 1994). The fear of not being able to meet nursing-home care costs in the future is an issue for 53 per cent of all Americans (Yankelovich Group, 1990). The financing of nursing homes, rather than their institutional structure, dominates the policy debate.

In general, whether nursing homes are voluntary or for-profit is not an issue as they have highly similar income streams; both receive similar shares of insurance-based, out-of-pocket, and public payments for their services. There are efficiencies of scale to be won in using this money. From 1985 to 1995 the number of nursing homes decreased from 19,100 to 16,700. This occurred as the corporate, profit-oriented nursing homes replaced the 'Mom and Pop' small business homes. The number of nursing homes run by public authorities has declined almost to non-existence (Table 6.2).

For a market-reliant society, a striking fact is the trivial share of long-term care which is paid for by insurance, either public or private. For the aged in the United States public insurance, Medicare,[2] pays for the acute care system in large measure. For long-term care that is not the case. Despite the fact that the United States has a long tradition of private insurance for all manner of life's troubles, only about 4 per cent of the elderly and a negligible share of the non-elderly currently have any kind of private insurance for the long-term care which is increasingly becoming a normal part of a life. While sales of such

Table 6.2 Patients in nursing homes and source of provision, United States, 1995

	For profit	Voluntary	Public
Facilities	11,000	4,300	1,400
Residents	1,549,000	990,000	421,000

Source: Statistical Abstracts, US Government, 1998, table 217, p. 142.

policies have increased, the number of policies in force is on the decline because of death and cancellations (Wiener and Illston, 1994). The cost of insurance varies with the age and health standard of the person being insured. This can range from one thousand to ten thousand dollars per year.

The Policy Context of Care for Children

While the long-term care system has its roots in the welfare policy debate; the childcare debate is almost ahistorical. The evolution of childcare in the United States is the combined outcome of several historiographies; of women, child welfare, families, education, anti-poverty measures, and the welfare state. As Michel (1999) has made clear, the disjunctures in these historical streams explain the curious development of child day-care policy. Childcare in the United States is based on three contradictory beliefs that appear to be central to choices now and in the past. These are: (i) mothers should stay home and take care of their children; (ii) poor mothers should work rather than go on welfare; (iii) the childcare system should function so that better-off women (married or unmarried, with children or without) can teach less-well-off mothers how to best care for their children.

Until the outbreak of the 1929 depression, the care of pre-school children was seen as an untouchable responsibility of the family. The very lack of a public policy debate about how to care for children while their mothers worked limited the range of options seen as open when child day care became a public issue. Changes in demography, changes in labour force practice, changes in family patterns have interacted to produce distinct patterns of child day care. For the United States the fundamental force changing the institutional pattern of childcare is the shift in labour market participation by married women. Families in their productive years are having fewer children and mothers are going back into the labour force sooner and staying longer. At its most basic level this is producing a set of shifts in childcare needs and responses.

A further driving force of change in the childcare system is a changing shape in the dependency ratios (Table 6.3). Since 1960 the United States has seen a dramatic improvement in the crude dependency ratio. There are more Americans in their productive years than there are dependent young or dependent old. This is a statistic that will continue well into the next century. It suggests that there will be fewer economic demands placed on the working-age population. However, despite the decline in the proportion of the population under sixteen, their care has had to be met in new ways. In the grand sweep of American history childcare was an 'at home' responsibility of mothers and adult daughters. The new circumstances of women in the labour force have prompted dramatic shifts in the pattern of care. When, for a complex set of circumstances, female labour force participation became the norm, women at work needed care for their children. Table 6.4 shows the resultant changes in public, voluntary and market responses to the need for social care arrangements outside the informal family sector.

Table 6.3 Age dependency ratios, 1960 and 1996

	Per cent 15–64		Per cent under 15		Per cent 65 or older	
	1960	1996	1960	1996	1960	1996
Finland	62.3	66.7	30.4	18.9	7.3	14.4
Germany	67.8	68.2	21.3	15.9	10.8	15.8
Japan	63.9	69.4	30.1	15.9	6.1	14.5
UK	64.9	64.9	23.3	19.3	10.7	12.8
US	59.7	65.5	31.0	21.7	9.2	12.8

Source: OECD, Social Statistics.

Table 6.4 The main providers of children's day care, United States, 1990

	Percentage share of total provision	Total for sector
Public		
Head Start	9.0	17.0
State school	8.0	
For profit		35.0
Chain	6.0	
Independent	29.0	
Not-for-profit		
Independent	25.0	48.0
Church	15.0	
Other	8.0	

Source: Willer, 1991, p. 21.

Current patterns of childcare

In the United States today most mothers of pre-school children are in the labour force at least part-time. Despite this the United States has no comprehensive system of childcare support for families. Children are cared for while their mothers work in many different ways. Those from poor and low-income families are eligible for a limited number of publicly provided and subsidized places. Children from middle- and upper-income households benefit from partial tax write-offs to purchase care from for-profit providers. Children from all income classes receive care in centres operated by churches and other non-profit centres. Children from all classes go to national chains of 'Jack and Jill's House'. The national chains, as a market mechanism, seek to provide the appearance of homogeneous care across the nation. In practice a part of this homogeneity is that most childcare, even by the voluntary sector, is segregated in terms of class and race.

Table 6.5 shows changes in the composition of the care-giver population for children. Grandmother coming into the child's home while the mother works has remained a stable care-giving arrangement. This amounts to one-quarter of the care for single mothers and 13 per cent of the care in two-parent households where the mother is full- or part-time in the labour force. In the past quarter century the change has mostly been within the market sector response. The for-profit and voluntary non-profit formal care centre has been replacing private paid arrangements in the homes of non-relatives, what in Europe is generally called childminding. In addition voluntary provision has been displaced by for-profit or employer provision.

One of the reasons that the child day-care provision is in such flux is that there is no one day-care problem but multiple day-care problems. A family's childcare needs will be very different depending on economic circumstance, family pattern, and the reasons for both parents being in the labour force. The reasons for a demand for outside child day care are limited only by the analyst's need to fix on a manageable number of classifications. So also are the responses. One reason for reliance on market-based provision is clearly this variety and complexity of demand. There is insufficient uniformity in the needs of families to build a successful political coalition behind any one public childcare policy.

Table 6.5 Working mothers: sources of childcare, United States

Family type	Year	Father	Mother	Grand-parent	Informal day care	Formal day care
All families	1993	15.9	6.2	16.5	16.6	29.9
	1990	16.5	6.4	14.3	20.1	27.5
	1985	15.7	8.1	15.9	22.3	23.1
	1977	14.4	11.4	na	22.4	13.0
Single mothers						
	1993	3.4	3.5	24.6	17.3	29.5
	1990	3.2	3.7	20.0	27.8	30.4
	1985	2.2	3.5	24.5	24.5	26.7
	1977	0.8	4.4	na	21.8	19.1

Source: US Department of Labor, Bureau of Statistics, 1996.

Table 6.6 United States: labour force participation by age of youngest child and marital status

	1960	1970	1980	1990	1996	Per cent change 1960–96
Married						
Under six	18.8	30.3	45.0	58.9	62.9	106.7
Six and over	39.0	49.0	61.8	73.6	55.9	
Separated						
Under six	na	45.4	52.2	59.3	63.1	39.0
Six and over	na	60.6	66.6	75.0	73.3	21.0
Divorced						
Under six	na	63.3	68.3	69.8	76.5	20.9
Six and over	na	82.4	82.3	85.9	85.5	03.8
Never married						
Under six	na	na	44.1	48.7	55.1	na
Six and over	na	na	67.6	69.7	71.8	na

Source: US Department of Labor, Bureau of Statistics, 1998.

As Table 6.7 shows, childcare costs are significantly different across income lines. The poor in America spend twice the share of their income as do the non-poor and the poor spend, as a share of income, fives times that of the rich.

Table 6.7 Child day-care costs, United States, 1993 (average weekly expenditures on pre-schoolers by family income)

	Per cent with costs	Of those with costs	
		Mean weekly cost, $	Per cent of household income
Poor	37	49.56	17.7
Non-poor	58	76.03	7.3
Monthly household income			
Less than $1,200	39	47.29	25.1
$1,200–2,999	49	60.16	12.0
$3000–4,499	57	73.10	8.5
Over $4,500	69	91.30	5.7

Source: US Department of Labor, Bureau of Statistics, 1998.

Current patterns of care for older people

In the US, long-term health and social care are initially the responsibility of the individual and the family and their needs are met by a health and social care market. However, ultimately a great deal of the provision is paid for by federal and state government subsidies, particularly through the programmes of Medicaid and Medicare (see notes 1 and 2 and Table 6.8). The individual patient typically goes through a progression from home care by a relative, to privately paid home care, to publicly subsidized home care, to privately paid nursing-home care and ending with publicly paid care either in an institution or at home. A major policy problem is that the typical recipient of care enters a nursing home with sufficient resources to pay for his or her own care but, with an annual cost now of approximately $42,000, these resources are soon depleted and Medicaid begins to pay the costs. Coupled with this is a practice by which families of the patient artificially 'spend down' by reallocating the resources of the nursing-home patient within the family in order to qualify for Medicaid (Moses, 1990). Various proposals to stimulate the purchase of long-term care insurance through public subsidies have failed to generate wide-range support (Holstein and Minkler, 1991).

The distinction in care for the aged between acute care and long-term care is vague and is becoming more so with changes in the delivery system and changes in technology of care. For both acute care and long-term care many are concerned about a two-class system. The dominance of the market model means that it is commonly assumed that the quality of nursing-home care increases from public, through voluntary to private provision, but there is little evidence to support this. There is such a large range of quality within each class that generalization has little real meaning. It is also sometimes asserted that even within the same institution the quality of care differs by the source of

Table 6.8 Sources of payment for elderly care, 1997 (billions, nominal dollars)

	Nursing-home care	Home health care
Medicaid	24.2	4.3
Medicare	8.4	14.3
Other federal sources	0.7	1.7
State and local sources	0.6	0.5
Out of pocket	30.0	5.5
Private insurance	0.4	0.3
Total	64.4	26.5

Source: House Ways and Means Committee, 1998, Green Book: Background Material Programs under the Jurisdiction, p. 1057.

payment. Politically these issues express themselves in different ways. For example, the advocates of health and social care services for the aged poor search for ways to keep a programme for the poor from becoming a poor programme. This involves constructing mechanisms for providing means-tested support that are seen by middle and upper class constituencies as complimentary rather then threatening to their own future care needs (Meiners, 1996). It is impossible to reform the funding and provision of social care in the United States without allaying the fears of the middle to better-off that their benefits under the present system will be undermined by more generous provision for the poor.

Medicaid (see note 1) is administered by each state and funded jointly by federal and state governments and is structured to provide greater federal aid in states with lower per capita incomes. Eligibility is based on means tests. Many older people pay for their own long-term care until they have 'spent down' their assets to become eligible for Medicaid. In any given year half of the persons in long-term care facilities have their bill paid by Medicaid and half of the remaining half will spend down their resources to become eligible by the end of a twelv- month period. To prove financial eligibility for Medicaid-funded nursing-home care is inordinately complex. State variation makes a commentary on standard practice almost meaningless.

Ever since the passing of the Social Security Act in 1932 a long series of political battles have been fought both to control public expenditure on long-term health and social care and to shift the balances between federal and state contributions. Nonetheless, the public contribution has risen steadily. In the United States, nursing-home and home-health care accounted for 12 per cent of the total personal health care expenditure bill in 1995. Federal and state governments paid for 58 per cent of nursing-home care and 56 per cent of home care. The overall cost and the public share have increased substantially since 1970, when the government was paying for only 40 per cent of nursing-home care (Harrington, 1998). In 1998 initiatives to cut Medicaid payments for long-term care and to shift to more reliance on health management organizations were pushed off the legislative agenda by the Monica Lewinski affair. In the State of the Union Message of 1999, President Bill Clinton announced a new federal government initiative to address the problem of long-term care. The centre-piece was a $1000 non-refundable tax credit to families who are paying for care. Also planned was a demonstration programme of long-term care insurance for federal employees. This latter was to serve as a demonstration project to other employers. However, the question of the future of long-term care was relegated to a minor issue in the presidential election of 2000 and remains lost from sight at the time of writing (2002).

One critic has suggested that when it comes to long-term care the invisible hand of Adam Smith turns out to have all thumbs. Most observers believe that as necessary as a new policy for long-term care is, it is irrevocably linked to the larger reform of health care as a whole. With the current emphasis on cost cutting and federal devolution the prospects of health care reform are low. Thus change, should it occur, is more likely at the state level. Long-term care policy is resistant to change at least in the short run, but as Table 6.9 shows, expenditure is projected to continue rising.

Table 6.9 Projected spending in 2018 on nursing-home and home health care, United States

Source of payment	2018, $ billions	Per cent increase since 1993
Nursing-home		
Medicaid	49.0	118
Medicare	10.0	132
Out of pocket	69.2	147
Home health		
Medicaid	5.2	45
Medicare	19.0	102
Other government	4.3	92
Out of pocket	11.5	109

Source: OECD, 1996, *Caring for the Frail Elderly*, Social Policy Study 19, Paris: OECD Publications.

Laying aside the intrinsic difficulties of long-term projections, it is clear that the cost of eldercare will increase. Only the magnitude and the sources of payment are in doubt. Wiener and his associates at the Brookings Institute estimate that nursing-home clients will increase from 2.2 million to 3.6 million while home care numbers will go from 5.2 to 7.4 million (Wiener, 1994). The magnitude of these projections is clearly conservative. The policies that are logically implied by these rising numbers are: (i) an intensive educational programme so that people are more aware that nursing care and home health care are increasingly likely to be a normal part of life and need to be privately planned for; (ii) greater availability of catastrophic care insurance; (iii) the encouragement of preventive healthy lifestyles among both younger and older people.

HOW THESE PATTERNS DEVELOPED

Long-term Care

Long-term care in the United States cannot escape its history. First, it is important to recognize that for early US welfare history there was no sharp distinction between the public response for the medical needs and the welfare needs of the poor, the old and the sick. During the first economic recession in the then young country the states reviewed colonial welfare practice. Massachusetts and New York both commissioned studies of their nascent welfare systems. The 1821 Massachusetts Quincy Report and the 1824 New York Yates Report reached the same conclusion. (In today's world you would have thought both were written by the same consulting agency.) Both reports found outdoor relief to be prohibitively expensive and both located the cause of indigence, even chronic medical indigence, as the consequence of individual failure. Both reports had policy suggestions: the development of an institutional response at the local level.

An earlier 1817 report on the conditions and causes of poverty was based on the views of those who cared for the poor (Heffernan, 1968). It found want, including want in old age to be the consequence of:

- ignorance
- idleness
- intemperance
- imprudent marriage
- prostitution
- pawnbrokers
- lotteries
- want of economy
- war
- benevolent agencies

Variously labelled almshouse, poorhouse, poor farm, workhouse and county farm, the idea was to create a local government residence where the work of the residents would cover part of the costs of their upkeep. Designed by poor relief administrators the workhouse would cure the poor of their habits, punish them for their dependency and be sufficiently undesirable that the able bodied poor would shun it. Care was to be so meagre as to discourage families from abandoning their old to the county. At the same time it would save the county money. Welfare reform has a long history of promising all things to all people. In these institutions the poor, the indigent aged without family support, the chronically ill, the mentally ill, the retarded and others rendered dependent on the public sector were to be housed. The poor farm and the community-supported old-age home were one and the same place (Holstein and Cole, 1996, p. 22). As 'indoor relief', as it was then called, became the main public response to indigence and chronic care needs so all care became the responsibility of the overseer of the poor who was also the manager of the poor farm. Those too ill to be cared for at home and whose families were unable to pay for a 'rest home' met a common and undistinguished fate. The Southern states, with their more homogeneous non-slave population, maintained a higher standard of public care. The treatment of the aged slave was at best highly diverse (Genovese, 1974). In New England, New York and the Middle Atlantic States, care fell more frequently to denominational institutions established for this purpose. In the north as well as the South women were cared for better than men. Women turned to organizations like the Association for the Relief of Respectable Aged Indigent Females where care could range from a kind of foster care for the aged to institutional care in what we would now call a hospice.

After the Civil War of 1861–65 social care varied dramatically between the North and South. In the South under Reconstruction few lived well and the aged were no exception. In other parts of the nation, specialization in the care of the dependent populations was increasingly the norm. The mentally ill went to asylums, the physically and developmentally disabled to state schools, the able-bodied adult poor went to the workhouse. There was a 'greying' of the almshouse. As it became more like a long-term care facility the quality of life in it changed. As the South recovered, conditions in almshouses improved while conditions in the rest of the nation deteriorated. Standards became very poor very quickly and in many states there was a return to outdoor relief. It became increasingly the norm for states to run facilities for care by clear categories alongside the early development of separate income assistance programmes for the aged, the disabled and single-mother families. This separation of the poor into worthy and unworthy became a major feature of US welfare. There was great variety in costs and consequences across and within the states.

Theda Skocpol (1995) in her examination of the development of US social policy makes much of public institutional structure as a determinant of policy. Perhaps the most important feature of this in US welfare development is that the federal constitution does not grant any specific welfare responsibility to the national government. This omission, if it were that, was reinforced by the famous veto of Franklin Pierce of the first effort of the national government to assume even modest social care responsibility by granting national lands to the states for the care of the mentally ill. As a consequence, until 1935, a hundred and fifty years into the existence of the United States, there were no national laws to do with the structure and distribution of social care services. The United States had no legal codes of social welfare except that established by state legislatures and state courts. The concept of subsidiarity was effectively by indirection and inaction. It led to maximum flexibility. It also led to uncertainty, inefficiency and, to use Trattner's term, 'a certain public tardiness' in matters of social care (Trattner, 1999).

From the ending of the Civil War to the onset of the American depression US social policy was positively anti-state. The clear and dominant belief was that while the nation was far from indifferent to the plight of the dependent it was also the dominant view that public interventions, such as the poorhouse often made things worse (Heffernan, 1968). This being so, the period between 1865 and 1929 witnessed many changes, which fundamentally shape the structure of long-term care in the United States today. First, by 1929 the greying of the alms-house was complete. Virtually all classes other than the indigent ill aged had gone elsewhere. Second, the moralizing and punitive environment of the alms-house stimulated the development of mutual aid societies. These established ethnic and denominational long-term care homes in all parts of the United States for Jewish, Catholic, or Lutheran aged and so on. There were also homes for the widows of craftsmen and mutual benevolent societies, such as the Elks, cared for their own members. Simply put, the inadequate almshouse now became the storage facilities for aged indigent while the benevolent mutual aide societies together diverted attention away from the development of home care. The 'county old-age home' became the image supporting the re-emergence of outdoor relief for the aged, allowing them stay in their own homes and purchase care. Old-age pensions on a universal or categorical basis became the political enemy of a comprehensive public old-age care system (Holstein and Cole, 1996).

Long-term Care, 1935–2000

The passage of the Social Security Act in 1935 by indirection rather than direction shaped US long-term care in a number of ways. First, the federal assumption of some responsibility for old-age assistance and of full responsibility for old-age insurance gave the aged a new income stream for the purchase of care. The decision of Franklin Roosevelt's New Deal administration to leave health care insurance out of social security reform was a direct consequence of a desire to make its passage more acceptable to the powerful American Medical Association (Starr, 1992). The 'off limits' approach to health care stimulated the development of market-based, privately owned aged health care facilities. Further, the decision to deny old age assistance payments to those in publicly run care facilities perhaps more than anything else stimulated the development of voluntary and privately owned nursing-homes.

In the 1950s, national support for long-term care came in two forms. Care of veterans, largely of the First World War, was turning the Veterans' Administration into a major operator of care for old men. The Social Security Act prevented the states from using old-age assistance funds to fund directly the public county old-age homes or pay fees on behalf of people living in them. The individual recipient of Old Age Assistance or Old Age Survivors' Insurance could purchase care in a private old-age facility. Over time the county homes were phased out and replaced by privately run facilities. Initially these were little more than family-owned enterprises where 'board and care' was provided but the income stream to the facility was indirectly from government assistance and insurance benefits. They were profitable. Soon doctors and nurses began to form small local corporations to provide some convalescent and long-term (terminal) medical care along with the room and board. Gradually, through amalgamation these grew into regional and then national corporations providing medical care, assisted living, home health care, and convalescent services. Public care and voluntary (non-profit) care facilities did not keep pace. By the 1950s a three-level system of old-age long-term care emerged. At the bottom was the old poor farm. Here long-term care was meagre and the facilities inadequate by almost any measure. At the second level somewhat better facilities were available to members of particular religious, ethnic, or fraternal groups. These facilities were highly varied; high socio-economic denominations had very classy facilities while lowly socio-economic denominations had facilities only marginally better than the old poor farms. At the top of the system were privately owned, fee-for-service, proprietary facilities where first-rate care was available to those with the ability to pay.

This pattern of dominance by the corporate facility was started in the 1950s, expanded in the 1960s and 1970s, and locked in by the 1980s and the 1990s. The voluntary agencies had a strong tradition against direct receipt of public funds. To do so would cause a loss of autonomy over care and the selection of persons admitted. Thus a combination of the character of the non-profit agency themselves and public regulations regarding direct fees meant that the charitable sector could no longer compete with the more flexible profit-oriented providers. Public homes disappeared as the expansion of Medicare, Medicaid and legislation for purchase of service by government allowed the poor to receive care in private homes. It is now clear that long-term care is a serious problem within the US health and social welfare system. The belief that national policy could solve the long-term care problem by indirection has not worked. Greater public subsidies through Social Security, Medicare and Medicaid reflected a belief that long-term care could be left to the market if cash transfers dealt with the income problems of older people.

Long-term care expenditure amounts to nearly 20 per cent of total health care expenditure in the United States. Medicaid funds half of this amount. Solutions to the problems of long-term care wait upon successful reform of the whole health care system. This challenge has been avoided by most administration except that of Clinton in his first term. But he too failed to find a way through the political maze of professional and corporate vested interests. In

2000 the organization, Physicians for a National Health Program, proposed a more comprehensive long-term care policy. It would be integrated with a national health plan in a single comprehensive public programme for acute and long-term care. All health payments would be channelled through a single agency in each state that would contract directly with both for-profit and voluntary providers. But this proposal sparked no interest from the two main presidential candidates.

The Development of Day Care for Children

Long-term care has been shaped and constrained by its history, child day care by its lack of a history. For most of America's history care of pre-school children has been seen as a family affair. Intervention by market, voluntary agency, and certainly public sector providers has been and remains strongly resisted. There are some historically interesting precursors to contemporary provision of day care outside of the traditional family arrangements but they amounted to a tiny fraction of all childcare until well into this century (Steinfels, 1973). In the nineteenth century and early third of the twentieth there was, after slavery, a widespread system of extended family care among African Americans and a very tiny market structure of day care for middle-class employed women. State and local government involvement was limited to regulating child welfare and to the child protection functions of government.

The clear preference has been for 'mother care' and it remains very much alive in any public debates about the future of public-sponsored or public-subsidized childcare (Berry, 1993). The purpose of a nineteenth century day-care centre was to provide childcare to prevent a mother going to the poorhouse or turning to prostitution (Michel, 1999, p.31). The mission statement of the Philadelphia Home for Little Wanderers says in part, '[but for our help] many mothers with their families must have gone to the almshouse, or done worse. We have saved them from this, and from the mortification or disgrace of being cared for by the commonwealth' (*The Little Wanderer*, 1868, cited by Michel, p. 320).

Ninety years later, in 1958, President Dwight Eisenhower called to order the White House *Conference on Children and Youth* with this warning:

> [women work] because they have to keep the wolf from the door...But if there is only a tiny percentage doing this because they prefer a career to an active real career of real motherhood and care for the little child, I should think they would have to consider what is the price they are paying in terms of the opportunity that the child has been denied. Certainly no one can do quite so much in molding the child's habits of thinking and implanting certain standards as can the mother. (Michel, 1999, p. 220)

A few years later John Kennedy's carillon call to his *President's Commission on Status of Women* contained this note: 'It is regrettable when women with children are forced by economic circumstance or by the regulations of welfare agencies to seek employment when their children are young' (ibid., p. 239). Richard Nixon at first supported the Childcare Development Act of 1971, which was designed as a first step toward the establishment of a universal federally subsidized childcare. After it had received bipartisan support in both houses of Congress, there was a right-wing republican reaction. Nixon responded by using the presidential veto and by invoking the cold war rhetoric of childcare centres as places where a classless society would be inculcated and which might even 'Sovietize' American youth (ibid., p. 251). Childcare became a 'third rail' issue in American politics, touched only by feminists on the left and fundamentalists on the right. Childcare did not return to the political agenda for more then a decade.

This had been the pattern until the New Deal in the 1930s. Before then the main state intervention was the 'mother's pension', a pitifully small means-tested benefit for single mothers. Despite the fact that these mother's pensions were subject to stigma and most often administered in a condescending and discriminatory way, women's groups by and large preferred public expenditure on the pension to any direct provision of childcare, such as a daycentre. Essentially, political progress on childcare was prevented by class differences. The poor sought free day care and quality was not a significant issue. The middle class sought a heavily regulated system so that there would be an assurance of quality. The upper middle class sought tax rebates and freedom to select care on an open market. And the rich opted out and sought immigrant nannies. Unlike public and elementary schools, the great melting pot of the first half of the twentieth century, child day care was always heavily segregated by race, class, and even gender (Michel, 1999, chapter 4). In the absence of a stable coalition in support of any one solution, childcare policy could make no progress.

The federal government finally entered the childcare business during the New Deal and its employment creation programmes. Under the auspices of the employment-centred Works Projects Administration federally-funded nursery schools were established for low-income children and known as the Emergency Nursery School Program or ENS. The policy intent was not to provide child day care for working mothers but to provide employment opportunities for single women as teachers, social workers, nurses and other female professions. An only slightly less explicit purpose was that upper-middle-class women should take the lead in child day care so as to simultaneously teach low-income mothers how they should care for their children.

The second stage of national government involvement in child day care occurred during the Second World War. This time the main object was to encourage women to enter the labour force as part of the war effort. The wartime childcare centres spent a great deal of time and effort on programmes to counter the 'trauma' children experienced simply by the unfortunate fact that they were in a childcare centre. The expectation was that women would return to homecare responsibilities at war's end. This shift did not occur. Labour force participation rates for women with children under the age of six, the normal starting age for school, actually increased by about 2 per cent between 1945 and 1950. Since 1950 the rate of increase has been about 1 per cent per annum.

The reasons for this steady growth in the employment rates of married women with young children are complex and not easily unravelled. Almost an example of Gresham's Law, the last quarter of the twentieth century has seen a geometric increase in demand for childcare alongside an only arithmetic increase in supply. There has been demand for safe, adequate and affordable child day care but no mechanism available for a supply response. And what little supply there was has encouraged further demand. The simple presence of some day-care facilities has been a stimulus to new entry into the labour force. Additionally, the growth in single parenthood has been a significant driving force behind demand. Single divorced mothers were the most likely to use non-family childcare. The substantial growth in the share of families that are mother-only families has changed the structure and composition of demand. However, the largest increase in labour force participation rate and hence for demand for day care came from two-parent families. These three sources of demand; from single never-married mothers (mostly poor), divorced mothers (across the full income spectrum) and from mothers in two-parent households (mostly middle income and higher) placed different constraints on a supply-side response. Government at all levels also faced heavy political pressure from the private profit-oriented providers, such as the National Association of Child Care Management, who have wanted lower mandated standards and weaker regulation. In contrast, the associations of non-profit providers not surprisingly prefer supply-side subsidies to demand-side subsidies. In this context the United States has made little progress towards a 'universal childcare system'. The simple fact is that with the interested constituencies in the childcare debate so divided there is no agreement over what a universal system would look like.

CONCLUSION

In any comparative examination of social care it is important to make distinctions between production, distribution and source of funding. In the United States, social care is mostly produced and delivered by both voluntary and profit-oriented providers. The distinction between the voluntary provider and the profit-oriented provider is now hard to discern even to those consuming the product or service. However, the government is often the source of funding, either through cash transfers or tax credits to the client who pays for the service or through direct contracts with the provider to deliver services to specified classes of clients. This combination of demand and funding has led to steady and substantial growth. For example, since 1967 the number of agencies providing not-for-profit services has increased from three hundred thousand to just under one million (Weisbrod, 1998, p. 2). Their total revenues have risen from 6 per cent to 10 per cent of GDP. About a tenth of these revenues are spent on social care (Salamon and Anheier, 1996, p. 148). The voluntary social service sector depends for about half of its revenue on payments by the state and for about a fifth on user fees (ibid., p. 152). In the delivery of care services for children and older people both the non-profit and market sectors are growing, while the distinctions between them are almost disappearing. Why is this so? Clearly a lack of faith in government in general is a factor. This is important both historically and as an outcome of more recent politics. As more women enter the labour market and as the dependency ratio shifts from youth to age, so demand for social care services will continue to grow. Weisbrod has shown that when governments provide care services in quantity and kind close to the needs and tastes of the median citizen then the number of dissatisfied people is small and there exists little role for a voluntary sector. Put another way, the more homogeneous a society is, and the more similar are its citizens' preferences, the smaller the need for a non-profit sector (Weisbrod, 1977). The same logic may influence the size of the for-profit sector. The United States is a less homogeneous society than the others described in this book and the demand for social care services is more diverse. It is safe to say that the growth of social care provision, delivered through varieties of the market mechanism outside of the public sector and outside of the informal sector, is certain to continue.

NOTES

1. Medicaid is a federal/state entitlement programme that pays for medical assistance for individuals and families with low incomes and resources. The programme became law in 1965 as a cooperative venture jointly funded by the federal and state governments. Medicaid is the largest source of funding for medical and health-related services for America's poorest people. Each state establishes its own eligibility standards, determines the type, amount, duration, and scope of services, sets the rate of payment for services and administers its own programme. Eligibility, services and payment vary considerably. Thus, a person who is eligible for Medicaid in one state may not be eligible in another state, and the services provided by one state may differ considerably in amount, duration, or scope from services provided in a similar or neighbouring state. Over the years Medicaid eligibility has been incrementally expanded to include increasing numbers of the poor. Legislative changes have also focused on increased access, better quality of care, specific benefits, enhanced outreach programmes, and fewer limits on services. Long-term care is an increasingly important provision of Medicaid as the population ages. Medicaid now pays for almost 45 per cent of the total cost of care for persons using a nursing facility or home health services. For those persons who use more than four months of this long-term care, Medicaid pays for a much larger percentage. In 1998 there was an average

expenditure of $12,375 per long-term care recipient (see the United States Health Care Financing Administration website: www.hcfa.gov).
2. In 1965 Medicare legislation established a health insurance programme for older people. Medicare covers most persons aged 65 or over. It pays for care in hospital and for treatment as outpatients and for seeing the doctor. Medicare consists of three parts: Hospital Insurance (HI), Supplementary Medical Insurance (SMI), and the Medicare+Choice programme, which was established by the Balanced Budget Act of 1997 and allows for participation in private sector health care plans. When Medicare began on 1 July 1966, approximately 19 million people enrolled. In 2000, about 40 million people were enrolled in one or both of HI and SMI, and 6.4 million had chosen to participate in a Medicare+Choice plan. HI is generally provided automatically, and free of premiums, to persons age 65 or over who are eligible for Social Security benefits. People over 65 and still in work are also generally eligible as are the long-term disabled. In 1999, the HI programme provided protection against the costs of hospital and specific other medical care to about 39 million people (34 million aged and 5 million disabled enrollees). HI benefit payments totalled $129 billion in 1999 (see the United States Health Care Financing Administration website: www.hcfa.gov).

REFERENCES

Berry, M.F. (1993), *The Politics of Parenthood: Child Care, Women's Rights and the Myth of the Good Mother*, New York: Viking Press.
Binstock, R.H, Cluff, L.E. and von Mering (1996), 'Issues Affecting the Future of Long-Term Care', in R.H Binstock, L.E. Cluff and O. von Mering (eds), *The Future of Long-Term Care: Social and Policy Issues*, Baltimore: Johns Hopkins University Press, pp. 3–18.
Darney, A.J. (1994), *Statistical Record of Older Americans*, Washington: Gale Research.
Dionne, E.J. (1991), *Why Americans Hate Politics*, New York: Simon and Schuster.
Drew, E. (1996), *Showdown: The Struggle between the Gingrich Congress and the Clinton White House*, New York: Simon & Schuster.
Esping-Andersen, G. (1990), *The Three Worlds of Welfare Capitalism*, Cambridge: Polity Press.
Genovese, E. (1974), *Role Jordan Role*, New York: Random House.
Hacker, J. (1997), *The Road to Nowhere: The Genesis of President Clinton's Plan for Health Security*, Princeton: Princeton University Press.
Harrington, C. (1991), 'A national long term care program in the US', *Journal of the American Medical Association*, No. 266, 3023–29.
Harrington, C. (1998), 'Decentralization and Privatization of long-term care in UK and USA', *The Lancet*, **351** (9118), 1805.
Heffernan, W.J.(1968), *An Historic Preface to Welfare Reform*, Madison: Institute for Research on Poverty, University of Wisconsin.
Holstein, M. and Cole, T. (1996), 'The Evolution of Long Term Care in America', in R.H Binstock, L.E. Cluff and O. von Mering (eds), *The Future of Long-Term Care: Social and Policy Issues*, Baltimore: Johns Hopkins University Press, pp. 21–36.
Holstein, M. and Minkler, M. (1991), 'The Short and Painful Death of the Medicare Catastrophic Coverage Act', in M. Minkler and C. Estes (eds), *Critical Perspectives on Aging: The Political and Moral Economy of Growing Old*, Amityville: Baywood Publishing, pp. 47–72.
Johnson, H. and Broder, D. (1996), *The System: The American Way of Politics at Breaking Point*, Boston: Little Brown.

Kamerman, S.B. and Kahn, A.J. (2001), 'Child and family policies in the United States at the opening of the twenty-first century', *Social Policy and Administration*, **35** (1), 69–84.

Mead, L. (1997), *The New Paternalism*, Washington: The Brookings Institute.

Meiners, M. (1996), The Financing and Organization of Long Term Care', in R. Binstock (ed.), *The Future of Long Term Care*, Baltimore: Johns Hopkins University Press.

Michel, S. (1999), *Children's Interests – Mothers' Rights: The Shaping of America's Childcare Policy*, New Haven: Yale University Press.

Moses, S. (1990), 'The fallacy of impoverishment', *The Gerontologist*, **30** (1), 21–5.

OECD (1996), *Caring for Frail Elderly People: Policies in Evolution*, Paris: Organization for Economic Cooperation and Development.

Salamon, L. and Anheier, H.K. (1996), *The Emerging Nonprofit Sector*, Manchester: Manchester University Press.

Skocpol, T. (1995), *Social Policy in the United States: Future Possibilities in Historical Perspective*, Princeton NJ: Princeton University Press

Skocpol, T. (1996), *Boomerang: Clinton's Health Security Effort and the Turn against Government in US Politics*, New York: Norton.

Starr, P. (1992), *The Logic of Health Care Reform*. Knoxville: Whittle Direct Books.

Steinfels, M. (1973), *Who's Minding the Children?*, New York: Simon & Schuster.

Trattner, W.I. (1999), *From Poor Law to Welfare State: A History of Social Welfare in America*, 6th edn, New York: Free Press.

Weaver, K. (1998), 'Ending Welfare as We Know It', in M. Weir (ed.), *The Social Divide*, Washington: The Brookings Institute.

Weisbrod, B. (1977), *The Voluntary Nonprofit Sector*, Lexington: D.C. Heath.

Weisbrod, B. (1998), *To Profit or Not to Profit: The Commercial Transformation of the Nonprofit Sector*, Cambridge: Cambridge University Press.

Wiener, J.M. and Illston, L. (1994), 'Health care reform in the 90's: where does long term care fit?', *The Gerontologist*, **34**, 402–8.

Wiener, J.M. (1994), *Sharing the Burden: Strategies for Public and Private Long Term Care Insurance*, Washington: The Brookings Institute.

Wilensky, H.L. (1975), *The Welfare State and Equality: Structural and Ideological Roots of Public Expenditures*, Berkeley: University of California Press.

Willer, B. (1991), *The Demand and Supply of Child Care in 1990: Joint Findings of the National Child Care Survey, 1990 and a Profile of Child Care Settings*, Washington: National Association for the Education of Young Children.

Yankelovich Group (1990), *Long Term Care in America: Public Attitudes*, Washington: American Association of Retired Persons.

7. Patterns of Social Care in Five Industrial Societies: Explaining Diversity

Anneli Anttonen, Jorma Sipilä and John Baldock

INTENTIONS AND ACHIEVEMENTS

As authors of this book, and as participants in the research and analysis upon which it is based, we set ourselves ambitious targets. As the first chapter explains, we wished to correct what we perceived as an imbalance in much comparative social policy: a preoccupation with those aspects of welfare systems more likely to be similar, particularly social insurance and cash transfer arrangements. Instead, we suggested, attention should be paid to those arenas where the state comes into direct and practical contact with individuals and families, particularly the provision of support for the care of the two largest groups of dependent people found in industrial societies, children and older people. Here a much greater variety of social policy arrangements is both logically possible and actually to be found. We further suggested that from these arrangements one might deduce some of the essential qualities of welfare systems: the degree to which they accord accessible rights and entitlements to their citizens and the degree to which they entail responsibilities and obligations. Additionally, in so far as social care has been shown to be structured in terms of class, gender, age and ability and disability, it appeared to offer the potential for richer and more nuanced understandings of welfare systems. Lastly, we wished to capture in a more systematic way something of the moral quality of welfare systems: the degree to which they accord both status and stigma and so different forms of citizenship in similarly industrialized, contemporary societies.

The countries chosen for study, Finland, Germany, Japan, the United Kingdom and the United States, were selected largely because they presented a reasonably full range of the regime types generated by comparative research on state welfare (see Chapter 1). In particular they provided standard examples of Esping-Andersen's now classic division of the welfare systems of industrialized states into three main types: the conservative-corporatist, social democratic and liberal forms (Esping-Andersen, 1990). We knew from previous work that this would not be enough, that welfare regime types, based primarily on social security systems, do not capture the greater internal variety and complexity of national care systems (Anttonen and Sipilä, 1996). Nonetheless, we hoped to construct and then elaborate a taxonomy of the main variables that could be used to describe the forms of care policy and delivery found in each country. Implicit in this goal was an assumption that national social care systems might exhibit clusters of characteristics related to the regime types found in the mainstream literature.

However, the work described in the core chapters of this book has to a significant extent undermined our initial assumptions about how social care is patterned. Two main complications have arisen, one to do with how social care is consumed, the other to do with how it is produced. First, the manner in which the citizens of any one country use or consume a particular form of care is rarely standardized in some monolithic or dominant manner. The take-up and use of particular social care services is highly varied, even among those with broadly similar care needs. In this sense the nature and quality of a social care system is, to a much greater extent than a health or an educational system, mediated by the degree of homogeneity or differentiation in the ways it is consumed. Second, on the production side, nations do not exhibit coherent patterns of social care in terms either of the principles that inform them or the ways in which they are delivered. A country may simultaneously provide or support care services that are universal and appear to confer genuine citizenship rights alongside others that are selective and sharply rationed. Equally, there is within each country, and even within the provision for a particular form of care, a considerable variety of delivery mechanisms. In some aspects of a nation's care services, direct public provision may be the rule, in others contracting out to the private or voluntary sectors, the use of tax credits or payments for care may be the dominant method. A search for national patterns was clearly going to be particularly difficult.

DIVERSITY IN THE CONSUMPTION AND PRODUCTION OF SOCIAL CARE

Differentiated and Segmented Consumption Patterns

In the case of childcare provision in all of the five nations there are variations and gradations of use from those households where parents 'choose' to stay at home to care for their pre-schoolers, through those who use complex combinations of family and part-time nursery care, to those who depend entirely on public childcare while they are in full-time work. Patterns of choice in the use of childcare vary, even within one economy, in terms of region, occupation, levels of education and the degree of segmentation of the labour market (Elias, 2001). There is continuing debate about how and why these choices are made. They are influenced by a range of factors, many of which are locally determined: labour market participation, costs and availability of childcare, family structure and informal alternatives to parental care and, perhaps most importantly, by what Hakim (1995; 1996) has defined as 'female heterogeneity' in work-life preferences that are independent of labour market or care opportunities. For example in Finland, where parents of pre-school children are able to choose between municipal day-nursery care or a home care allowance, the pattern of take-up has both differed from policy makers' initial expectations and varied over time according to the economic climate and the availability of employment. In 2000 roughly half of all mothers chose to stay at home and the other half to work mainly full-time. However, this balance has been different at other times as families have variously negotiated the balance between income, job availability, services, costs, entitlements to parental leave and their own lifestyle preferences.

Similarly in Britain the introduction of Child Care Tax Credits to help pay for nursery care has not had simple or clear effects on women's decisions to return to the labour market. Some, particularly lone mothers, have been drawn into paid work but others indicate that the benefit has not affected their decisions either way (McLaughlin et al., 2001). Rather there is evidence that individual preferences for paid work, or even for part-time or full-time work, often pre-date care responsibilities and can be unchanged by them (Muehlberger, 2000, p. 20). The United Kingdom, like the United States, has comparatively high levels of female participation in the labour market, admittedly more commonly part-time, despite a limited and variable supply of out-of-school childcare facilities.

Many of the same points and parallel examples can be advanced in the case of older people's use of care services. Older people with comparable needs make an almost infinite variety of choices that cannot be wholly explained by costs and service availability. Responses to care reforms are consequently hard to predict. In both Germany and Japan, for example, the take-up of the new services made available under universal social care insurance schemes has been less than predicted (Peng, 2001). In Britain and Finland, as the chapters in this book show, the use of public care services is only loosely structured by type and severity of need or the availability of family support. Individual preferences, on the part of both users and carers, as to care they are willing to use are an important mediating factor between what is available and what is taken up.

DIFFERENTIATED POLICY LOGICS AND MODES OF PROVISION

Most countries can be shown to be pursuing both 'progressive' and 'regressive' policies, that is to say both policies that accord care entitlements to individuals and others that support or even enforce family and community obligations and which may impose degrees of shame and stigma linked to their poor law origins. For example, while in the United States the public sector offers limited, tax-based recognition of the pre-school care needs of children whose parents go out to work, provision for retired people with health and social care needs is relatively generously funded in largely non-stigmatizing ways through Medicare. In Finland, in contrast, citizenship-based childcare provision sits alongside a system for providing home care to older people which is comparatively partial in its coverage, geographically unequal in its generosity, and which traces its form and procedures back to selective poor law provisions (see Chapter 2).

Local and regional differences remain significant features of social care systems, so much so that it is often rather inappropriate to draw any conclusions from national figures. Thus, for example, in the United States where public social care is funded by the states, cities and counties and supported by federal subsidies, there is great diversity in types and levels of provision. The reasons for this variation are largely the product of local political histories. Occasionally differences may be more systematically arranged, such as the continuing gaps in childcare provision between the former East and West of Germany. In the United Kingdom, as well as a pronounced history of territorial inequality (see Chapter 5), political devolution has now led to quite different principles of support for home care in Scotland compared with England and Wales. Our main empirical observation is of variation and diversity not only between national care systems but also within them.

The four main modes of social care provision set out in Chapter 1 — informal, voluntary, commercial and state (Table 1.1) — remain useful as ways of understanding the range of actors, mechanisms and rationales that combine together in social care systems. Relatively 'underdeveloped' care systems may, through lack of choice, lock users predominantly into one mode of social care arrangement: the commercial in the United States; the informal in Japan. Paradoxically, better public services or financial supports appear to invigorate all four of the main modes and to increase the diversity of care arrangements. The use of social care services then becomes highly differentiated and segmented according to complex patterns of consumer preference which are both fluid and difficult to explain, often at other than the individual level. Nor is it possible to read off from basic data such as rates and forms of women's labour market participation, or the type and volume of care services available what the patterns of use will be. Better and more generous services provide more choice but do not necessarily determine the directions of choice. This may in part explain Esping-Andersen's finding that the probabilities of both high levels of welfare support for families and high levels of family welfare burden do not differ markedly between Southern Europe and Japan compared with the continental (conservative) countries of Europe (Esping-Andersen, 1999, pp. 93–4).

However, the reasons for variety in service use are not crucial at this point in the argument, rather we wish to make the case that the absence of monolithic, dominant modes in the consumption and production of personal services makes it unwise to construct typologies of social care systems that are comparable to those developed in the welfare regime literature. It remains possible, and sometimes necessary, to characterize social care systems in broadbrush ways. But what has become clear from our study of the five national 'systems' is that to suggest that nations are even preponderantly of one mode of provision or another (Finland/state; United States/market; Germany/voluntary; Japan/informal) is to underestimate diversity in each country, the degree to which systems are changing and the amount of choice that people exercise in opting into or out of what is available. There are also limits to which it is useful, or even possible, to document this complexity; the result is a very detailed institutional description of little analytic usefulness. Rather we seek in the remainder of this account to justify an alternative way of understanding social care, that is in terms of how policies and provisions change over time. We have found it helpful to use a dynamic even evolutionary analysis rather than one based on relatively static, cross-sectional description.

PATTERNS OF SOCIAL CARE DEVELOPMENT

Among the countries studied here there is a surprising degree of uniformity in the historical origins of the state's role in social care. Initially at least, industrialization appears to have stimulated the state to intervene in very similar ways. In all the countries, though at different times, some version of the Victorian poor law was to be found. As economic change, particularly urbanization, led to more instances in which family or community supports failed, so the local state began to intervene to shore up traditional institutions and obligations. It did so largely by offering stigmatizing and punitive alternatives, whether they be forms of out-door relief or, increasingly, subsistence within institutions. These traditions of local and stigmatizing personal services usually remained institutionally and ideologically separate from the national schemes for income replacement that began to develop in the late nineteenth century, paradoxically first of all in the United States with the pension and disability schemes for Civil War veterans and their families (Skocpol, 1992; Aspalter, 2001) and secondly in Bismarckian social insurance legislation (see Chapter 3). These are not original insights on our part but simply reflect a number of classic statements of the pattern found more generally in the histories of welfare systems (for example, Esping-Andersen and Korpi, 1987). There is order to these histories, which fits tidily with functionalist theories, whether they are Parsonian or Marxist, of how societies reproduce themselves and their labour power. All public social care systems started roughly in the same way. The distance travelled since then is a function of particular national histories. This analytical framework builds in an idea of linear development that strongly suggests a model in which countries do not represent different types of social care but are simply at different stages along a single path of progress. Whereas the welfare regime approach to comparative social policy produces horizontal classifications of different but equivalent types, the study of comparative social care tends to imply vertical classifications ordered in terms of more or less development. In principle, teleological analysis such as this is bad social science. However, in this case, used with due caution, it does help expose some distinctive aspects of social care development.

Three main dimensions of change are revealed in the histories of these five countries:

1. A long-term historical dimension in which an increasing proportion of the social care functions of a society are removed from the entirely private domestic economy of the household towards a greater overlap with the formal economy of the market, the voluntary and charitable sector and the state. Using a phrase coined by the Norwegian political scientist, Helga Maria Hernes (1987, p. 39), we call this the process of social care 'going public'.
2. A dimension along which publicly funded or provided care services move from being entitlements that are available to families, or to individuals because of their role or status within the family, to becoming services that are available simply on the basis of individual citizenship. We call this the process of the individualization of social care. It is related to but not quite the same as the idea of 'de-familialization' used by other authors.
3. A dimension along which publicly funded or provided care services move from being selective, usually in terms of income, or contingent upon some form of behaviour, often labour market participation, to their being genuinely universal in availability and take-up. This is the process of universalization.

These dimensions of change and development can be combined to generate a three-dimensional understanding of the evolution of social care, shown in Figure 7.1.

In principle, Figure 7.1 creates eight segments or categories into which a social care provision might be placed. At one extreme are the discretionary,

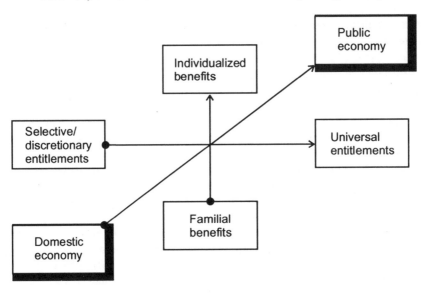

Figure 7.1 Dimensions of change in social care

charitable handouts more typical of nineteenth century philanthropy and intended to encourage families to attend to their needs in ways more acceptable to the donor; and at the other is public, professional help provided to individuals in proportion to their need and entirely independently of their household or family circumstances. However, because, as we have pointed out earlier, countries' social care systems are highly segmented and differentiated, no nation's care arrangements can be placed at one single conjuncture of these three intersecting dimensions of change. Different aspects of a nation's care arrangements tend to be positioned at different points. There is a lack of synchronicity as social care evolves along the three dimensions. Thus, for example, in the United States care provision for older people has to a significant extent been accepted as a public responsibility and benefits accrue to individuals rather than according to household resources or capacities and the care that follows is produced through market-based arrangements which are part of the public economy. However this assistance is substantially selective in terms of incomes and co-payments. Pre-school childcare in the United States, on the other hand, remains fundamentally a household responsibility in terms of its costs and organization and much is purchased through the private market. Where public help with childcare is available it is selective and granted in terms of family rather than individual entitlements. The ways in which social care arrangements for older people and for pre-school children can be positioned in terms of this model are further illustrated below in more detailed discussion of the three dimensions of change.

'GOING PUBLIC': LOCUS, PROCESS AND AGENCY

Within the overall dimension of change in which care 'goes public' by moving from the domestic to the formal economy, we have observed three subsidiary forms; shifts in the *locus* of care, in the *process* by which it is resourced and delivered and in the *agency* that takes ultimate responsibility for it. These three concepts, of locus, process and agency, have long been used in sociological analysis and so provide a degree of conceptual security. Another advantage in using them, as we seek to outline below, is that they allow a dynamic under-standing to the ways in which care is going public, as change in each of the forms impacts upon and alters the significance of the others. A crude, but not entirely inaccurate, summary of the development of public social care in all five countries reveals that in the early history of the development of social care, shifts in locus, process and agency tended to take place simultaneously. It was unusual for the family and the state to share care across any of the forms and where it went public it did so entirely or not at all. In contrast the more recent histories are typified by efforts to separate out locus, process and agency and, in particular to construct arrangements where care can continue to take place within the home but with shared outside intervention in its provision and management.

Thus the purely domestic and the entirely public forms of care for children and older people are relatively easy to distinguish. On one hand there is the care that takes place within the private home, is resourced by the household and where ultimate responsibility for the welfare of the child or older person lies beyond the public gaze and solely with the family. At the other extreme is the case where the child or older person is cared for wholly outside the family and the household, in a public place, at public expense and in a manner for which the state is responsible. In between these two poles are potentially an almost infinite variety of combinations of the domestic and public. We have sought to disentangle this variety for two reasons; first in order to determine significant criteria by which national care systems might be said to be similar or different; and second because behind the variety lies a more fundamental aspect of 'going public': the renegotiation of the balance of care responsibilities between the state and the citizen.

Historically, legal and cultural conventions about the primacy and privacy of the family meant that within most cultures there existed an invisible but unbreachable wall between care in the domestic environment of the family and the public world beyond it. This implicit rule remains strong in the United

States and Japan where the insertion of practical or financial support directly into the household to assist in the care of pre-school children or older people remains muted. Where financial help is available it mainly takes the form of tax credits, in the case of pre-school day care in the United States, or health insurance payments to older people themselves, in the case of both Japan and the United States. Where practical assistance beyond family care is added in the United States or Japan it is generally bought directly from the market by the family or older person themselves. In other words, responsibility and control (agency) remain within the household and the family. Similarly in these countries the state has tended rarely to enter the household as a provider (process) or organizer (agency) of childcare and when it has done so it has been in fulfilment of a social control rather than a welfare function; because family care is judged inadequate or economically dysfunctional. As Chapter 6 points out, in the United States '[w]hile there is some agitation for public provision of child day care, it is for the most part a subtitle in how to move single mothers off welfare rather than a debate over how to provide a more substantive, adequate and affordable child day care to everyone' (Chapter 6, p. 147).

In Japan direct state intervention into the household 'has not entirely been freed from stigma and social welfare tends to be associated in the minds of many citizens with means-tested benefits for the poor (Chapter 4, p. 83). Until recently both the provision of care, and responsibility for it, remained tied to a particular, external location. Thus where the state shared practical responsibility for the care of older people it did so outside the home, in the form of health care and largely in hospitals. The development of public help for Japanese families looking after dependants was impeded by values that made '[t]he idea of home care supported by non-family help...hard to grasp in a society in which the idea of the family remains strong even if the reality is rather different' (Chapter 4, p. 90).

In Finland on the other hand the invisible wall between the worlds of household and public care has been greatly reduced, allowing more complex and shared mixes of locus, process and agency. Chapter 2 describes the political accommodations that led in 1985 to legislation that 'took Finland a unique step further than any other nation in public support for childcare...the state arrived at a position where it actually funds parenthood itself' (Chapter 2, p. 40). In this sense the boundary round the private household has ceased to be a barrier to variety in the care process or to a degree of shared responsibility between the parent and the state. A consequence of the undermining of the significance of locus is that in Finland the proportion of pre-schoolers cared for outside the home is less than in other Nordic and Central European countries: 'a clear majority, three-quarters of Finnish children under three, are cared for at home, as are a third of those aged three to six' (Chapter 2, p. 43). This has been made possible by the intervention of the state in the process of childcare both through the provision of home care allowances and parental leave benefits. The boundary between the household and the outside economy has become porous. In Finland, '[e]ffectively the parent never leaves the labour market completely and is merely absent from work for a few years' and engaged in carrying out what is in part recognized as a public function (Chapter 2, p. 43).

In Germany, in contrast, childcare up to the age of three has historically been dominated by provision inside the home by mothers, with limited use of crèches (*Kinderkrippen*) and *Kindergärten*. Thus among the under-threes much care still takes place within a grey market of childminding (Chapter 3, p. 58) and the one in twenty children who do receive formal day care are from 'families defined as in social need and who pass a means test…[thus] the traditions of poor relief are still visible' (ibid., p. 72). The development of a public responsibility (or agency), on more universal grounds is relatively recent. Since 1986 childcare leave (*Erziehungsurlaub*) and income-tested childcare pay (*Erziehungsgeld*) have been available, and from 1999 children have had a right to a kindergarten place from age three to starting school. In the United Kingdom and Japan too, where childcare has also traditionally been regarded as a family matter, governments have now drawn up ambitious programmes for increasing and subsidizing, either directly or through family-based tax credits, the number of day-care places. They are, however, not ready to pay parents to stay at home to care for their children.

'Process' in the provision of care is concerned with the ways in which services are resourced or funded and with the delivery mechanisms that are used. These issues have received more attention than any other aspects of the increasingly public nature of social care. This has been due to political and academic interest in the 'mixed economy of care' and in welfare pluralism of various sorts (see Chapter 1, pp. 11–14). A principal focus has been on who pays for care and on where it is provided and by whom. However, this work has tended to neglect the relationship between process and agency, or, in other words, the consequences of welfare pluralism for the distribution of ultimate responsibility for the welfare of children and older people. We would suggest that comparisons of the degree of welfare pluralism in different countries can be unrevealing unless the mixture of the public and the private is also analysed in terms of how responsibility for determining and managing care is shared. In the United States and Finland there are great similarities among the over 65s in the balance between living at home (93 per cent) or in an institution (7 per cent), among children under seven in the use of day care (29–31 per cent) compared with some form of care at home (69–71 per cent), and in the proportions of women in full-time (53–57 per cent) or part-time (14–19 per cent) work (Tables 2.3, 2.7, 6.6, 7.1 and p. 150). However, the sources of these similar patterns are very different: in Finland because process and agency in social care are shared with the state but in the United States largely because they are not.

A key consequence of a change in the locus of care from family to the other sectors is that it it becomes monetized; it has to be paid for and its costs are revealed. This form of going public may happen quite independently of social policy simply as more households need or choose to buy or it may be a consequence of greater state participation. Monetization is seen everywhere: in the social care insurance systems for older people recently developed in Germany and Japan; in state support for social care costs in Scotland; in the expansion of coverage of Medicare in the United States; and in the widespread growth of pre-school childcare outside the family in all the nations we study here.

It is important to note that going public through monetization is not the same as, but is linked to, the dimension of commodification/de-commodification that was central to Esping-Andersen's analysis of welfare capitalism. There the key process of 'de-commodification' is defined as occurring when meeting a need or even sustaining a whole existence becomes possible 'without reliance on the market' (Esping-Andersen, 1990, p. 21), generally because the state takes responsibility for financing and possibly producing a service. In this sense in Finland, for example, childcare has to a degree been both de-commodified and at the same time monetized as the state now either pays for or provides a significant proportion. Paradoxically, and that is the point here, this de-commodification of the function of childcare is achieved precisely by detaching it from the privacy of the household and monetizing it, either by paying parents or by paying staff in day nurseries. The de-commodification of care is associated with the increased 'commodification' of (particularly women's) care work (Ungerson, 1997).

Our attempts in this section to find a way of conceptualizing and analysing the process of care 'going public' are not entirely satisfactory or complete. The descriptive material in the country-based chapters demonstrate that, one way or another, families are providing less of total care solely within the domestic sphere and 'buying' more of it as taxpayers, insured persons and as private purchasers. At the same time the state is accepting a more explicit role in stimulating, restricting and otherwise directing these changes. These tendencies appear to indicate a common pattern in the development of national care systems and are broadly understood as the growth of pluralism in social care. However, we suggest that, at least at an analytical level, by distinguishing between locus (where care is provided), process (who resources and provides it) and agency (who is ultimately responsible for ensuring the care of a child or older person) we are better able to understand the continuing variety within the growing publicness of social care systems. These are further complicated by the second and third dimensions of historical development we emphasize, individualization and universalization, and which are discussed next.

THE INDIVIDUALIZATION AND UNIVERSALIZATION OF SOCIAL CARE

While these two dimensions of change are analytically distinct they are better treated together when selecting examples from the five countries studied here, for in practice they are often related. In its earliest forms, social care from the state was often an individualized welfare benefit, a form of rescue for those old people or children who had no family that might be defined as or legally even morally liable to support them. The absence of family was the main criterion of selection. However, as poor law assistance evolved into various forms of domiciliary care, so entitlement to them became increasingly family or household based, both in terms of the objectives of the services (to strengthen family caring) and the criteria for selection (usually household income). Most social care services became forms of selective assistance to families. The opposite of these, social care entitlements that are entirely non-selective and based on individual need, remain rare today but can be seen as the endpoint of the two processes of individualization and universalization. It might be noted that there is an element of completing the circle here. In early industrialization, as the landless moved to the factory towns, the single, adult worker model of the labour market predominated. Later the concept of the family wage and the male-breadwinner model took hold, at least to a degree, particularly in the post-war welfare settlements. Now the forces of global competition are recreating the individualized adult worker; the family wage, and with it the family-based benefit, may both ultimately mark a brief interlude in the development of capitalism.

'Progress' towards Individual Rights to Social Care

The childcare literature has a distinctly evolutionary tone, with some public care systems being described as 'laggard', 'backward' and others 'exceptional' and 'progressive' (Donzelot, 1980; Gauthier, 1996; Millar and Warman, 1996; Kamerman and Kahn, 1997; Pringle, 1998). The ultimate destination is sometimes explicit, usually strongly implied. It is a state whose social policies recognize and support entitlements to care that are framed in terms of individual parents' and children's rights. These are generally contrasted with policies at the other end of the continuum of progress, those that seek to enforce traditional and collective obligations to care and which most often reside within the family and are almost always gendered. This is a powerful normative model of development. Not only does it contain the ideas of progress and even historical inevitability, but it also allows for the fact that welfare systems are rarely consistent and often contain contradictory and countervailing policies. Thus governments do simultaneously pursue policies that provide or fund services based on individual entitlement, as well as others that seek to shore up weakening patterns of obligation and reciprocity within the family or community. Compounding this complexity is the fact that a high degree of both localism and selectivity in social care systems tends to hide inconsistencies and anachronisms among policies and mechanisms that would be more obvious and unacceptable at a national level. Or, while the selective and family-focused services continue to evolve locally, universal citizenship-based entitlements are developed at a national level, often creating complex boundary problems between the two systems and, for the individual user, odd inconsistencies and inequalities.

Sometimes these tensions between local selectivism and national universalism can become politically and administratively unsustainable and wholesale national reform follows. This is more marked in the case of entitlements for older people than it is for childcare provision. The social care insurance system in Germany is a clear example of the extension of the principles and mechanisms of citizenship-based health care into the context of hitherto family-focused, selective and local home care. The Golden Plans in Japan and Medicare in the United States, particularly where the latter supports home care services, are varieties of the same development path. In the UK, in contrast, the Royal Commission's recommendations for universal care entitlements have been resisted in England and Wales, because of fears that they would undermine family care, but accepted by the new Scottish parliament (see Chapter 5, pp. 114, 120) which agreed that it was inequitable to provide free care within the National Health Service but charge for it in nursing homes and at home. The long-term trend would appear to be irresistible. Finland is paradoxically a 'laggard' and resists universal and individualized care entitlements for older people. Home care services remain local and selective, and focused mainly on those without family support. They have been 'protected' from reform by their relative abundance and the widespread development of generous local authority home care allowances (see Chapter 2, pp. 32–4). In a political culture in which universalism at the local level is much more marked than in the other countries, our analysis would predict that some rationalization of these Finnish anomalies is likely in the longer term.

However, it is not always clear which policies are progressive and which conservative. 'Traditional policies' are sometimes dressed in the guise of progress, such as some 'payment for care' programmes which may bind women more tightly to responsibility for looking after older people, or childcare programmes that merely rearrange the structures within which women do the work. A review of British policy on care and employment concludes, 'Enhanced access to childcare merely recreates the gender template by promoting low paid jobs for women as paid carers who are predominantly providing care services for other women' (McKie et al., 2001, p. 233). Paradoxically the process of de-commodifying access to childcare or eldercare has the effect of re-commodifying some aspects of women's labour.

Equally, some 'reforms' merely substitute new types of informal obligation for now less fashionable ones. Millar and Warman (1996) suggest that while the individualism of modern family policies may have undermined the traditional obligations of marriage and its links to nuclear and extended families, it has done so by giving a new primacy to the relationship of parenthood and to servicing the rights of children rather than husbands or wives. 'Relationships between adults are seen as fundamentally private, but this does not mean that the state is unwilling to intervene in family life, and, enforcing parental obligations [to care] while seeking to recognize children as individuals with rights of their own, can create some tensions in policy' (ibid.). A decline in state-sanctioned obligations of one sort is replaced by new forms of duty of another.

Only in Finland has a non-contingent parental right to time off from childcare been realized in a society that is the clearest example in our selection of an emphasis on individual entitlements independent of family relationships. Thus in Finland adults have a right to work and children have a right to state-aided care without these two entitlements being linked. In the UK, in contrast, the National Childcare Strategy will only provide childcare help to parents who are in work. The relatively new system of Child Care Tax Credits may have been a national reform but it is much like local welfare in that it involves both a means test and a work test and it affords parents a 'right' to work rather than a right to childcare. Germany too has adopted relatively narrowly focused family policies. Linda Hantrais (2001) points out that 'while policy actors in Germany explicitly recognize the legitimacy of state involvement in family affairs, overall policy lacks coherence, and its main object continues to be the conjugal relationship rather than the family as a unit, as demonstrated in tax system'. In the United States, Aid to Families with Dependent Children (AFDC) emerged as a form of temporary support during the New Deal era but lasted until it was replaced by Temporary Assistance for Needy Families in 1996 (see Chapter 6). Both, however, are essentially a benefit aimed at the 'family' defined only as motherhood, and AFDC in particular had the effect of driving parents apart so that mothers could remain eligible for the benefit. Missing from our group of countries is an example of a social policy system, such as exists in France for example, that deliberately and without systemic contradictions promotes the family, rather than the individual, as the fundamental object of welfare entitlement and help from state policies and provisions. But then France has an exceptional history: the Napoleonic administrative reforms completely replacing local systems of individual poor relief.

Trade-offs within Individualized Citizenship

The risk of trade-offs between one person's new right to care and another's new obligation is one of the characteristics that makes social care more complicated than other forms of welfare. For example, improving some individuals' entitlements to social security payments does not generally imply constraints for others beyond the generalized payment of taxes or contributions. In contrast, guarantees of personal care for some people may disadvantage others in a whole range of ways. This 'zero-sum' paradox derives in part from the fact that, in most of its aspects, providing social care involves people performing menial tasks. Care is labour intensive and there are few opportunities for the technological and productivity gains that generally provide the bases for reform in other sectors of the economy. An individual right to care means someone else must be found to do the caring. Thus the decline of informal childcare by mothers or of children's (daughters') time spent tending their parents has generally been achieved by creating new forms of low-paid and insecure employment for women (Brannen et al., 1994; Ungerson, 1997). Another example lies in our finding that one of the sources of the growing amounts of paid care observed in all the nations surveyed here has been the greater availability of immigrant workers. Without them the growth of relatively affordable nurseries for children and domiciliary workers for older people in Germany, Britain and the United States would probably not have been possible. The relative 'backwardness' of Japan in terms of individual rights to care outside the family may in part be due to the absence of new sources of cheap labour. Finland, however, presents a contrary case. Only one and a half per cent of its women workers are immigrants (Table 7.1 below) and care workers are not particularly low-paid.

Another 'right' that imposes costs on others, however willing they may be, is the right to home care for older people. This has been a powerful idea, indeed almost a social movement, in all the five nations. Home care is presented as the logical outcome and happy coincidence of a whole range of contemporary techniques, interests and ideologies: better drugs and treatment, new assistive and monitoring technologies, professional care-management techniques, the improved housing and income of older people, anti-institutionalism and the politics of public expenditure all conspire to make home care a 'good thing'. However, research reports from all the countries studied here show that home care services are rarely a complete substitute for the round-the-clock support of an institution. Home care is rarely a '24/7 service'. Instead home care policies tend to impose more specific obligations on informal carers by either, at best, incorporating them into managed care plans or, more often, treating family support as the more flexible backstop that will fill the gaps left by partial or unreliable formal provision (Twigg, 1989).

Universalization: From Services of Last to First Resort

Not only are there progressive and retrograde implications for citizenship that flow from the individualization of care entitlements but, within all the nations we studied, there are culturally well-understood hierarchies of care services in terms of their ability to confer esteem or stigma. Again this appears to be a product of the uneven development from a poor law base. We found that some social care services are highly valued and are readily turned to when there is need; others are seen almost entirely negatively and are only used when no other source of help is available. This difference might be characterized as the difference between services of first and last resort. It is a distinction which is fundamental to understanding the quality of social welfare in a country and at the same time it is a distinction that is very hard to capture and evidence.

Public services are not always those of last resort. An important distinction appears to be whether they are simply modern versions of previously selective, poor law-based provision or rather formerly 'middle-class' market-based services made public and universal. At one extreme having to avail oneself of a service can be shameful and stigmatizing, a reflection of personal and family failure. At the other extreme, access and use may be perceived as desirable, even an example of good fortune. Only in Finland are social care services largely status neutral and this appears to be a consequence of the particular history of the Finnish state which allowed it to break most links with a class-based past. Elsewhere, however, status hierarchies among services are the rule and they are hard to read by those outside the culture or even the locality. They certainly cannot be deduced from comparative statistical data. For example, among working parents living in large cities in Japan, winning a place for one's pre-school child in an officially authorized day-care centre (*ninka hoikusho*) would be regarded as good fortune. Compared with a place in one of the unauthorized centres (*munika hoikusho*), the costs are likely to be lower, because they are subsidized by the state, and the quality higher, because the nurseries are required by municipalities to meet specified staffing and building standards. However, the places are relatively scarce and there are waiting lists. In 1994 the system (*sochi seido*) through which the central state tightly rationed places within the public childcare system was loosened to allow more parental choice and larger role for private providers. This has led to more nursery places but less confidence in quality (Peng, 2001). In the United Kingdom, on the other hand, places in public local authority nurseries are allocated by social workers according to assessments of social deprivation. They are primarily given to children defined as having 'special needs' of an individual or family nature. In the United States there may be distinct a ethnic bias in the use of public pre-school programmes.

Alternatively some service developments have been successfully presented and understood as the extension to all of provision that was once the prerogative of the wealthy few. This was how Aneurin Bevan sought to present the 'new' residential homes for old people in Britain in 1948 (see Chapter 5). It was certainly how the public perceived the National Health Service. It is the mode in which kindergartens became universal in Germany (as education rather than care) and local authority nursery care in Finland. There is a difference in social valuation to be found in all the countries we have studied between those services that are aspects of the poor law made universal and those that amount to the democratization of services formerly reserved for the better off.

Extremes of social valuation are less common where services for older people are concerned, partly because dependency in old age is of itself not to be desired. However, it is again true that the social implications of use cannot be easily read off from the bald figures of expenditure and provision. For example, in the United States, retired citizens of all classes and background use Medicare funding where possible to assist with health and care needs. A retired university professor would see the contribution to costs from federal funds as a right and entitlement won through many years of social security contributions and would expect the quality of the service received to be indistinguishable from those that a wholly private payment would obtain. In the United Kingdom, on the other hand, older people who use home care or a nursing home paid for by the state might well not wish their neighbours and friends to know. They might also be concerned that being a 'DSS' (Department of Social Security) funded user will mean that they will get services of a lower quality.

In short, unlike the use of more 'mainstream' welfare services such as pensions, schools and medical care, take-up of publicly provided or publicly-funded social care services is accompanied by complex constructions of status and stigma which enhance or contaminate the very use of the service itself. These valuations are not revealed in comparative tables setting out data on services and their coverage, nor are they easy to evidence through research. They remain implicit or even hidden behind rather than revealed in statistics published by the OECD or the European Union. These cannot show, for example, the way in which public domiciliary services for older people in Finland are often status neutral, a citizenship right, while in Germany local state services can still carry poor law connotations and come with a range of social significations depending on their cost and source and which, in turn, have played a part in the preference for cash from the social care fund rather than for 'more valuable' services from local care providers. These are social valuations that are well understood in the everyday culture of society. They are also valuations that could be argued to contribute to the essence of daily, lived citizenship.

Richard Titmuss famously and powerfully argued that it was primarily the use of means tests that affected perceptions of services and their users: 'virtually all types of means tests…and all schemes for charges with a related right to permission…run into problems of moral values, incentives and equity' (Titmuss 1968, p. 120). For Titmuss the detailed texture of citizenship represented within a nation's social services was closely related to the forms of means-testing used to finance them. Means tests are an 'assault on human dignity,...socially divisive and...lead to the development of two standards of services for two nations', that is to say poorer services for poor people (ibid., p. 122). To some extent Titmuss's abhorrence of means tests was a product of his time and its folk memories of the 1930s. His opposition to all forms of selectivity has rendered some of his arguments less relevant to contemporary debate (Reisman, 1977) but his consistent focus on the social construction of welfare, and not simply on its measurable material forms, remains useful. We would argue that more recent developments and wider-ranging comparative work (Titmuss tended to focus only on differences between Britain and the United States) show that the issue is less one of the means test *per se* but more to do with the wider context of meaning within which selectivity is embedded. Titmuss saw selection as a source of inequality. Instead it is now clearer that it is often inequality that makes selection stigmatizing. Means tests and selective services appear to be more socially divisive the more unequal the society. Thus, although there are income-based charges for municipal day-care in Finland and Japan, they do not lead to the negative images for the services and their users that Titmuss's argument would suggest. Indeed while debates about the reform of social care in Finland and Japan are generally cast in a form that assumes they are about what will be available to and be used by everyone who is eligible, and are therefore national issues, in Britain and the United States those who argue over and administer social care policy often would not expect themselves to use the services involved, and, partly as a result, the issues are rarely at the centre of political or media attention. The class-based history and politics of social care and the ideological frameworks within which they take place are central to the uneven development of entitlements and patterns of use.

EXPLAINING THE UNEVEN DEVELOPMENT OF SOCIAL CARE CITIZENSHIP

The tendency to a lack of coherence within social care systems, both in terms of their policy structures and the ways in which services are actually allocated and consumed, has made it difficult to explain their evolution other than through the particular histories of individual services. This tendency to resort to history in order to explain social care is clearly demonstrated within this study. While it was our initial intention to construct more generalized taxonomies, in practice the authors of each national study found themselves driven to write summary histories of childcare and eldercare. In this sense our project has failed; we were largely unable to move beyond the particularist accounts that have already been more thoroughly presented by social historians.

The most powerful non-historical accounts of social care are those built round the concept of the 'male-breadwinner model'. While not intended solely as an explanation of the nature of social care citizenship (indeed the literature tends to focus more on income maintenance systems), this analytical approach, explicitly proposed by Carole Pateman (1988) and most vigorously developed by Jane Lewis (1992), is now the most widely used to understand the character of national care systems. Lewis describes the male-breadwinner model as 'a set of assumptions about male and female contributions at the household level: men having primary responsibility to earn and women to care for the young and the old' (Lewis, 2001, p. 153). Social care policies can then be categorized according to how nearly they represent this model in practice or are consistent with other forms of female labour marker participation. Lewis and others (Orloff, 1993; Scheiwe, 1994; Ostner, 1994; Sainsbury, 1996; Daly, 2000) have gone on to develop a substantial literature describing the forms in which gender relations are implicit in social policies and to elaborate typologies of welfare systems organized in terms of assumptions about women's work and care roles that are embedded within them. Male-breadwinner assumptions can be found in the post war arrangements for both income maintenance and the delivery of social care in most industrialized countries, particularly Britain and Germany but to a much lesser extent in the Nordic nations where, at least after the Second World War, a 'dual-breadwinner' model is often apparent both in the reality of the labour market and the logic of policies. The United States is also a difficult case to classify as its income maintenance and care-funding systems have tended to focus more on individuals than on families, though certainly not always (Skocpol, 1992; Berkowitz, 1991). What is less clear is the causal argument implied by the male-breadwinner/dual-breadwinner continuum. Lewis accepts that 'a pure male breadwinner model never existed; women always engaged in the labour market. But there were historical periods in some countries and for some classes for which the model more accurately described the social reality than others' (2001, p. 153). However,

> crucially, the male breadwinner model also worked at the level of prescription. Policy makers treated it as an 'ought' in terms of relationships between men and women, and in many countries it served to underpin both social policies that assumed female dependence on the male wage and family law... (ibid.)

This approach is therefore primarily an ideological explanation of social policy. Put crudely, it is strongly suggested that, because of a dominant idea in the heads of legislators and administrators, it is quite possible for policies to be out of line with the actual participation of women in the labour market and therefore their ability to perform the social care functions expected of them. In the article that is being quoted from here, Lewis allows for this possibility suggesting that 'when the gap between changes in behaviour and the pattern of gendered assumptions following from the model became too great, the rupture led to a new set of policy assumptions' (ibid., pp. 157–8). Here she is focusing particularly on the UK case where she suggests, in the article cited, that New Labour's policies may even have run ahead of real labour market change and come to assume a universal dual-career model of labour market participation when in fact only a minority of wives and mothers actually work full-time.

The labour-market based account of social policy appears to suggest that there are likely to be causal relationships between all the three factors described in Figure 7.2 and that, empirically, these linkages can vary over time and in terms of the direction of cause and effect. Thus, while female participation in the labour market is usually ahead of policy assumptions, it may also occasionally lag behind them. Equally changes in policy, such as improved access to childcare, may have diverse and even unexpected effects on labour market participation. For example, in Finland the effect has varied over time depending on the strength of the job market. Lastly there may be periods when public policies have little direct impact compared with a direct connection between the labour market and care patterns; when more women do enter paid work, care patterns may change quite independently of public policy. This has been the case in both Japan and the United States where the absence of public support for care has forced women to find new sources in the family or in the market. Thus the actual forms of care in a society, that is to say the balance between informal provision by the family and public provision by the state or market, together with the balance of female and male roles within the household, may at times be out of line with both labour market participation by women and the current intentions of policy makers. These complications are not necessarily weaknesses in the explanatory framework. The looseness of the linkages may indeed be an

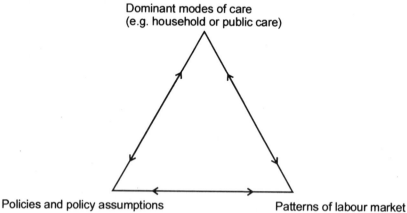

Figure 7.2 Links between social care, policy and the labour market

accurate portrayal of social reality. What the labour market theory of social policy appears to be saying is that, while in the shorter term there are tensions between the three dimensions of analysis, that is to say policy, care and labour market, over the longer term they will tend to congruence.

Table 7.1 summarizes the recent patterns of women's participation in the labour markets of the nations in our study. Overall, the levels of female involvement in paid work are very similar. What mainly varies are the proportion and degree of part-time participation. One might expect part-time work to be more often selected by women in those countries where social care services are less available or flexible. The table supports the argument except in the case of the United States. As Chapter 6 shows, the high level of full-time work by women in the US is sustained both by a greater use of market-based childcare and by the availability of state-funded social care for older people. In both cases the availability of cheap, female and often-migrant labour, plays a significant role. As Lewis has pointed out, policy in the US has long implied an adult-worker model of labour market participation but largely without the social supports that back a similar assumption in Sweden or Finland. In most nations there are also contradictory pressures from within social policy itself. In Britain, various policies introduced by New Labour and designed to help women with dependants move into the labour market (the National Childcare Strategy, the New Deal for Lone Parents, and Child Care Tax Credits) are to a degree countered by an income maintenance system that is still concerned with household income and withdraws benefits sharply once family earnings increase. In Japan too, the pattern of causality between policy assumptions and women's labour market participation has to be understood in the context of a society with high levels of co-residence with older people and distinctly low levels of non-domestic social care. These factors affect the detailed distribution of part-time and full-time work within the female labour market but still do not entirely compensate for what

Table 7.1 Women's labour market participation 1999, as per cent of women aged 15–64

	Finland	Germany	Japan	United States	United Kingdom
In paid work	71.3	62.8	63.8	71.5	67.5
Part-time[a]	13.5	33.1	39.7	19.0	40.6
Migrant workers	1.5	9.1	1.0	11.7	3.7

Note: a Less than 30 hours per week.

Source: Labour Force Statistics 1979–1999, OECD, Paris, 2001.

are simply higher levels of the work-plus-care burden for women. The lack of congruence in Japan (and also in a number of Mediterranean countries) between policy assumptions, care services and the proportion of women in paid work has triggered falling levels of marriage and fertility among younger women, now a matter of great concern in public debate about the future of the Japanese economy, and the emergence of protest movements among older women who cannot so limit their caring obligations.

> Toward the end of the 1980s, Japan's postwar welfare régime, well known for its re-markable capacity to impose much of the burden for social welfare and care on the family (namely, women), began to crumble...Those most affected were middle-class women in their forties and fifties, who had formed the base of Japan's family-centred welfare...As their double burden increased, these women began a social and political mobilization to protest against the LDP government's policy...They took advantage of the LDP's electoral decline in the 1990s to strike for their demands. The impact of women's social mobilization was huge. Most of the social policy reforms in elder care, including the two most important, the Golden Plans and long-term care insur-ance, would not have been possible without women's political work. (Peng, 2001, pp. 191–92)

Overall, explanations of social care in terms of the gender structure of the paid labour force, both actual and implicit, are useful for capturing linkages between political ideology and the structure of social care policy but they lack specific explanatory power. Simply to suggest a particular constellation of wel-fare policies demonstrate that a prevailing ideological model of women's eco-nomic role is the determining factor is not to show how the process of determi-nation works. At worst there is a risk of tautology: because these policies exist, this mind-set must too. What is necessary is a greater understanding of how the politics of social care produces diverse responses to the need to reconcile the actual pattern of women's (and men's) labour market roles and caring functions within a society. As global economic competition forces all nations to treat all adults as individual workers, so striking this balance in a sustainable way becomes more critical for national economic and political success. We have drawn a number of tentative conclusions about how and why particular 'solu-tions' have evolved.

THE STRUCTURAL SOURCES OF SOCIAL CITIZENSHIP

As pointed out earlier, in writing the accounts of social care policies in the five countries studied here, the authors found themselves forced to engage in sum-marizing their policy histories. In none of the countries did it appear possible to portray the existence of a distinct social care regime type; the variety of services, in both quality and volume and the logics informing them, was too disorganized to justify this. The descriptive literatures tend to characterize and explain only discreet parts of countries' social care arrangements in terms of the histories that led to them. Different parts of care systems have different histories. Key shifts in state support for, and provision of, social care are explained in terms of particular political conjunctures, often almost unexpected and accidental compromises and settlements. There is also a strong dose of path dependency in many accounts. Histories of social care services are generally couched in terms of the journey from their poor law origins. Change tends to be incremental and fundamental innovations and reconfigurations of policy are relatively rare. However, cumulatively, qualitative shifts in the assumptions behind policies do occur as nations 'progress' towards universal social care citizenship. We have sought to highlight the historical circumstances that make these shifts more likely.

Three aspects of social care histories appear to be particularly conducive to change: sharp breaks in the evolution of a nation's constitutional and social character, what we call 'clean breaks' in social care histories; a dominance of centrally rather than locally determined policies; and the appearance of a democratic (that is, bottom-up) rather than administrative (top-down) politics of care. We explore each of these briefly here since they are covered in greater detail in the country-based chapters.

The Importance of a 'Clean Break' Social Care History

Paradoxically it is the nations that have had the more disrupted, even traumatizing, twentieth century histories that have been more likely to develop universalist social care systems. Continuity of social institutions appears to be bad for social care innovation while discontinuity is positive. Finland is really the only clear example of this and it is least marked in the case of the United Kingdom. In Finland the post-war state was created almost as the antithesis of all that had gone before. The civil war that broke out in the young state almost immediately after independence in 1918 was both a class war and a severe setback for the modernization of social policy (see Chapter 2). The defeat of the Finnish working class meant that the systems of local poor relief were sustained for another generation. However, the end of the Scond World War marked a complete reversal of this history and the appropriation of the state by the ordinary Finnish people. The post-war Finnish state was essentially an entirely new creation, representing in itself the essence of a new more democratic citizenship and one in which social policy was of the greatest significance. The principle of social citizenship became embedded in the very nature of the state. The child benefit system, introduced in 1948, marked the beginning of a universalist social and family policy. In addition, the women's movement, well represented in parliament, played a central role in the construction of care policy. Full-time female employment was already the norm in the 1950s and the 1960s brought even more mothers with small children onto the labour market. Migration from the countryside to the towns and cities quickly revolutionized the care and support relationships between the generations and this was reflected in the transfer of care functions from the domestic to the public arenas: in the 1950s old-age welfare was modernized and the home care service became a municipal service but based on national legislation; the National Health Act came into force in 1972 and the Day Care Act in 1973. Social care reform may have come late in Finland but the factors that had caused its delay also allowed a clean break with the structures and values of the past.

In Britain in contrast, the historical continuity of the constitutional and political character of the nation is very marked, particularly at the local level. As Chapter 5 seeks to show, the Second World War and the Beveridge welfare settlement slowed rather than encouraged reform of social care provision. Local social services continued to evolve within their long-established discretionary and selective framework. Continuity at the local level is also a feature of the social history of the United States. Although it is now generally accepted that the US was in many ways the first welfare state this was largely a product of federal programmes following the Civil War and the introduction of universal white male suffrage. 'In the year 1890, one third of the federal budget was consumed by post-Civil War welfare programs for the veterans, their wives and some cases their children' (Aspalter, 2001, p. 6). However, at the level of the county, city and state the traditions of minimal and stigmatizing welfare soon reasserted themselves and this was to remain the pattern throughout the twentieth century. Reform came only at the federal level and almost always in the form of programme funding that must be annually re-voted by Congress: the social security provisions, including Medicare, born out of the New Deal and the Johnsonian 'War on Poverty' programmes of the 1960s. In Germany, as Chapter 3 shows, social care politics exhibited less of a clean break with the past than might have been expected. The Nazi period was seen as so aberrant that post-war reconstruction in the West was interpreted as the reinstatement of systems that had their roots in the Bismarckian state at the national level and the church-based arrangements that had reached their peak at the local level under Weimar. Japanese post-war constitutional arrangements were a clean break with the past but again only at the national level where the American authorities had set up a liberal, market-friendly system designed to contain the authority of the state and which ensured one-party domination for many years. At the local level, however, the pre-existing poor law based systems tended to fill the vacuum and reassert themselves. Nonetheless, public pre-school daycare is preferred to its private alternatives and public social care for older people, admittedly delivered through the health care and hospital system, has certainly not been reserved for the poor. This universality of state services may be because, unlike the cases of Britain and the US, the links between contemporary Japanese welfare services and poor law past were ruptured by the Second World War. Social provision has subsequently been defined in terms of universal rights that apply equally to all classes but which are contingent upon entitlements constructed through labour market participation and mediated by a distinctly traditional conception of the role of the family. Japanese social care is universalist but, because supply is low relative to population, it has not gone public but remains largely in the domestic sphere. Care in the Japanese family remains a function of gender, but there is no significant tradition of domestic labour based around differences in class and race as there has been, and continues to be, in the US and Britain.

Localism and the Trend to Centralization

While a 'clean break' political history is a key platform for social policy reform in industrial societies, it is less commonly so at the level of local government where social care is most often located. Social divisions in the use and evaluation of services are more pronounced when they are local. To put it crudely but largely accurately, in Germany, Britain and America local generally means selective and reserved for the poor while national is much more likely to imply universal provision used by all. The point can be extended by observing that in all the countries we studied, social care provision rarely progresses to the status of citizenship entitlements without becoming a centralized, national government responsibility, even if delivery is then devolved to the local administrations. This is partly because where social services remain entirely local there is institutional continuity in their evolution from means-tested poor law provision while, in contrast, a National Health Service or Medicare, among other examples, are relatively immaculate conceptions at the national level and less tainted by the signs of deterrence and stigma of the past. In Finland and Japan, while many social care services are similarly rooted in local poor law provisions, twentieth century history appears to have undermined and replaced their automatic associations with status and desert.

Finland has assumed the role of the benchmark in our study; the key point of comparison with which the other social care systems are usefully compared. Essentially Finland demonstrates the possibility of social care services which are both local and universal; the unique example of the transformation of the municipal poor law into a set of citizenship-based entitlements.

A Democratic rather than a Bureaucratic Politics of Social Care

One of the consequences of social care services' links to and evolution out of various forms of local poor law assistance is that they rarely escape into the arenas of democratic politics but remain services whose development is dominated by the professionals and bureaucrats who deliver them. In contrast, social care which is generated by democratic politics tends to universalize middle-class standards and expectations, whereas bureaucratic politics merely rationalizes provision for the less eligible. Chapter 5 describes how in Britain the experience of the Second World War and the politics that followed it sustained the continuity of a subject political culture and ensured that social care services remained outside the Beveridge settlement and were determined by evolutionary bureaucratic politics rather than by political competition. In contrast, in Finland day care for children was 'one of the most debated social policy issues of the 1960s and early 1970s' (Chapter 2, p. 39). Once included within the diet of party political competition and the resulting compromises and trade-offs, universal Children's Home Care Allowances available to all parents of children under seven emerged relatively unplanned out of the democratic political process, in particular out of trade-offs between the ruling Social Democrats, the rural Centre Party and informal coalitions of women members of parliament (see Chapter 2, pp. 38–44). These were almost accidental conjunctures of political interest. In Germany and Japan the extension of the universalism and standards of the health care insurance system to social care has similarly been a product of democratic politics, the issues being debated both in the legislatures and the wider community. In contrast, in the UK, the recommendation of the Royal Commission on Long Term Care that there be universal public funding of social care needs was not taken up by the parliamentary political processes, at least not in England, and has emerged as a set of bureaucratic rules and regulations generated after debates hidden within government and the civil service (Chapter 5).

In Finland a significant added factor pulling care issues into party and parliamentary competition has been the effective political power of women. As pointed out in Chapter 2 (p. 28), Finnish women were among the first to win the vote, in 1906. Subsequently Finland's particular experience of rapid urbanization and industrialization meant that full-time work became the normal form of women's labour market participation. Significant representation in the trade unions and in all political parties followed. These factors combined with the system of proportional representation to allow cross-party coalitions to pursue women's interests in parliament.

POLITICS AND THE PLASTICITY OF SOCIAL CARE

This book set out to describe and explain how social care is organized and understood in five industrial societies. Our analysis suggests that in most countries governments can be shown to be pursuing both 'progressive' and 'regressive' social care policies at the same time, that is to say both policies that accord care entitlements to individuals and others that support or even enforce family, gender and community obligations. We argue that while care policies tend in the longer term to develop along a set of key dimensions (from the domestic to the public, from the familial to the individualist, and from the selective to the universal), they do so in highly varied and unsynchronized ways even within one country. What determines the pattern and speed of change is largely a matter of the particularities of national political histories. However, we would add a further aspect of social care that makes it especially vulnerable to this chequered historical development; what we call its 'plasticity'. This refers to the properties of social care that make its production and consumption highly substitutable between the domestic and the public spheres. Constraints in one sector are balanced by a greater output in another. In this sense there is a degree of 'plasticity' to social care that is not true of other key areas of personal welfare provision like health or education services.

Richard Rose (1989) was among the first to show how human welfare is supported by the production of goods and services within three distinct sectors of modern economies, the household, the market and the state. Rose goes on to argue that a decline in output from one of these sectors can sometimes be offset by a rise in another. However, most goods are produced primarily within only one, or at the most two, of these sectors and it is difficult to shift production from one to the other. Goods that can be readily produced by all three sectors are relatively rare: Rose lists alcoholic drink, meals and cleaning as examples of goods where there is what he calls 'high substitutability' between the public and the household economies (ibid., p. 127).

Rose might well have added social care to his list of substitutable goods. Social care displays a very high degree of substitutability across economic sectors in both its production and its consumption. It is often to be found being produced and consumed entirely within each of the household, market and state sectors and also by complex combinations of these. One of Rose's key points is that this is why it is so difficult to measure the volume of care within a society. While a monetary figure can be put on the services provided by the state and to a lesser extent those bought and sold in the market, social researchers can do no more than make broad assumptions about the volume and cost, in labour time, of care services produced within the household sector. It is this that undermined our efforts to place valuations on the volumes of pre-school and elderly care in the societies we have studied (see the discussion in Chapter 1). Furthermore, as the proportion of time spent in paid labour falls in most industrial societies, though with gendered differences, so the domestic sector, always the largest in terms of labour time available, continues to grow. Rose uses data from studies of the household economy to estimate that even in 1981 more that 52 per cent of labour time was to be found in the domestic economy in the UK. To an extent it is this sheer size of the domestic economy that both demonstrates the relative insignificance of the public care sector in the overall scheme of things and also explains why policy makers can manage it so variously and erratically. The domestic economy acts as a vast buffer absorbing the mistakes and inadequacies of the social care policies.

Because there is high substitutability between sectors in the case of care there is also more room for difference between nations as well as more opportunities for politicians to tinker with its forms of production and consumption. One reason why social care policies in industrial societies sometimes shift with surprising abruptness may be that politicians know, or at least can implicitly assume, that if the state role changes, the market and household sector will adapt. As a result of the essential plasticity of care, the constraints on the range of possible care systems are almost solely political rather than economic. The extension of the state into the arena of social care need not involve coherent and substantial reform, as it necessarily must, for example, in the cases of social insurance, education or health care. If spending on acute treatments in a health system is insufficient the results will be visible in a way that does not apply in the case of social care. Rather the evolution of a public role in social care can be local, partial, piecemeal, disorganized and even accidental. Many forms of public help first evolved for one particular group in society that posed social problems beyond the control of the domestic sphere. Thus home care services, now mostly used by older people and common to all the countries we studied, often began as local initiatives for particular sections of those with disabilities or, in the case of the UK, for nursing mothers. Similarly some childcare services have their roots in specialized state protection for the orphaned and the troublesome, others in the provision of kindergarten education for middle-class children.

CONCLUSION

In this study we have sought to highlight a range of user-related qualities that characterize the social care systems of the countries studied: the degree to which services are either rationed to selected categories of people or are available universally to all with a particular need; the degree to which services are actually used by all social classes or are in practice accessed mainly by excluded sections of the community; the related question of whether services are those of first or last resort and which services attach either stigma or status.

We have shown, as many researchers before us have found, that these qualities are very much a product of distinct service histories and their links to the particular evolution of welfare provision in each nation. Despite a considerable degree of similarity in the origins of national care services, for they almost all grew out of local poor law administrations, the pace and trajectory of their development has varied considerably from nation to nation. We have argued that there is linearity to these development trajectories; that the idea of progress is often explicit and almost always implicit. However, there is no one route of development followed even at a different pace in each country. Rather the evolution of social care services can best be described in terms of a set of intersecting pathways. Historically nations have moved along these at very different rates and the resulting positions we now find them in are more akin to positions on a map of social care than categories in a typology of social care systems. The political economy of social care may be making 'care go public' but the mechanisms through which this is happening remain complex.

All the country-based chapters in this book have spent a good deal of space on the history of their social care systems and in explaining how they are bound up with the nations' political and economic development over the last hundred years or more. This was not a pattern of explanation that we had wished to focus on when we began our comparative work. Contemporary regime theory, which we saw our accounts as paralleling, pays relatively little attention to the detail of national historical factors. While political and social histories may be needed to explain when and how income maintenance systems came into being, they are not the keys to their nature. Social insurance systems exhibit coherent technical and organizational logics and, depending on their structures and goals, they can be shown to represent distinct models of welfare. However, in seeking to explicate the rationales and textures of social care services we found that diversity was more common than pattern. With each round of our research, and our reports to one another on the nature of the national systems, we were introducing ever more history to explain these variations. Only history, and particularly political history, appeared able to communicate why the services were structured and delivered in what appeared to be idiosyncratic national forms. Paradoxically however, while there is a lack of pattern to the services themselves, there is at least a degree of pattern to the histories. We have argued that despite the intrinsic plasticity of care, there is a longer-run trajectory that all social care reform will tend to follow in order to reconcile social reproduction with global economic competition. There is a certain inevitability to state-regulated, universal social care services based upon individual citizenship entitlements.

REFERENCES

Anttonen, A. and Sipilä, J. (1996), 'European social care services: is it possible to identify models?', *Journal of European Social Policy*, 6 (**2**), 87–100.

Aspalter, C. (2001), *Different Worlds of Welfare Capitalism: Australia, the United States, the United Kingdom, Sweden, Germany, Italy, Hong Kong and Singapore*, Graduate Program in Public Policy, Discussion Paper No. 80, Canberra: Australian National University.

Berkowitz, E.D. (1991), *America's Welfare State: From Roosevelt to Reagan*, Baltimore: Johns Hopkins University Press.

Brannen, J., Meszaros, G., Moss, P. and Poland, G. (1994), *Employment and Family Life: A Review of Research in the UK (1980–94)*, Department of Employment Research Paper No. 41, London: HMSO.

Daly, M. (2000), *The Gender Division of Welfare: The Impact of the British and German Welfare States*, Cambridge: Cambridge University Press.

Donzelot, J. (1980), *The Policing of Families*, London: Hutchinson.

Elias, P. (2001), 'Female Employment and Family Formation in National Institutional Contexts', in L. Hantrais (ed.), *Researching Family and Welfare from an International Comparative Perspective*, Brussels: Directorate for Technology Foresight and Socio-Economic Research, pp. 33–8.

Esping-Andersen, G. (1990), *The Three Worlds of Welfare Capitalism*, Cambridge: Polity Press.

Esping-Andersen, G. (1999), *Social Foundations of Postindustrial Economies*, Oxford: Oxford University Press.

Esping-Andersen, G. and Korpi, W. (1987), 'From Poor Relief to Institutional Welfare States: The Development of Scandinavian Social Policy', in R. Erikson, E.J. Hansen, S. Ringen and H. Uusitalo (eds), *The Scandinavian Model*, Armonk: M.E. Sharpe, pp. 39–74.

Gauthier, A.H.(1996), *The State and the Family: A Comparative Analysis of Family Policies in Industrialized Countries*, Oxford: Clarendon Press.

Hakim, C. (1995), 'Five feminist myths about women's employment', *British Journal of Sociology*, **46**, 429–55.

Hakim, C. (1996), *Key Issues in Women's Work*, London: Athlone.

Hantrais, L. (2001), 'Improving Policy Responses and Outcomes to Socio-Economic Challenges: Changing Family Structures, Policy and Practice', in L. Hantrais (ed.), *Researching Family and Welfare from an International Comparative Perspective*, Brussels: Directorate for Technology Foresight and Socio-Economic Research, pp. 39–45.

Hernes, H.M. (1987), *Welfare State and Women Power*, Oslo: Norwegian University Press.

Kamerman, S.B. and Kahn, A.J. (eds) (1997), *Family Change and Family Policies in Great Britain, Canada, New Zealand and the United States*, Oxford: Clarendon Press.

Lewis, J. (1992), 'Gender and the development of welfare regimes', *Journal of European Social Policy*, **2** (3), 159–73.

Lewis, J. (2001), 'The decline of the male breadwinner model: implications for work and care', *Social Politics*, **8** (2), 152–69.

McKie, L., Bowlby, S. and Gregory, S. (2001), 'Gender, caring and employment in Britain', *Journal of Social Policy*, **30** (2), 233–58.

McLaughlin, E., Trewsdale, J. and McCay, N. (2001, 'The Working Families Tax Credit: some issues and estimates', *Social Policy and Administration*, **33** (2), 168–81.

Millar, J. and Warman, A. (1996), *Family Obligations in Europe*, London: Family Policy Studies Centre and Joseph Rowntree Trust.

Muehlberger, U. (2000), *Women's Labour Force Attachment in Europe: An Analytical Framework and Empirical Evidence for the Household*, IRISS Working Paper Series No. 2000-07, Brussels: Directorate General XII.

OECD (2001), *Labour Force Statistics 1979–1999* (2001 Edition), Paris: Organization for Economic Cooperation and Development.

Orloff, A.S. (1993), 'Gender and the social rights of citizenship: the comparative analysis of gender relations and welfare states', *American Sociological Review*, **58** (3), 303–28.

Ostner, I. (1994), 'The Women and Welfare Debate', in L. Hantrais and S. Mangan (eds), *Family Policy and the Welfare of Women*, Loughborough: European Research Centre, pp. 35–52.

Padfield, I. and Proctor, M. (1998), *Young Adult Women, Work and Family: Living a Contradiction*, London: Mansell.

Pateman, C. (1988),'The Patriarchal Welfare State', in A. Gutman (ed.), *Democracy and the Welfare State*, Princeton: Princeton University Press, pp. 231–60.

Peng, I (2001), 'Women in the middle: welfare state expansion and devolution in Japan', *Social Politics*, **8** (2), 191–96.

Pringle, K. (1998), *Children and Social Welfare in Europe*, Buckingham and Philadelphia: Open University Press.

Reisman, D.A. (1977), *Richard Titmuss: Welfare and Society*, London: Heinemann.

Rose, R. (1989), *Ordinary People in Public Policy: A Behavioural Analysis*, London: Sage.

Sainsbury, D. (1996), *Gender, Equality and Welfare States*, Cambridge: Cambridge University Press.

Scheiwe, K. (1994), 'Labour market, welfare state and family institutions: the link to mothers' poverty risks', *Journal of European Social Policy*, **4** (3), 201–24.

Skocpol, T. (1992), *Protecting Soldiers and Mothers: The Political Origins of Social Policy in the United States*, Cambridge, MA: Harvard University Press.

Titmuss, R.M. (1968), 'Universal and Selective Social Services', in R.M. Titmuss (ed.), *Commitment to Welfare*, London: George Allen & Unwin, pp. 113–23.

Twigg, J. (1989), 'Models of carers: how do social care agencies conceptualise their relationship with informal carers', *Journal of Social Policy*, **18** (1), 53–66.

Ungerson, C. (1997), 'Social politics and the commodification of care', *Social Politics*, **4** (3), 362–81.

Index

206 *The Young, the Old and the State*

childcare provision 116–17, 134,
150–56, 161–3
compensatory education 136
Congress 145, 162, 190
consumption patterns 169
economic growth 110
female labour market 103
House of Representatives 148
individualization and universalization
181, 182, 184
institutional and home care 119
–Japan Security Treaty 99
labour market participation of older
people 106
locus, process and agency 174–5, 176,
177
long-term care 157–61
Medicare 123
older people, policy context of care
for 148–50
patterns of social care development
173
policy logics and modes of provision
170, 171
political life 124
Senate 148
social care citizenship, uneven
development of 185, 186, 187
social citizenship, structural sources of
191
welfare mix 11, 29
universal rights 25
universalization of social care 178–84
Urponen, K. 30

Vaarama, M. 33
Verba, S. 111–12
Veterans' Administration 159
Vihma, L. 40
'Vision of the Welfare in the 21st
Century, A.' 82

Volksgemeinschaft 68
voluntary care 31–4
von Bruch, R. 62

Waerness, K. 3, 6
'War on Poverty' programmes 190
Ward, C. 116
Warman, A. 4, 16, 178, 180
Wasoff, F. 115, 117
Weaver, K. 145
Wedderburn, D. 131
Weisbrod, B. 164
Welfare of the Aged Law (1963) 99
welfare centres 91
Welfare of Children Law (1947) 86,
98
welfare mix 28–9
Welfare of Mothers and Children Law
(1964) 99
Welfare of the Physically Handicapped
Law (1949) 98
Western Europe 15, 17
Wiener, J.M. 150, 156
Wilensky, H.L. 144
Willer, B. 151
Wilson, E. 135
Wintersberger, H. 11
Wistow, G. 12
Wittenberg, R. 122
Wollasch, A. 66
Women's Voluntary Service 129
Workers' Aid 65–6
'workhouse test' 28
Working Families Tax Credit 118, 136
Works Projects Administration 162

Yamanoi, K. 90
Yokoyama, K. 82, 99
Youth Department 66

Zenkoku, H.D.R. 84, 86, 88